Plantation Crisis

ECONOMIC EXPOSURES IN ASIA

Series Editor: Rebecca M. Empson, Department of Anthropology, UCL

Economic change in Asia often exceeds received models and expectations, leading to unexpected outcomes and experiences of rapid growth and sudden decline. This series seeks to capture this diversity. It places an emphasis on how people engage with volatility and flux as an omnipresent characteristic of life, and not necessarily as a passing phase. Shedding light on economic and political futures in the making, it also draws attention to the diverse ethical projects and strategies that flourish in such spaces of change.

The series publishes monographs and edited volumes that engage from a theoretical perspective with this new era of economic flux, exploring how current transformations come to shape and are being shaped by people in particular ways.

Plantation Crisis

Ruptures of Dalit life in the Indian tea belt

Jayaseelan Raj

First published in 2022 by
UCL Press
University College London
Gower Street
London WC1E 6BT

Available to download free: www.uclpress.co.uk

Text © Author, 2022
Images © Contributors and copyright holders named in captions, 2022

The authors have asserted their rights under the Copyright, Designs and Patents Act 1988 to be identified as the authors of this work.

A CIP catalogue record for this book is available from The British Library

Any third-party material in this book is not covered by the book's Creative Commons licence. Details of the copyright ownership and permitted use of third-party material is given in the image (or extract) credit lines. If you would like to reuse any third-party material not covered by the book's Creative Commons licence, you will need to obtain permission directly from the copyright owner.

This book is published under a Creative Commons Attribution-Non-Commercial 4.0 International licence (CC BY-NC 4.0), https://creativecommons.org/licenses/by-nc/4.0/. This licence allows you to share and adapt the work for non-commercial use providing attribution is made to the author and publisher (but not in any way that suggests that they endorse you or your use of the work) and any changes are indicated. Attribution should include the following information:

Raj, J. 2022. *Plantation Crisis: Ruptures of Dalit life in the Indian tea belt*. London: UCL Press. https://doi.org/10.14324/111.9781800082274

Further details about Creative Commons licences are available at http://creativecommons.org/licenses/

ISBN: 978-1-80008-229-8 (Hbk.)
ISBN: 978-1-80008-228-1 (Pbk.)
ISBN: 978-1-80008-227-4 (PDF)
ISBN: 978-1-80008-230-4 (epub)
ISBN: 978-1-80008-231-1 (mobi)
DOI: https://doi.org/10.14324/111.9781800082274

*To Bruce Kapferer
teacher and friend*

Contents

List of figures, maps and tables	ix
Acknowledgements	x
Preface	xii
Introduction	1
1 Pre-crisis: the making of a moral order	23
2 Workers: stay on, move out	45
3 Retirees: failed attempts to stay on	64
4 Youth: hidden injuries of caste	80
5 'Dam'ned in dispute	98
6 Crisis of relations	118
7 Rumour and gossip in a time of crisis	143
8 New companies, new workforce	164
9 The social consequences of crises	181
Appendix: A short history of the Peermade tea belt	193
References	200
Index	209

List of figures, maps and tables

Figures

0.1	A tea estate in the Peermade tea belt	18
1.1	Hill Valley estate outline	39
2.1	A ruined tea factory in the Peermade tea belt	48
5.1	Protest in a plantation town in the Peermade tea belt	102
6.1	Ruined medical dispensary on the Hill Valley estate	129
6.2	A crèche converted into a Christian prayer house in 2011	133
6.3	The same prayer house in Figure 6.2 in 2019	133
6.4	A muster office converted into a Christian prayer house in 2013	134
6.5	Self-constructed house of a temporary worker	135

Maps

0.1	Location of major tea belts in India	17

Tables

1.1	Types of contracts of tea plantation workers, Hill Valley estate, Kerala	29
2.1	Ten case histories of tea worker households, Hill Valley estate, Kerala	55

Acknowledgements

I have accumulated a huge intellectual debt over the years I spent on research for this book. I am deeply grateful to my doctoral supervisor, Bruce Kapferer, who constantly pushed me to think critically and carefully. He was always accessible and welcoming whenever I was stuck trying to formulate ideas or to express them logically. His comments were invaluable in strengthening and sharpening the arguments presented in the book. I cannot thank enough Andrew Lattas for generously commenting upon previous versions of the chapters. His support and encouragement helped me navigate through the years of PhD writing. Although conceived in Bergen, the book matured in London, at the LSE and SOAS, through the 'underbelly of the boom' research project. I received a great deal of encouragement from my colleagues in the project: Alpa Shah, Jens Lerche, Richard Axelby, Vikramaditya Thakur, Brendan Donegan and Dalel Benbabaali. In particular, I want to thank Alpa and Jens, who led the project and have been a constant support in finishing this book. I am grateful to Jonathan Parry, Caroline Osella, Geert De Neve, David Mosse, Gill Shepherd, Faisal Devji, John Chr. Knudsen, Vigdis Broch-Due and Kathinka Frøystad for their interest in my work and the stimulating discussions that always made a difference.

I owe special thanks to Sumeet Mhaskar, Bhawani Buswala, Murali Shanmugavelan, Gajendran Ayyathurai, Bjørn Enge Bertelsen, Sruthi Herbert, Nithya Natarajan and Shreya Sinha for their friendship and support over years of research and writing. I express my sincere thanks to my fellow graduate students in Bergen, particularly Laura Adwan, Sajan Thomas, Dag Erik Berg, Reshma Bharadwaj, Dinesan Vadakkiniyil, Elias Bedasso, Espen Helgesen, Carmeliza Rosario, Mehmonsho Sharifov, Tord Austdal, Thor Erik, Thomas Mountjoy, Mads Solberg, Samson Abebe and Kjetil Fosshagen, for engaging with my research in different contexts. In CDS, I would like to thank Umesh Omanakuttan, Abhilash Thadathil, Thiagu Ranganathan, Mythri Prasad Aleyamma, Sunandan Ghosh, Aritri Chakravarty, Thirtha Chatterjee and Ritika Jain for their friendship and encouragement.

Chris Penfold, the commissioning editor at UCL, and Rebecca Empson, the series editor, believed in this project from the outset. I am grateful to them and the UCL editorial team. I also want to thank the two anonymous reviewers who offered perceptive comments that significantly improved the manuscript. An earlier version of sections of Chapter 3 was published in an article, 'The crisis and the retirement: Alienation in Kerala's tea belt', in *Focaal: Journal of Global and Historical Anthropology* 86 (2020): 84–96. Chapter 7 is an extensively revised version of a 2018 article, 'Rumour and gossip in a time of crisis: Resistance and accommodation in a South Indian plantation frontier', published in *Critique of Anthropology* 39(1) (2009): 52–73. I thank the editors and publishers of *Focaal* and *Critique* for permission to revise the manuscripts for this book. My deepest gratitude goes to the plantation workers in the Peermade and Munnar tea belts, although my relationship with them goes beyond a word of gratitude since I am part of them. And finally, I express deep appreciation to my family, particularly Amma and Appa, for their love and support. My biggest debt is owed to my wife Aswathy and our daughter Diya whose affection provided me with the strength to complete this book.

Preface: Fieldwork in a time of crisis

Ethnographic accounts are generally written by anthropologists outside their own community. I had the rare opportunity to carry out ethnographic fieldwork in the very micro community into which I was born. While I carried out systematic ethnographic fieldwork, this book also draws on my experience growing up in a workers' household as a plantation boy. An extended embodiment of the plantation community has shaped my world views and my anthropological approach to the study of human beings. I had the profound advantage of speaking the same language as my interlocutors, their dialect, but also their style of speech, its oratory with all its proverbs, aphorisms and short stories through which the sociocultural world of the Tamil plantation workers are articulated and transmitted. I was able to grasp subtle and implicit aspects of sociocultural life which might have gone unnoticed by anthropologists from outside the community. For instance, I was attuned to the differences between people belonging to different castes, which are sometimes transmitted in non-verbal embodied ways through etiquette, politeness, avoidance and abstinence. These can often be difficult for a foreign anthropologist to recognise, although long-term field immersion is intended to overcome this. This does not in any way suggest that my information is necessarily superior to that gained by a non-native anthropologist. However, the quality and sense of significance may be distinct. The importance that I give to identity, to its complexity and to certain principle values, I suggest, derive from my day-to-day experience as a member of the very community that I was studying.

Although there are clear advantages to being a native anthropologist – especially in giving me a deep sensitivity to the economic crisis that the workers confronted – in certain ways I was also restricted in the kinds of information I was able to gather. For the plantation workers, a foreigner is simply a foreigner; they do not care whether the particular researcher is from (another part of) India, North America, Europe or Australia. But the cultural capital of upper-caste urban India, or of whiteness and the colonial heritage, has its own hierarchy within which foreign researchers become positioned. Plantation workers are not concerned about foreign researchers publicising their personal life because they stay in the field for only a short period of time and disseminate the information gathered to a distant and unknown audience.

The fear was that I would share local knowledge (to which I was privy through my web of personal relations), with significant implications for a local audience. The expectation was that information presented in newspapers or academic articles that I wrote would feed back into the local situation, with negative consequences. As such my position was neither neutral nor outside. I was regarded by many as too close, too intimate with the events, and people were concerned that I might divulge too much. My positioning created in certain circumstances an ambivalent caution. People would test me by teasing, responding ironically or being extremely hesitant and even avoiding interaction with me. This became even more true as the workers were increasingly affected by the uncertainty that the crisis in the tea industry had generated.

I realised that, even when I was part of the plantation community, participant observation transformed me, in a way making me more intimate with the life in the tea belt. Over time I realised that I had come to know more about some people than most of their own neighbours did. Many told me stories of poverty that they would not share even with their close relatives or neighbours. Sometimes they described their poverty objectively to others, yet not with the kind of emotion they employed with me. These were organic moments of sharing the inner experience of poverty, not merely the daily routine of collecting information. When I met people in the street after long conversations, the way they greeted me expressed that intimacy, precisely because they had told me many things that they might not have told anyone else. And, as it happened with more and more people in the village, I became something like a sorcerer, one who knows a great deal about everyone – a person who holds the secrets of plantation life. The workers and their families had experiences that were overflowing through my fieldnotes. At the same time, it was paradoxical that those overflowing experiences were indicative of what many of them thought of as the futility of human life. As many workers told me, they had to sustain their lives 'for their children even if not for themselves'.

I do not presume to speak on behalf of the workers, although I was born and raised in a Tamil Dalit plantation household. My intention is simply to lay out the stories as told to me over years of living and doing fieldwork. As a 'native' researcher, my approach to ethnography is mindful of the postmodern critique of participant observation (Geertz 1972; Clifford and Marcus 1986) and also of the importance of Bourdieu's phenomenologically reflexive approach (Bourdieu and Wacquant 1992). The significance of this is crucial whether the observer is an outsider (which is Bourdieu's reference) or an insider. Perhaps there is a greater onus on the native researcher to be cognisant of her or his own common-sense assumptions that may mask the effects of other processes. As the foreign researcher must critically interrogate the nature of her or his positioning, so must the native researcher. I have tried to take both the position of an outsider – where nothing can be taken for granted or assumed – and that of an insider, one who has lived the structures of which she or he may not have hitherto (prior to engaging in anthropological research) been fully aware. My critical approach combines the intimate experience of the insider with the more distanced reflexive orientation of the outsider. Part of such a critical approach is attending to structural processes that are not necessarily reducible to individual subjectivist terms – an emphasis of postcolonial and postmodern perspectives.

At the same time, my description of my positionality in the field should not be interpreted as a mere addition to the postmodernist 'anthropological critique' that has been dominating anthropological writing for the last quarter-century. This critique, rooted in textual analysis of every component of anthropological research, occasionally becomes a self-centred analysis that downplays broader structural hierarchies and inequalities. Some of the recent 'turns' in anthropology, such as the 'ontological turn', seem to reinforce this self-centric analysis of ethnographic situations. While I agree with the significance of thick descriptions of ethnographic situations, I believe that a holistic approach is required to fully understand the ontological transition, or the repositioning of self of the plantation workers and the changes in the perception of self and others due to structural transformations in the dominant social identities (of class, gender and caste) in the crisis context.

Alienation of the workers is at the centre of this ontological transition. At the same time, in my exposition of this ontological transition and the phenomenology of crisis, I was careful not to deny the social dimensions in which the crisis unravels. It may appear therefore that my focus on the alienation and powerlessness of the workers overshadows their creative engagement, or their 'agency'. Such celebrations of agency have become a dominant orientation in anthropological literature after the 'crisis of representation' discourse (Clifford and Marcus 1986; Marcus and Fischer 1986). In my view, the celebration of the workers' agency, without examining the true liberatory potential of workers' actions, is myopic and does not allow the fieldwork-based knowledge to examine the structures of exploitation. It is important to understand that the social process goes beyond the rhetoric of agency and individual, which may themselves be produced out of structural forces rather than the other way around – often the perspective of individualist and ego-centred perspectives (Kapferer 2005a). Further, the fieldwork on the lived experience of the tea workers demonstrates that they 'speak' of their alienation as the core phenomenon of their lives. They were impassive whenever I tried to 'appreciate' them for their 'creative engagement' with the crisis. Therefore, not recognising their recognition of alienation would be to deny their agency.

Walking through the crisis was emotionally taxing for me as I have experienced sleepless nights pondering the crisis and the hollowness it produced for the workers' families. Despite being from a family of plantation workers, the ethnographic fieldwork has radically transformed my own cosmological and ontological understanding of human life in the plantations. Now the difficult part was to come to terms with how I wanted to lay out their lives in the text with the highest regard for their dignity and the ways they experience the dimensions of the economic crisis. Perhaps one thing I paid the utmost attention to was to unpack the crisis in a way that de-naturalises the marginal life of the Tamil Dalits in the plantation frontiers of India.

Doing fieldwork in one's own community is a challenge not only in terms of how you choose to position yourself in it, but also how you are already positioned within the plantation cosmology and its categorical relationships. As a native anthropologist, I was subjected to structures of social and political significance that were different from those to which a foreign anthropologist might be subjected. Foreign anthropologists would not be personally confronted on a daily basis with the subtleties underpinning the dynamics of identity and relations in the contexts they enter. I was constantly enmeshed in the complexities of identity as I negotiated my path through plantation life. In distant tea estates where I did not know the people, I would be asked leading questions indicative of my caste and social origin (whether my ancestors were from northern or southern Tamil Nadu, for instance). I was often asked by the workers if I had any relatives in the tea estates that I visited. Giving the names of my relatives living in their estate would position me in terms of caste and family reputation.

This was mainly done by the upper-caste managerial staff, trade union leaders, government officials and merchants in the nodal towns, who often wanted to put me in my place. The coerced embodiment of a particular identity ascribed to me by the upper caste occurred through their narratives of incidents in which plantation people from my kinship networks sought their help in sorting out issues with the labour conflicts in the plantations. Their narratives were often filled with sarcasm and stereotypes about Tamil plantation workers. Some would invoke incidents in which they had helped the workers and would link that to my kinship networks, as if I should be obliged for their assistance to the plantation workers. Whenever I left the offices of these non-plantation people who were somehow connected to the plantation business, I would ask myself what the relationship would have been between Sidney Mintz and Don Taso if Mintz had been a Black anthropologist. Or, for that matter, if M.N. Srinivas and André Béteille had been Dalits trying to walk though Brahmin streets to conduct research on caste.

Anthropologists critically discuss their privileged position and the power they hold in 're-presenting' the lives of people they engage with. Such discussions do not pay due attention to the vulnerability of those ethnographers who are not treated on a par with some of the population within the socio-political hierarchies of the society they write about. The precariousness of being a Dalit while doing fieldwork in the Indian countryside is indeed revealing. Such dehumanising experiences push us to be much more intimate to the stories of those who suffer at the bottom. This poses a challenge to the detachment from the field that is supposed to be required to finish writing, for example, this book. This challenge is augmented by the call for reflexivity and positioning of oneself in describing plantation life in a crisis. Perhaps, in the course of becoming an anthropologist, I recognised more the mutuality of being with the plantation community, thus continually becoming a plantation boy.

Introduction

Many people have grown up, lived, worked and died on Indian tea plantations. Although a small number have left in search of a better life elsewhere, they have often been replaced by their relatives. However, most workers have not experienced a life outside the plantations, which have cocooned their families for generations. Therefore, when long-standing owners began to shut down plantation production as the tea industry entered a period of crisis in the late 1990s, it represented a moment of unprecedented social and economic disruption for the workers. In the Peermade (Pīrumēdu) tea belt in the southern Indian state of Kerala,[1] as in the other tea belts of India, the workers, who descended from the indentured workforce of the colonial period, were the victims of economic and political forces beyond their control. In Kerala, these workers were predominantly Tamil-speaking Dalits (ex-'untouchables'), the poorest and the most oppressed community within India's caste hierarchy. What was worse than being socially reproduced within the plantations was being forced into a liminal juncture when the plantations were abruptly shut down.

The tea industry in India boomed in the first three decades of the postcolonial period, roughly between 1950 and 1980. By the late 1980s, India was second only to China in the production of tea globally, responsible for nearly 25 per cent of global tea production and employing 1.26 million people on tea plantations and another two million indirectly. However, the collapse of the price of tea in the international market in the early 1990s led to a major crisis in the Indian tea industry. Arguably, this was due to neoliberal structural transformations in the international tea trade. Trade agreements between countries conditioned the tea trade between 1950 and 1990, but this changed by the early 1990s as a few major corporate firms that controlled the industry began to intervene much more in determining the price of tea (Neilson and Pritchard 2009). The transition of the tea market from a state-regulated to a free market was part of larger transformations in the international political economy of trade. Similar changes occurred in other major agricultural commodities such as coffee and cocoa. Accordingly, the decline of the agrarian economy in the global South is directly linked to the globalisation of neoliberal capitalism.[2]

Bound up in the triumph of global capitalism, specific changes in customary markets had particular impacts on plantations in India: the collapse of the Soviet Union, India's main trading partner for tea, augmented the crisis. Iraq then became the major buyer for Indian tea but this new market was lost following the Gulf War of 1990–1. The rising cost of production, decreasing productivity of tea bushes and the heavy export duty in India are cited as other factors that precipitated the crisis. In 2008, Indian tea earned only USD 590.23 million in foreign exchange, in comparison with USD 506.832 million at its height in 1981 (Jain et al. 2008; Mishra et al. 2011, 2012), a drastic decline in real terms. The percentage share of tea in total agricultural export was 19 per cent in 1981. It declined to 3.41 per cent in 2008 (Mishra et al. 2012). Still, India continued to be the second largest producer of tea following China and the fourth largest exporter of tea following Kenya, China and Sri Lanka. This shows the significance of tea in India's economy and the extent to which it could affect the lives of the thousands of tea workers.

The crisis made a deep impact since it marked the end of the relatively encapsulated and isolated contexts of plantation life. Until the crisis, the plantations were largely socio-economic systems unto themselves and separated from the wider economic and cultural settings within which they were located. Having lived on the tea plantations for as many as five generations, in the aftermath of the tea industry crisis, Dalit labourers were suddenly pushed into the informal economy outside the plantations. Although some people had chosen to move out of the plantations in previous generations, it is only since the crisis that they have had to seek work outside en masse. Many went to work in the agricultural, construction and garment sectors in their ancestral villages and industrial townships in the two southern states of India – Kerala and Tamil Nadu. Although some of these jobs came with higher wages than those in the tea plantations, they also came with the new insecurities that accompany casual labour.

Outside the tea plantations where they had been relatively isolated from other communities, many Dalits faced overt caste discrimination for the first time. As for those who remained in the plantations, the men became labourers in the booming construction industry (mainly commuting to work in lowland cities and towns), while the women became contract workers on the plantations and/or were employed in the government-supported rural employment guarantee scheme. These new patterns of mobility were highly gendered as Dalit women tried to stay behind and keep their houses and jobs on the tea plantations, as low paid as they were, while the men moved to work outside.

Trade unions, an important functional unit under the plantation production system, were taken over by caste and religious groups expressing their sectional interests. While unions were still active on the plantations, they had become instruments connected with religion and caste identity that were previously marginalised. The workers were further divided by the redrawing of boundaries of tea estates and the workers' settlements when new companies took over some of the plantations. What was previously a single village was now split into two, and the workers had to fight among themselves over control of socio-religious institutions such as the temple.

The plantation owners undertook major reforms in both land and labour regimes that dramatically affected the fate of the work force. The planters used the crisis as an opportunity to diversify the economic activities on the plantations. The Kerala Land Reforms Act of 1963 had previously made it illegal to use land under monocrop plantation for any other purposes. These legal restrictions had been enacted primarily to guarantee jobs for the permanent workers. They also ensured that the plantations were exempt from land ceiling restrictions. In the name of the tea crisis, the planters lobbied for a significant amendment to the Land Reform Act which enabled them to use 5 per cent of their land for non-plantation purposes such as tourism, renting to property developers for new resorts and cultivating other agricultural crops. The Kerala government claimed that this new amendment was enacted to 'rescue' plantations from the crisis, and the opposition front, comprising leftist parties, raised concerns over fragmentation and misuse of plantation land in the longer run (*The Hindu*, 24 September 2012). The new amendments, however, were silent on the demand for land by the plantation workers. Furthermore, again using the justification of the crisis, welfare benefits were suspended, eroding the hard-won gains of the preceding decades. In 2011, when some of the plantations in the tea belt were reopened under new ownership, they preferred to employ a casual workforce. Those long-serving workers who were looking forward to becoming permanent were denied their due promotions. Accordingly, the economic crisis became a decisive event in plantation life and society, inducing transformations in the existing plantation order and social institutions, producing new institutions/practices in plantation life and, more crucially, exposing plantation workers to the outside world.

The crisis was further exacerbated by conflict over the control of Mullaperiyar Dam between the states of Kerala and Tamil Nadu. The governments of both states claimed control over the dam and expressed conflicting opinions on its safety and economic purpose. Ethnicity inevitably became caught up in the dispute, aligning the Malayalis of Kerala against the Tamils of Tamil Nadu. The linguistic minorities of Malayalis and Tamils were targeted in Tamil Nadu and Kerala respectively. In Kerala, antagonism and discrimination against Tamils mostly targeted the plantation Tamils, which added insult to injury for they were already suffering from the crisis and the subsequent closure of the plantations. The dispute reactivated sub-nationalist ideologies according to linguistic identity, which effectively alienated the plantation Tamils in Kerala.[3] This left the plantation Tamils not only having to find ways to survive the crisis through locating new means of subsistence, but also having to fight against anti-Tamil ethnic prejudice and antagonism.

In the context of both the tea crisis and the dam conflict, various dimensions of plantation Tamils' identity assumed new significance that resulted in their further stigmatisation. Their wider conception of being Dalits (meaning 'oppressed') combined with other aspects of their identity – the history of many as having once been bonded labourers, a low status by virtue of their Tamil linguistic identity in Kerala and being from the 'wild' highlands rather than from the settled and 'civilised' lowland valleys – operate to give them a low and stigmatised social/cultural worth. Such reduced value is highlighted when contrasted to the high socio-cultural value accorded in Kerala to those conceived of as being high caste, upper/middle class, Malayalam-speaking and living in the lowland villages and towns. Critically, caste,[4] both as an identity and as a relational organising principle, achieved new significance, suppressing the class relations relevant to the industrial system of the relatively enclosed plantation system, or discovering (for the plantation workers) a reinvented import in its meshing with the class processes of the world external to the plantations. The plantation workers thus encountered dimensions of the stigma that was attached to Dalit as well as Tamil identity, as the workers were exposed to the new forms of subsistence relations. The sense of stigma is reinforced by the relative lack of control that the workers had over their life situations.

The collapse of the plantation economy resulted in the breakdown of the workers' socio-economic relations. A moral society among the workers was largely built on the moral economy of the plantation. None of the groups in the workers' community – the youth, the workers and the retirees – were able to fulfil their moral responsibility within their kinship and social relations of the plantations. As the crisis led to the fracturing of social relations, the workers and their families desperately competed with each other to acquire social status by claiming that they were more 'decent' (meaning civilised and aspiring) compared with others who were 'failing' in building their life after the crisis. This phenomenon of accepting the capitalist values of individual achievement is what I call the 'politics of decency': it was oriented towards finding solace in comparing one's life situation with those who are perceived to be stuck within the plantation order.

Around 2011–12, the new companies which took over the erstwhile closed plantations started to recruit new Adivasi (indigenous/tribal) workers. These migrants from the northern Indian state of Jharkhand were a mobile labour force who did not speak the local languages and who were not given permanent or even temporary contracts and thus formed a super-exploitable casualised labour force. Caste, ethnicity and region are thereby used to divide labourers and make them more vulnerable and exploitable. It is against this backdrop of an increasingly neoliberal regime, strengthening the position of the planters while state control over plantations declined, that we must understand the fate of Dalit tea plantation labour.[5]

Plantation Crisis documents this moving episode of capitalist abandonment of the Tamil Dalit plantation labourers at a critical juncture of political-economic transformation, their experience throwing into relief various dimensions of the crisis, and the way it affects them. The crisis exposes the workers to a wider system in which they re-encounter, in a vastly different historical situation, a socio-political order from which they had been shielded in their protected plantation enclaves. In doing so, the book captures what Bruno Latour (2005) might address as the disassembling of the social: the fracturing of the social relations of the plantation system and their reassembling in the context of the crisis and the conflict. Going beyond the conventional focus on the causes and the consequences of economic crisis for the economy as such, this book asks: what is the nature of the intimate experience of extraordinary crises by the poor such as the workers in the plantation frontiers?

Much of the anthropological literature on the plantations in South Asia meticulously examines various aspects of the plantations, including how the tea-plucking women endure the gendered plantation system reproduced through caste–gender–ethnic hierarchies (Chatterjee 2001;

Besky 2014; Chaudhuri 2014; Jayawardena and Kurian 2015; Jegathesan 2019). Some have also looked into the functional aspects of caste and ethnicity for the plantation system (Hollup 1994; Bass 2012). The radical rupture that the crisis generated in the South Asian plantations has not received much attention.[6] Those who have written about the crisis have approached it in terms of its material aspects – tea as a commodity and tea plantations as a sector of the economy (Jain et al. 2008; Mishra et al. 2011, 2012). Such focuses override the concerns of workers within the plantations. They mainly appear as an abstract category of labour, as a factor of production.

The reduction and abstraction of the marginalised human beings is also evident in the analysis of economic crises elsewhere. For instance, studies on the 2008 financial crisis have mainly focused on examining what went wrong in terms of mainstream economic logic and the political economy of power and corruption on Wall Street. Such a focus fixes the working poor's suffering as inherent to the logic of neoliberal capitalism. This fixing of the workers within the production relations provides a space to rationalise their abandonment during crises. If we are to unpack the diverse aspects of the rupture that the crisis created for the workers, we need to locate them within broader socio-cultural contexts within which the crisis unfolds and also pay attention to their intimate experience of crises. This focus is extremely important as the crisis of the tea industry encompasses, translates and feeds into a number of other crises for the plantation women and men.

On that account, *Plantation Crisis* moves beyond concerns about how the crisis came into being, how it can be resolved or the sociology of errors examining what went wrong in the larger political economy that led to the crisis. Rather, it provides an intimate account of a crisis that emphasises its structural and phenomenological aspects, keeping the workers' lives at the centre of its analysis. Such a focus has become more relevant as the poor in different parts of the world are increasingly coerced into the ethical project of forging life out of the ruins of extractive capitalism (Tsing 2005, 2015; Martínez 2007; Li 2014; Empson 2020). In the following chapters, an attempt is made to unearth the complexities of the crisis through understanding the logical connection between rhizomic formulations that are intensified in moments of crisis and conflict.

Ethnographic fieldwork for this book was carried out between 2009 and 2015 in a plantation I call the Hill Valley estate in the Peermade tea belt owned by the True Life Company. Here I carried out participant observation, key interviews, generational histories and a household-level survey of the workers' shacks, called line houses.[7] I followed Dalit workers to their new sites of labour in Coimbatore, Tirupur and to villages back in Tamil Nadu to better understand their situation there and conducted interviews with them. And, lastly, I drew on the ethnographic research I conducted with the Adivasi labourers from Jharkhand who were based on a neighbouring plantation in the Peermade tea belt, about 12 miles from the Hill Valley estate, in what I call Top View estate owned by the Auburn Company, and a two-week visit to some of their homes in the Santhal Parganas in Jharkhand to better understand their background.

Plantation capitalism and the logic of crisis

Strung along the high reaches of the Western Ghats, the plantations that are the subject of this book are geographically located far away from the urban financial centres that connect and control global capitalism. Those who are employed in the plantations – whether Tamil Dalits or Adivasis from Jharkhand – come from communities that were socially marginalised and stigmatised in their wider societies. Yet, as Sidney Mintz and others have shown, the plantation workers were at the heart of capitalism, for they produced commodities mainly for the international market.[8] This means that even while living on the margins in the highland frontiers, they were highly vulnerable to the shocks of the global market (Wolf 1982; Mintz 1985). As the capitalist commodity markets for colonial plantation products were globally interlinked, they generated recession in one place and boom in another with aggressive price fluctuations. The emergence and demise of plantations at the frontiers of global capitalism and the abandoning of its workforce in different parts of the world are therefore closely interconnected historically (Wolf 1982). With the triumph of globalised neoliberalism, the unfair terms of trade for agricultural goods have meant that the disadvantaged position of nations in the global South was permanently entrenched. It becomes important then to situate the plantation crisis within larger crises generated by the neoliberal political-economic transformations that expediated economic decline in the global South (Ferguson 1999).[9]

Around the world, poor countries have been locked into a system where they must compete to become the cheapest to produce for the international market. The contemporary crisis in the tea industry, therefore, resulted from the global neoliberal policies of the continuous search for, and making of, cheaper places for the production of tea. For the tea companies, market failure in one place opens up possibilities for business somewhere else. These companies have shut down operations in

India, citing the increased cost of production, and have either invested in plantations in African countries or have outsourced production to other firms and concentrated on the retail market as in the case of Tata Global Beverages. This is the process through which plantation frontiers are connected to the network of rhizomatic capitalism. At the same time, the way global plantation capital is moved from one place to another is highly brutal as it had not reckoned with the workers' economic suffering, let alone the social consequences of the crisis.

To reiterate the point, the movement of capital under extractive plantation capitalism pushes for local specialisation of commodities according to global needs, and within this system, crisis was understood as a transition to an economy in which one has a comparative advantage. According to this logic, Kenya, Indonesia, Vietnam and Sri Lanka had a comparative advantage over India as they had a cheaper labour force, higher productivity and lower opportunity cost. Insistence on the comparative advantage led Indian plantations to seek out other options, such as plantation tourism and further mechanisation of the production process. The transition cost of this shift, however, was passed on to the workers and undermined the position of the established labour.[10]

This means that the crisis in the Indian tea plantations was caused not by speculation, panic and errors in the calculation of the global economic system, but rather by the very logic of the system which wanted to have the plantations cultivating something in which they have a 'comparative advantage' in the global market. That is to say, neoliberal capitalism has employed this logic of comparative advantage to perpetuate ruptures and crises as a way of further disadvantaging and extracting profit from the plantations in the global South, as convincingly argued for so long by Caribbean political economists (Best 1968; Beckford 1972). The crisis of plantation capitalism, then, assumes a life of its own as it becomes internal to the neoliberal logic of crisis as generative and integral to the long trajectory of capitalism. This structural logic of contemporary capitalism naturalises, and therefore invisibilises, the suffering subjects, as reiterated recently by Rebecca Empson (2020). Extending this structural logic of crises to a poststructural narrative, Janet Roitman (2014, 3) has examined how, 'through the term "crisis," the singularity of events is abstracted by a generic logic, making crisis a term that seems self-explanatory'. In the Peermade tea belt, crisis as a historical condition justifies its actuality and normalises the closure of plantations and the abandonment of the workers.[11]

While crisis as a phenomenon itself is rationalised, the crises of industrial capitalism in the global South have received much less attention from the global North, probably also because the operation of industrial capitalism does not seem to be its major concern. As Gilles Deleuze explained the emergence of neoliberal capitalism three decades ago, 'capitalism (in the first world) is no longer involved in the production which it often relegates to the Third World even for the complex forms of textiles, metallurgy or oil production. It's capitalism of higher production … what it wants to sell is services and what it wants to buy is stocks' (1992, 6). As a consequence of this outsourcing of industrial production, the exploitative dimensions and the abandonment of the workers in industrial/agrarian capitalism is imagined to have less impact on the global North vis-à-vis financial crises. When financial meltdowns and contagions become the contemporary face of crony capitalism, industrial capitalism is unintentionally missed from the radar of resistance movements such as the Occupy protests. At the same time, this 'Eurocentric' understanding of what contemporary crises mean somewhat vindicates the predatory forms of capitalism not only in the capitalist frontiers in the global South, but also in the global North, for example in the steel factories of Sheffield as noted by Massimiliano Mollona (2005). Neoliberal capitalism attacks formal employment relations wherever it finds them and replaces them with precarious informal arrangements. Although this phenomenon is seen everywhere as the poor across the world are simultaneously included and excluded from global capitalism (Sassen 2014), those who are at the extreme lower rung of the global commodity chain in the plantations become much more vulnerable to global economic distress, with highly unstable inclusion and exclusion.

The workers' suffering is an externality – the outsourcing of the true costs of production onto those who receive the least profits. Their liminal position in this sense is completely anticipated within the market arrangements of extractive capitalism. The tea companies argued that the 'cheapening of labour' was imperative to overcome the crisis and to be able to compete in the international tea market. The companies recruited a large number of casual workers and denied permanent status to the temporary workers. They cited crisis to further cheapen the labour and to reap higher profits. While the workers were forced to bear the brunt of the crisis and the failure of the market, the heyday of the tea boom in the pre-crisis period did not add any benefit to the workers except that their employment was secured. The plantation wage was the lowest for any manual labour in the highlands, which ensured that the life of the workers was precarious at all times. The low wage was justified by the companies by citing the provision of free line houses, which were often built by encroaching on the land owned by the state. State institutions often turned a blind eye to such encroachments. In fact, the state institutions provided very generous assistance to the smooth functioning of the plantation system. In the crisis context, the state institutions that functioned within the logic of corporate structures (Kapferer 2005c) became more capitalistic, as they focused on the revival of tea production rather than rescuing its workforce.

The logic of saving a 'commodity' rather than 'people' had also penetrated the local discourses of tea companies, union leaders and government officials in the Department of Labour. The union leaders and the government officials too often stressed that for the workers to survive, plantation production must thrive in the first place. The unions and the state did not hold the plantation companies responsible for abandoning the workers. In effect, they considered the workers' suffering during the crisis as inevitable and as integral to the ups and downs of the plantation economy. Here, the existence of plantation production becomes a primary condition for the existence of the workers. It seems a rational argument from an economistic point of view. This rationale, however, facilitates the status quo and disallows the workers' resistance against the tea companies and the corporate state which abandoned them. In an attempt to save 'tea' and the 'plantation system', the unions and the state bureaucracy gave a silent nod to the further casualisation of labour and the suspension of labour laws as an attempt to cheapen the cost of production. This logic is a contemporary neoliberal derivative of what Marx referred to as commodity fetishism.

In both the transnational and local discourse on the crisis and the suspension of labour laws, the state officials, the unions and the tea companies offered a nationalist discourse that workers need to make some sacrifice in the interest of the nation. During our conversations, the union leaders and the government officials often evoked the significance of the plantation sector in India's foreign exchange as the export brings in foreign money and therefore the commodity (tea) serves the interest of the nation. The 'sanctity' of the plantation system was repeatedly evoked by these non-worker-stakeholders in the tea belt throughout my fieldwork.

Within this logic of the tea companies, the state and the unions, the workers' subjection to exploitation became a patriotic act. They have been contributing to the prosperity of the nation, and thus have been integrated into the nation, but paradoxically only by becoming more alienated. It is by evoking a national interest that the plantation enclaves of the international system are reproduced. The nation is indebted to tea, and the tea production is indebted to the nation, whereas the plantation workforce is subjected to the interest of the nation and tea production. To reiterate, by perfectly associating neoliberal economic growth with nationalism, the impeccable blend of tea companies, unions and the state legitimises the reproduction of the plantation system even when the workers suffer because of the crisis.

In September 2015, in the neighbouring tea belt of Munnar, the workers, most of them women, fought against the plantation company–union–state nexus. The strikers' group, called Pembillai Orumai (Women's Unity), demanded a higher bonus rate than the company offered (Raj 2019). The company claimed they did not have money for the fair bonus. The workers did not believe the balance sheet and financial statement provided by the management, as the workers pointed to the contradictions of the management practices, including the fact that the company had allocated millions of rupees for buying luxury cars for the top managerial staff. Finally, the company agreed to pay the fair bonus. The peculiar feature of the strike was that it was organised outside and also against the conventional trade unions who, according to the strikers, took a cut from the plantation company and agreed to a lower bonus rate. They also came out against the wage negotiations between the state representatives, unions and the tea companies' associations in which the workers were not allowed to participate.

Categorical oppression, alienation and the phenomenology of crises

The plight of the workers in the crisis context is in many senses an extension of a history of alienation, which I consider as a function of the workers' 'stigmatised' categories of identity, including being an underclass. I define this phenomenon as categorical oppression (Raj 2020), a term that captures how the workers' categories of identity, having been located at the bottom of the hierarchy of such categories (or categorical relationships), make their existence painful (Mitchell 1956).[12] To be sure, categorical oppression refers to how different categories of identity of the workers, including caste, class, ethnicity, language and place of origin, are stigmatised, inferiorised and lived through by the workforce in the context of the crisis. It is through categorical oppression that the workers are reproduced both as a source of cheap labour and as one of the most stigmatised groups within the larger social hierarchies.

The ideology of caste is a central element of the categorical oppression of the tea workers. As mentioned in the beginning, most of the workers are from Dalit communities, who continue to experience discrimination, violence and untouchability. Therefore, the workers' experience of the crisis and the new social conditions that it generated for them need to be understood also within the context of the caste society in India. The capitalist plantations took root in a casteist society that not only offered a cheaper labour force but also legitimised it. At the same time, the potency of the caste system should not be reduced to it being a facilitator of divisions of labour in capitalist settings. The capitalist ideology has used caste structures but to be deployed only within the ideology of caste.[13] Caste, as an encompassing ideology, is still a dominant force of the social organisation and relations within the broader Indian society, both rural and urban. This becomes more explicit in the crisis context, specifically in the way the workers experienced the stigmatised categories of identity of Tamil-speaking Dalit working class living in the highlands. In fact, their linguistic identity as a Tamil-speaking minority is stigmatised mainly because of their caste, as will be discussed later in the book. For the workers, other categories of identity thus also feed into the stigmatisation of caste.

In the next chapter, I discuss how the caste system was used to generate the class order within the tea belt that offered Dalits in plantations a degree of protection against explicit ritual-based discriminations in comparison with other Dalits in Indian villages. The intensity of caste outside the plantations became evident when the workers moved out and were caught up in it. When I asked them about their efforts to secure a livelihood, their struggle with everyday caste discrimination too often appeared in our conversations. Caste had followed them wherever they moved in search of a livelihood as India's 'footloose labour' (Breman 1996). This burden of caste that they have to carry becomes too much to bear as the struggle for a livelihood is combined with the struggle for a decent life. In other words, the Dalits have to struggle not only for economic security, but also for social dignity within the Indian caste society. The experience of the Dalit tea workers, as discussed in the book, shows that the moment we introduce them into the discussion on the transformation of caste and class, it becomes difficult not to see the primacy of caste. For the Dalit women from the crisis-ridden plantations, gender dimensions add further layers in their categorical oppression and struggle for a decent life.

In the crisis context, the workers experience and embody categorical oppression through a condition of being totally alienated. By alienation I refer to a thorough lack of control that human beings may come to have over their socio-economic situation and by extension even over the most basic circumstances of existence itself. The workers in the Peermade tea belt, as evident in the following chapters, experience a lack of control over and detachment from their life situations. The factory-like system of plantations here over time developed a production system that objectified labour and alienated the workers from, to evoke Marx, the products of their labour, self, other human beings and nature. Marx (1959 [1844]) fundamentally located alienation in the separation of the product from the producer that occurs as a result of private property, commodity fetishism and the objectification of labour (Marx and Engels 1964 [1846]; see also Mészáros 1970; Israel 1971; Lukács 1971 [1923]; Ollman 1971). The Marxian approach to alienation, as a separation of the producer from the product, has been a popular orientation in anthropological research as well. Steven Sangren (1991, 2000), for instance, examines how Chinese worshippers produce the power and divinity of deities (territorial cult gods) as part of the production of cultural symbols, which in turn becomes central to the reproduction of society at large. However, the worshippers attribute their own existence to the power of deities, thus alienating themselves from their product – the power and divinity of deities. Sangren thus defines alienation as the inversion of subject and object in the reproduction of society.

Michael Taussig (1980) discusses the alienation of peasants that occurs when they become wage labourers in the sugar plantations in Colombia and in the mines of Bolivia, separated from their product in the process of capitalist development. Following Marx, Taussig examines the processes through which the workers are related to the objects of their labour as alien and potentially self-destructive objects. At the same time, Taussig recognises the significance of cultural forms beyond their function as a facilitator of capitalism. Taussig also moves beyond the plantation/mine production spaces in understanding the workers' alienation, looking at their ritual and religious practices, whose transformations are partly indebted to the emerging capitalist economy in the region. Having explained categorical oppression before, the point I take from Taussig is that alienation occurs not only from capitalist production per se but also from other processes of the workers' lives, such as the stigmatisation of identity categories both inside and outside the sites of production and its holistic experience by the workers.

In this direction, I extend alienation beyond its economistic usage as a mere consequence of capitalist production and its division of labour to address the qualities of social relations. I regard such processes connected to the values of caste, ethnicity, gender and language to have alienating effects. These are further facilitated in the productive context of the plantations and in the economic forces affecting the wider society.

While their alienating force can operate independently of other considerations, in my analysis I consider the intermeshing of socio-cultural dimensions of the identities and relations of plantation workers with political and economic processes. Thus, I explore the ideology of caste in the context of the class relations of plantation life and their transformations during the crisis and the inter-state conflict. The focus here is on the *intense experience* of their multiple alienation and *reduction* to non-being, which is so pervasive that alienation becomes a naturalised condition of the workers' existence (see Fanon 1966, 1967).

Crisis as situated event

In this book, I have approached the tea crisis and the dam dispute as events in the anthropological sense. The anthropological studies of events focus on situations which have the potency to reconstitute structural relations. My approach to events is primarily shaped by the 'situational analysis' of the Manchester School (Mitchell 1956; Gluckman 1958 [1940]; Van Velsen 1979; Kapferer 2005b, 2010).[14] A major point in situational analysis is that the event is not understood as a mere illustration of social reality, but as a generative moment (Kapferer 2005b, 2010; Meinert and Kapferer 2015) where prevailing social processes are significantly refigured in opening up new potentialities in the formation of social realities (Kapferer 2010). The Manchester School approach places emphasis on both situations and events – the situation is the context in which the event takes place, and that event in turn restructures the context. This approach is useful to understand the contexts of crises and conflicts that potentially create new institutional and customary orders. The situated event also reveals what everyday social practices tend to obscure. It is exemplified by the replacement of a class order with an institutional structure that emphasises caste hierarchy and by the upsurge of caste/racial discrimination during the economic crisis and dam conflict.

In this sense, the crisis opens up the internal contradictions, such as the caste hierarchy and fraudulent welfare claims, that were submerged in the reproduction of the plantation system. Along the line of the economic crisis, the dam dispute should also be considered as a situated event where both the Tamil (Tamil Nadu) and Malayali (Kerala) identities gained importance, with disadvantageous effects on the Tamil plantation workers. The dispute brought to the surface prejudices and stereotypes that Malayalis had towards Tamils but which had hitherto been subdued.

It gave these prejudices greater agency in the structuring of socio-political relations with Tamils and especially Dalits, who are the particular objects of Malayali prejudice. The dispute, in the same way as the crisis, is part of the continual formation of realities for the workers.

The crisis and the dam dispute have had repercussions beyond the plantation context as they draw on cultural elements such as ethnic stereotypes and prejudices which were functional in everyday life prior to the crisis. That is to say that the crisis as an event 'likely reveals the social and political forces that engage in the generation or production of social life' (Kapferer 2010, 2), although its importance lies in being a 'dynamic process that in itself constitutes an original structuring of relations' (Kapferer 2010, 12). In view of that, I observe that the situation of Tamils in Kerala during the crisis period makes explicit two aspects related to their marginal life. Firstly, the various miseries suffered by Tamils in the period of tension reveal the hidden domains of prejudices and discrimination they face for being a 'Dalit cum underclass cum linguistic minority'. Secondly, this discrimination against Tamils exposes the imprints of unrecognised discriminatory processes within the claimed egalitarian system that marks Kerala's projection as an 'enlightened' state.[15]

Following the Manchester situational analysis, I observe that various social categories (of greater or lesser inclusion) such as Tamil, Dalit or specific caste identity (Dalit is an inclusive identity covering a differentiation of outcastes), or class association, become relevant or irrelevant in the structuring of social relations according to the logic of the situation. The logic of the situation in the relatively closed system of plantation production is such that Tamil or Dalit has modest meaning or relevance. In the outside field of socio-economic relations, however, and as I describe in the coming chapters, such identities are of acute relevance. In addition to paying attention to the situated meaning and contextualisation of the crisis and conflict, I also focus on how these situated events generate new discourses of hegemony and power but also new modes of resistance (see Foucault 1972, 24–6). For example, the circulation of rumour and gossip about the crisis and the identification of the plantation Tamils as the stigmatised Tamils during the conflict challenges a discourse of infinite continuity of the plantation system. This situational analysis approach that focuses on crisis as lived experience offers possibilities to critique a political-economic understanding of crises that treats crisis as an aberration to the structural readjustments in the economy, which could be resolved through analysing and deciphering it statistically (Mbembe 1995).[16]

The tea belt

The Peermade tea belt, known as the teapot of Kerala, is one of the most important tea-producing regions in South India. Located on the southern part of Western Ghats,[17] the tea belt comprises 36 tea estates with more than 10,000 hectares of tea bushes strung around the hill town of Peermade in Idukki, the second largest district of Kerala state. Peermade is known outside Kerala for its proximity to the Periyar Wildlife Sanctuary and to Sabarimala pilgrimage centre.[18] The tea belt is located close to a prominent border point between the states of Kerala and Tamil Nadu. During the pre-independence period, the princely rulers of Travancore had their summer palace in the tea belt. Its 'wild and exotic' landscape makes it an important tourist destination. The first 10 websites that appear in response to 'Peermade' in the Google search engine are websites designed for tourists. Peermade is presented as a popular hill station with beautiful tea gardens that tourists should visit.[19]

Despite the continuing importance of Peermade as a tourist destination, the region is popularly seen in Kerala as one of cultural and social backwardness. Widely accepted opinion in India is that civilisation took root in the fertile plains, whereas the forest and hill regions harbour 'primitive' tribal populations or else those of low social origin. This view is as much supported by common prejudice as it may be by scholarship because Dalits and Adivasis form the major share of the demographic composition of the belt. Around 60 per cent of the population in the Peermade *taluk* (an administrative unit of a district) are from Dalit/Adivasi groups, which also includes a large portion of plantation workers (National Census 2001). The remaining 40 per cent comprises other communities who have migrated to the Peermade region in the wake of the plantation development.[20] This means that those who inhabit the Peermade region are either the indigenous population (Adivasi community) or people brought to the region as part of the plantation development. The higher proportion of people from low-ranked communities among the inhabitants of the Peermade tea belt triggers the opinion that it is an area occupied by the backward, primitive and uncivilised members of Kerala society. While the region's economic backwardness and lack of infrastructural facilities relative to the plain is a fact, the stigmatisation of people from the Peermade region is more often the effect of social prejudice having to do with values of a caste and class nature.

There is no railway transportation in the entire Idukki district. The nearest railway station is located 55 miles away from the tea belt in the town of Kottayam. This is in contrast to the comparatively developed lowland

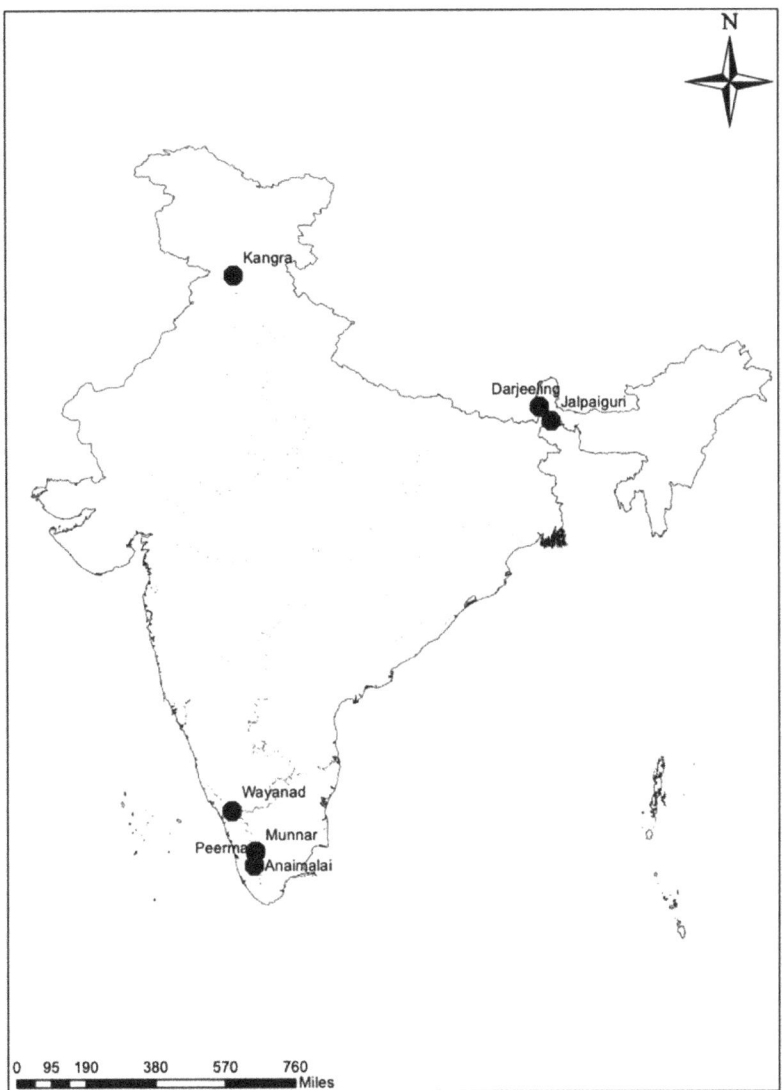

Map 0.1: Location of major tea belts in India. Source: Author.

region in Kerala. In the words of one of my informants, a young man from a valley town who pursued his bachelor's degree in an elite private college,[21] 'Peermade is a nice place to visit, but not to live in forever'. The reasons he cited include its hilly terrain, chilly weather, lack of proximity to urban centres, rural atmosphere and poor infrastructural/technical resources such as frequent (electric) power shortages and modest internet connectivity. It is no wonder then that a government posting to the region is often regarded as a bureaucratic disciplinary matter – a punishment for offences such as corruption. This stigma of the highland should be noted as paradoxical in Kerala's context as the gap between urban and rural in Kerala is the least pronounced of any state in India and thus the rhetoric of stereotypical differences attached to regions as developed or underdeveloped is least expected to dominate the popular culture.

The real distance between the towns and the tea estates is only 8 miles on average, but the extremely poor roads and transportation systems between the towns and the tea estates significantly decrease the accessibility of the tea estates to their satellite town. The tea estates are isolated from the local towns by having the workers' settlements in the very middle or on the frontier of the plantation, which further increases the distance between towns and the workers' settlements. The social life in the local towns of the tea belt should be understood as an elaboration of the plantation system (Thompson 1975). These satellite towns are products of the plantation development in the region and very much reflect its character as an auxiliary to plantation life; this means the periphery (towns) acts as a marketplace and a gateway for the plantation workers to the outside world. Plantations are a total institution-like regime that distinguishes plantation life from life on its periphery. In contrast, life in the periphery represents another world of an ordinary village or a semi-urban township that is marked by small land holdings

Figure 0.1: A tea estate in the Peermade tea belt

and heterogeneous occupations and that, in part, has organically evolved socio-economic institutions which are missing in the plantation system. Besides, it is life in the periphery that shows plantation workers an alternative life situation, or what is regarded as 'ordinary' life in the larger society outside. In other words, it is the periphery of the plantations that demonstrates that plantation life is peripheral to the larger social life.

Outline

In the chapters that follow, it becomes clearer how the colonial *race-making character* of plantations (Thompson 1975) becomes instrumental when the global economic developments connected with and intensified by existing cultural processes lead to the continuing abjection of plantation Tamils. In doing so, the chapters help us to conceptualise the processes by which plantation capitalism continues to produce the *imperial debris* in the global South with its 'racialised relations of allocations and appropriations' (Stoler 2008, 193). Accordingly, plantations are imperial formations that are continuously in the process of becoming. Chapter 1 recounts life within the total institution of the plantation before the crisis with a focus on the internalisation of the plantation order. It would be impossible to understand the nature of the abandonment without a sense of the plantation production order and its social relations before the crisis. Chapter 2 focuses on the struggles of the workers who were forced to seek other means of livelihood in the abandoned plantations. It examines the structural challenges they faced and the strategies they devised as they moved in and out of plantations in search of work. Chapter 3 moves on to the struggle of the retirees when their gratuity payments were deferred citing the economic crisis. For the retirees, the pay-out was the only means to retain respect, sustain kinship relations and engage with everyday sociality in the plantations. In other words, the pay-out was vital to fight the alienation resulting from being a Dalit-Tamil-underclass retiree in the plantations.

Chapter 4 follows the plantation youth to the immediate outskirts of the plantations, to the industrial belt of Coimbatore-Tirupur and to their ancestral villages in Tamil Nadu. It details their routine strategies to escape the crisis and how they eventually get trapped in the caste and ethnic oppression as they move to the cities in Tamil Nadu and Kerala. I argue that, for the Dalits, the economic and social mobilities need to be understood as distinct processes, as attaining economic mobility does not guarantee social mobility. Chapter 5 shows how the revival of a dispute between the states of Tamil Nadu and Kerala over the control and safety of the Mullaperiyar Dam further exacerbated the suffering of Tamil workers affected by the economic crisis. The rediscovery of Malayali nationalism (Kerala nationalism) in the dispute context (defined in opposition to Tamils or Tamil Nadu nationalism) has had damaging consequences for the plantation youth who sought work outside the tea belt. The ethnic stereotyping of lower-class/outcaste Tamils encapsulated in the inferior-*ising* ethnic slur *Pāndi* found more explicit use than ever before. The dispute became a decisive moment in which the prejudice which was relatively submerged was brought to the surface by the dispute.

Chapter 6 examines the changing social relations among the workers who continue to live in the plantations amid the current economic crisis. I examine the reconfiguration of social relations by discussing how the crisis led to the disintegration and destabilisation of the solidarity that existed previously. This fracturing of social relations involves in part the further alienation of workers from each other and thus aggravates the marginal and marginalised existence that has often resulted from the closure of the plantations. Chapter 7 explores gossip and rumours related to the economic crisis. I focus on that particular gossip in which the state of Kerala, the trade unions and the plantation management were blamed for the depressed condition of the plantation workers. I concentrate on the spread of the rumour concerning the possible takeover of the plantations by new companies. I observe that gossip and rumours in the crisis context have distinct effects when it comes to the question of resistance and accommodation. In this context, rumour is an effective instrument for the control and disciplining of workers. Conversely, gossip functions as a form and agent of resistance, which further shows that the workers were conscious of their exploitation.

Chapter 8 follows the labour regime under the new companies that took over some of the deserted tea estates in 2012. These companies, under the disguise of the crisis, deployed newer strategies of accumulation by replacing Tamil labourers with more vulnerable seasonal migrant workers from poorer regions of central and eastern India. All these migrant workers are maintained illegally as casual labour in order to cut the cost of production and undermine the power of labour. This chapter delves into the dynamics of the new labour regime in the tea belt by focusing on the newly recruited tribal workers from the central Indian state of Jharkhand.

Chapter 9, in conclusion, reflects on two interrelated questions that emerge out of the ethnography of the economic crisis: firstly, why were the workers abandoned by both the state and the tea companies to face the crisis? Secondly, what makes it possible for the plantation companies to just walk away from the plantation business with total impunity? By reflecting on these two questions, the Chapter 9 specifically looks at the stigmatised positioning of the workers as Tamil-speaking Dalits in the larger categorical relations in the Indian society on the one hand, and the possible economic rationalities and a supportive state bureaucracy that the tea companies rely on for the abandonment of the workers on the other. These are the interrelated processes that legitimise the abandonment of the workers and the impunity of capital in the crisis context. At the end, the chapter places the tea plantations and their workforces within the broader system of neoliberal production, the corporate state and stigmatised identities. The Appendix provides a short history of the Peermade tea belt.

Notes

1. Peermade means hill of Peer and is named after a Sufi saint, Peer Muhammad. Original names of the tea belt and a few other places are retained to identify the region. However, I have mostly used pseudonyms for the estates and the plantation companies to protect the identities of my informants.
2. A similar situation could be seen in the case of other plantation crops such as rubber, where the availability of cheaper as well as synthetic rubber from South-East Asia resulted in the collapse of rubber production in India. Therefore, the tea crisis can be viewed as part of a larger crisis in agrarian capitalism in the global South.
3. For instance, the government of Kerala passed a resolution demanding proficiency in the Malayalam language as a basic requirement for government jobs, which effectively closed government employment to Tamil-speaking plantation youth.
4. The caste system is mainly attributed to the social and ritual positions of different categories of people in relation to each other in Hindu cosmology. For major anthropological discussions on caste, see Srinivas (1952, 1966), Marriott (1955), Béteille (1965), Dumont (1980), Raheja (1988), Ilaiah (1996) and Dirks (2001).
5. Sara Besky (2008, 126–8) reported similar developments in north-eastern India, where the powerful planters' associations evade state control and get fair trade certifications even when basic conditions for fair trade are not met, such as safe working conditions and decent wages.
6. Mythri Jegathesan (2019) mentioned the economic crisis in the Sri Lankan tea plantations, but she did not engage with it in detail.
7. This covered all 136 labour households of the tea lines: 123 Dalit households (82 Paraiyar, 37 Pallar, 4 Arunthathiyar) and 13 general caste households.
8. Plantations were instrumental in the emergence of modern capitalism across the world. Anthropologists have written on how the industrial revolution was made possible through plantation capitalism in the global South (Mintz 1985; Wolf 1982, 335). In England, the commercialisation of agriculture and the dispossession of rural communities through enclosures was an important development that led to the growth of modern capitalism (Thompson 1963).
9. From Karl Marx onwards, scholars have examined the connection between capitalism and the endless crises that it generates. Marx (1981 [1894]) argued that crisis is inherent to the logic of capitalism, which opens up its internal contradictions, leading to its decline (see Schroyer (1972) for an analysis of Marx's theory of crisis). Following Marx, Rosa Luxemburg (2013 [1911]) examined market speculations, international credit systems and variations in production leading to a series of economic crises in the West throughout the nineteenth and early twentieth centuries. Drawing on this history of the crises, Luxemburg (2003 [1913]) too argued that capitalism would collapse, although she disagreed with Marx on its trajectory. For her, the non-capitalist economies (mainly the colonies) would be brought into capitalism, reach their high point and then collapse (see Koselleck (2006) for an etymological history of crises). Colonial plantations in India are clear examples of how non-capitalist societies were

brought into the capitalist system. However, we are yet to see the decline of capitalism in contemporary plantation society and beyond, where capitalism has pervaded all kinds of social relations and bodily practices (Deleuze 1992; Hardt and Negri 2000).

10 The Indian tea crisis unfolded in a similar fashion to that in the Zambian copper belt, where the slump in the production of copper effectively closed down the mines and resulted in massive unemployment, where a similar 'comparative advantage' logic of capitalism proved to be disastrous (Ferguson 1999, 239–40), not only to the workers but to the entire Zambian economy.

11 Rebecca Empson (2020) calls for paying attention to ethnographic heterogeneity as a way to challenge the homogeneous explanations that rationalise poverty and inequality as integral to neoliberal austerity measures.

12 Some of the concerns raised through categorical oppression in the book echo literature on intersectionality rooted in black feminist literature and critical race theory. However, categorical oppression as an idea is developed from the anthropological literature of Mitchell, Bourgois and others because it speaks directly to the social analysis of the migrant labour identity and their positioning within categorical relations in the host society. This anthropological approach was also well in advance of the otherwise highly influential concept of intersectionality in examining the interplay of identity categories.

13 This argument on caste does not underestimate the significance that capital had achieved since the second half of the twentieth century and the subsumption of the social into the capital, as highlighted by Karl Polanyi (2001 [1944]) and Louis Dumont (1977). However, as pointed out in the literature on racial capitalism (Robinson 1983), capitalism not only took root in the racial society but also advanced racial inequality through the racial division of labour. Similarly, capitalism in India developed within a caste society by employing and advancing the caste hierarchy (Shah et al. 2018).

14 There are differences within the Manchester School on the orientation they wanted to take in situation analysis, particularly between Max Gluckman and Clyde Mitchell (Kapferer 2010, 8), where Gluckman was more sympathetic to the consideration of social processes as systems, which allies more with a structural-functionalist position. In contrast to Gluckman, Mitchell conceived social processes as more open and continuously changing. My own orientation is closer to Mitchell's conceptualisation of social processes, while I also think that Gluckman's insistence on the representational character is significant, as also recognised by Mitchell (1956).

15 The Kerala development model was also significantly implicated in the persistence of Kerala's enlightenment ideology. This is because the Kerala development model is often attributed to the egalitarian developmental policies of Kerala, particularly to land reform. I elaborate on Kerala's claim of egalitarian ideology and its relation to the Tamil minority in Chapter 9.

16 Veena Das (1995) discussed the anthropology of critical events with a focus on India. She explored events that had transformed the national political scene, such as India's partition and the Hindu–Muslim violence that followed it. This is different from the participatory observation of events in micro-contexts that I am concerned with in this book. Participatory observation and contextualisation of events in their micro-contexts are central to the situated meanings of the events discussed in this book.

17 The Western Ghats are a series of mountain ranges approximately 1,600 kilometres long located in the western part of India. They are home to almost all the tea plantation districts in South India. This includes the tea plantations in Nilgiri in Tamil Nadu, Wayanad and Nelliampathy in the Malabar region, Ponmudi Mountains in the most southern part of the Western Ghats and the Kannan Devan Hills of Munnar.

18 Sabarimala is a famous Hindu pilgrimage centre for Lord Ayyappa devotees. It is one of the largest pilgrimage centres in the world, with an estimated 40 million devotees visiting every year.

19 Presenting Peermade as an idyllic tourist destination disguises the abjection and poverty among the plantation workers of the region. In tourist brochures, tea estates are deceptively called tea gardens (Daniel 1996).

20 Dalits form most of the plantation labour force in the Peermade tea belt. Managers, clerical staff and technical operators are mostly from the Syrian Christian, Nayar, Ezhava and Nadar communities. Members of these communities also own shops in the satellite towns of the tea belt.

21 Peermade and adjoining areas have highly respected educational institutions, but these are meant for students from affluent families from the lowland region. This is in parallel to famous international schools in other hill stations, such as Ooty and Kodaikanal, that cater for children from affluent families all over the world.

1
Pre-crisis: the making of a moral order

During our long conversations, the workers often portrayed the tea companies' abandonment of the plantations – and therefore of the workers – as a 'moral failure'. They explained how 'sincere and hardworking' they were during the heyday of plantation production. They used to work extra hours during high seasons of tea plucking to meet the demand from the company. Such exploitative relations were concealed in a discourse that the company's profit would improve the workers' situation – or at least that was the moral expectation. This expectation did not come from an emotional attachment to their labour or the plantations but from an implicit assumption of a subtle social contract between the company and the workers.

  The workers occasionally organised strikes demanding better wages and an increase in bonus rates. However, their protests for higher bonus rates, which were organised around the same time every year, often ended with the workers agreeing to the company's decision to offer the lowest bonus rate legally possible. The company sometimes accepted the workers' demands as communicated through the unions. However, the workers alleged that most often, this small success by the unions was part and parcel of the reproduction of the company itself as the union leaders who acted as the power brokers in the tea belt often turned out to be corrupt (Raj 2019). This reproduction of the production order paved the way for the imagination of a moral economy. It was not only the workers' subjugation but also their occasional victory over the company that was part of a moral relationship. In this sense, the moral relationship could be understood as an aspect of the reproduction of hegemony (Palomera and Vetta 2016). At the same time, this moral relationship in the plantations was integral to the larger social hierarchy (of caste) and capitalist class order that made the very establishment of the colonial plantations possible across the world (Bourgois 1989).

The discourse on this moral relationship was dominated and led by the group of workers who benefited more from the company in the form of light labour and promotion to semi-skilled work, such as field watchmen and supervisors. The argument is not that every worker in the plantations subscribed to these moral relationships and that the workers did not recognise the exploitative dimensions of plantation production. There were a few 'everyday rebels' who explicitly challenged the exploitative dimensions of the plantation system as a form of 'immediate struggle' (Narotzky and Smith 2006). The management often put them down by assigning them arduous tasks in the field and denying them welfare provisions whenever they could. The other workers also often talked to each other about the exploitation, yet those conversations did not translate into tangible actions.

The workers' complaint about a moral failure of the plantations in the crisis context can be understood only if we pay attention to relations that cut across the formal and informal dualities, as argued by Polanyi and others (see Palomera and Vetta 2016). These values and practices that facilitated the production of that moral relationship are also incidentally instruments of the reproduction of the plantation system. As Eric Wolf noted (1966, 2), 'the formal framework of economic and political power exists alongside or intermingled with the various other kinds of informal structure which are interstitial, supplementary, parallel to it'. Based on oral history and my observations before the crisis, this chapter examines the processes that reinforced the plantation order before the crisis,[1] specifically the insulated frontier, occupational hierarchy,[2] graded patronage and symbolic power,[3] spaciality, appropriation of the caste system and the intermediation of unions. These processes feed into each other and cut across the standard division of formal and informal practices. The translational nature of the processes emerges from the very nature of the plantation system with the workers living within their workplace. Most of the sections are based on the Hill Valley estate, although the description, I would argue, applies to the entire tea belt to some extent. This chapter also helps the reader get a sense of plantation life before the weakening of the plantation system and understand the extent to which the crisis caused a rupture in the workers' lives.

The insulated frontier

Plantations in the Peermade tea belt are apt examples of what Foucault (1980) referred to as spaces of enclosure with a complex disciplinary regime and a punitive apparatus. The plantation communities that I discuss – until the crisis wrought by neoliberal policies – were relatively independent socio-political enclaves within the larger society of Kerala and India. Most aspects of the plantation workers' lives were defined in relation to a political order structured by the plantation management. Indeed, the plantations are best described as a state within a state (Baak 1997) or a mimesis of the colonial state (Chatterjee 2001, 5), where all dimensions of the workers' existence were subject to plantation management control and regulation.[4] Further, the insulated nature of the plantations, coupled with a clear-cut division of authority and responsibility distinguished in terms of origin, social background and lifestyle (Baak 1997, 119), contributed to the plantation society assuming the form of a total institution (Goffman 1961; Smith 1967), where the plantation system of production primarily conditions everyday life.[5] This enclaving of plantation society also may have facilitated the shaping of a habitus (Bourdieu 1977) that sustained the reproduction of a rigid and stratified order of plantation society. Plantation society, in general, is confined within itself, and the social order of plantation life is conditioned by the all-encompassing system of plantation production that entered into all aspects of life, even those not directly connected to the production processes (Smith 1967; Genovese 1976). This peculiar insularity of the plantation society is what underpinned the formation of graded patronage that is consistent with the plantation class order.

In this total institution-like system, workers are denied the capacity to move out from the insulated space and are secluded from changes overtaking socio-economic circumstances in outside realities. The only connection to the outside world from the plantation is the satellite towns. The poor condition of the roads that connect the estates with the satellite towns and the inadequate transportation facilities further restrict the movement of the plantation workers to the satellite towns. At the same time, the insularity of the plantations was not simply an effect of the nature of the plantation economy. The insularity was exacerbated by an outside cultural imagination of caste that defined the plantation workers as low in the caste hierarchy. This spatial insulation and cultural alienation placed restrictions on the development of a powerful social and political consciousness among plantation workers to change their situation, unlike other sectors of the Kerala population. Consequently, opportunities open to other communities and groups in Kerala, often mediated by state intervention, are far more restricted for the plantation populations. The socio-geographical isolation of the workers in the Peermade belt operates to discourage or reduce the likelihood of organised political action or resistance in the plantations.

The rigid and internalised order of plantation production is noted in other plantation belts, for instance, in the banana plantations of Costa Rica (Bourgois 1989). It can be further likened to that described for mineworkers in Bolivia (Nash 1979) and in colonial Zambia (Mitchell 1956; Epstein 1958), whose social and political existence was defined by the mine authorities.[6] The major difference is that whereas in the Zambian case the mineworkers might be regarded as an African labour aristocracy, the tea plantation workers were/are a labouring underclass. The social and political factors that rendered them an underclass further intensified their dependence on and subjection to the regimen of the plantation industrial order and further operated to seal them off from the wider society. Of course, the plantation communities are nonetheless entangled in the wider socio-political field that extends around the plantations and whose life processes are not determined, even though they may be affected by the existence of the plantations and their communities. Plantation workers participate in this field – as persons of devalued status – and have come to depend on their relations with it as a function of the neoliberal changes affecting the plantations.

Although they live in the insulated space of plantations relatively sealed off from the surrounding realities of mainstream Kerala society, the dynamics of plantation life are not restricted to the insulated space, nor does it follow that its divisiveness or solidarity is explicable solely by forces that are internal to the community (Martínez 2007). Therefore, the insulated space and the rigid production relations obstruct rather than prevent the intrusion of outside realities and thus operate to produce a relatively closed-off system with few alternatives to imagine beyond the closed system. What I concentrate upon here is the social order of the plantations as conditioned by the plantation industrial system. Plantation systems in various historical periods and situations (colonial, postcolonial and neoliberal) had their own forms of control, both inherited and invented, but in a continuous variation (a process of *poesies* in Deleuzian terms). The forms of control discussed here, including spatiality, should be understood as elements of ideological values (Dumont 1980) aimed at the collective identity of workers and primarily shared by them in the engagement of their own hegemonic control.

Occupational hierarchy

Tea plantations in the belt were marked by a strict hierarchical ladder of authority (of power relations in the productive order) with the owner at the top, workers at the bottom and positions of greater to lesser authority and power strung between the two extremes (the absolute power of the owner at the top and the powerless worker at the bottom). The power gradient included the owner at the apex, followed by the manager, superintendents, field officers, factory managers, supervisors, office clerks, technical (skilled) workers and unskilled workers. The occupational hierarchy within the enclosed plantation is the basis upon which the required power relations are reproduced. A significant aspect of the occupational hierarchy in the postcolonial plantations is that there are too many internal divisions among the workers based on where they work (factory, field or staff bungalows), permanent or temporary, and male or female. These elaborate divisions run from the top of the management to the bottom among the workers. At the same time, the complex internal divisions appear cohesive and integrated from the point of view of the production relations.

In the Hill Valley estate, the person who managed the company was called the group manager (GM). The GM was followed by the managers of the different estates (the divided units of the plantation), and all of them were men. Although the GM was the apex authority in the plantation order, it was the estate manager who held the real authority since he was the one who lived on the estate and directly administered the daily production processes. He was assisted by two superintendents, each of whom had responsibilities for the production process in the field and the factory, respectively. The superintendents were usually young management/agriculture graduates appointed for the purpose of training and gaining work experience on the plantation. In addition to assisting the manager, their function included mediating the relations between the field/factory officers and the manager. They also took over the managerial responsibilities whenever the manager took leave or went on a business trip. The staff below the plantation director and the manager were divided based on their roles at the factory or in the field, the two domains of plantation production. This excludes office staff who take care of the paperwork concerning both the factory and the tea fields.

The field and the factory were under the direct control of the factory manager and field officer, respectively.[7] The role of the field officer in the entire production process was much more significant as he was also an administrative officer, a representative of the company to deal with workers' grievances and any dispute among workers within or outside the workplace that obstructed the plantation order. The field officer was responsible for maintaining the plantation infrastructure, which comprises the maintenance of buildings and the electrical and water supply to the estate. Below them in the class order were office clerks, who were followed by supervisors in the field and factory.[8] Supervisors (*Kankāni*), as the title implies, engaged in full-time supervision of the production process in the factories and the tea fields. They were also responsible for ensuring the workers' attendance in the workplace and for following the schedule. They also assisted the field officer in preparing the wage list and maintaining the attendance register. The supervisors mediated the relationship between the workers and the field officers. The supervisors were followed by the technical or 'skilled' workers, including mechanics in the factory, drivers, plumbers, carpenters, postmen and electricians. These 'skilled' workers and supervisors were treated as an upper class within the working classes. During the colonial period, they were called 'learned men'. The workers employed as housekeepers in the staff houses were considered 'skilled' workers.

At the same time, the workers at the bottom of the plantation structure were treated as 'unskilled' despite the sophisticated skill they possessed for the work in the fields and factories, such as tea plucking and sorting the powders in the factory. There are further categories within the group of 'unskilled' wage labourers, and the foremost one is the gender-based division of labour. Women were predominantly field workers plucking the tea leaves; men were employed as labourers in the fields or the factories. The women worked more hours than the men as the latter were often excused for one or two hours if the assigned work demanded arduous physical effort. However, the perception and categorisation of women's work in the plantation as 'soft work' facilitated their exploitation. Although workers could interchange workplaces, in most cases they tended to remain as either field or factory workers throughout their employment life. Factory work was divided into shifts and was done mainly by men, but the factories had been shut down in many estates. The workers were paid for an eight-hour working shift but had to work overtime during high plucking months. Their work was further differentiated in accordance with whether they were casual (*kaikāsu*), temporary (*vārthāl*) or permanent (*varushathāl*) and according to their place of work – field or factory. Table 1.1 provides the provisions for the various classes in the tea plantations.

Table 1.1: Types of contracts of tea plantation workers, Hill Valley estate, Kerala

Permanent	Temporary	Casual
Minimum wage.	Minimum wage.	Minimum wage.
Work is guaranteed throughout the year.	Work is not guaranteed. Any work in addition to that done by permanent workers goes to temporary workers.	Work is not guaranteed. Work when the supply of permanent and temporary workers is below the demand.
Eligible for provident fund.	Eligible for provident fund.	Not eligible for provident fund.
Eligible for medical care outside the plantations. The company will refund the medical bill if the company doctor approves it. Eligible for paid medical leave.	Not eligible for medical care outside the plantations. Can use local medical facilities within plantations, if available. No paid medical leave.	Not eligible for medical care outside the plantations. Can use local medical facilities within the plantations, if available. No paid medical leave.
Housing guaranteed.	Housing is not guaranteed. Will be considered if houses are available after providing for permanent workers.	Housing is not guaranteed. Will be considered only if houses are available after providing for permanent and temporary workers. In most cases, they must share with other casual workers' families.
Eligible for an annual bonus.	Not eligible for the bonus.	Not eligible for the bonus.
Eligible for retirement benefits (gratuity).	Not eligible for retirement benefits.	Not eligible for retirement benefits.
Eligible for weather protection including blanket and umbrella. Also eligible for free work tools, including bamboo basket and plucking machine.	Not eligible for weather protection and tools.	Not eligible for weather protection and tools.

Permanent workers were those workers who were guaranteed work at least at the minimum wage throughout the year and were entitled to welfare, including housing, medical care and sick leave, an annual bonus, a provident fund and retirement benefits. Temporary workers were not guaranteed work throughout the year but still lived within the tea estate and worked during the peak tea-plucking season. They were not eligible for retirement benefits, bonuses, medical care or sick leave, but they could access the provident fund. They were given housing that permanent workers did not take or were allowed to build small huts next to the permanent workers' settlement. The position of the casual workforce is the worst. The Plantations Labour Act allowed the employment of casual workers only for occasional work outside the everyday process of production (for instance, logging). Across India, the recruitment of casual workers for regular production/mundane tasks in factories or plantations employing more than 25 people is strictly illegal. Still, these rules are breached across the country and increasingly in the plantations. Since the employment of casual labour for mundane tasks is unlawful, and they also do not exist in the official registry of the company, they were in a most precarious situation and often had to find work outside the plantation as well. Another significant difference between the temporary and casual workers is that the latter were not eligible for the provident fund nor any social security benefits. However, even the permanent work on the plantation does not allow anything more than a precarious reproduction of life. Although they are regular permanent workers, they do not fall into the elite labour or aristocracy of labour like those in the public sector industries in other parts of India (Parry 2020). The wage rate of the permanent workers was much lower than the average wage for manual labour outside the plantation.

None of these workers were provided with protective gear such as gloves and masks, even for spraying pesticides. Many tea companies do not follow the safety standards issued by the Tea Board of India in taking protective measures for the workers. The women tea pluckers who work in the open tea fields develop serious health issues over, for many, their four decades of work in the plantations. They had to carry tens of kilograms of tea leaves on their heads on the steep slopes throughout the heavy monsoon and hot summer seasons. There are no latrine facilities. Often they had to have their lunch in the open fields, even when it rained. Only a very few tea fields have weighing rooms. They were exposed to leech bites during the monsoon leading to bleeding, itching and burning. Snakes that hide under the tea bushes are also a major threat to the tea-plucking women.

Caste in class

Under this rigid plantation production system, aspects of social processes outside the plantation system have become transformed to fit into the class order of the plantation production, as in the case of the caste system. In the Peermade tea belt, caste as a ritually structured system is redefined in the plantation productive system in that caste is perceived as an occupational category determined by the economic order. This was how colonial officials and entrepreneurs conceived of caste (Dirks 2001), and it was such a conception that was the logic underpinning the recruitment of indentured labourers. Such a construction perceived caste as equivalent to class identity or status, a culturally specific example of social stratification. This denied caste as a dimension of a ritually defined hierarchical system unrelated to the stratification system based on an economically grounded political order (see Dumont 1980). That is to say, caste identity was taken out of its ritual and cosmological context, and the role of caste in the plantation became distinct from its original function of maintaining a Brahmanical caste order. Caste in the plantation was an atrophied form which is not endogamous and had no connotations of ritual purity or pollution (Jayawardena 1963). So caste in the plantation was very different from the ritually defined hierarchical caste system within which economic functions are nested.

Within such a class order, as further discussed in Chapter 6, caste identity did not yield much superior status in everyday interactions in the plantation because the plantation system itself is the social system in the plantation, where everyday interactions were conditioned by the production process itself. This means that, although Nadars, Vellalas and Ezhavas are treated as higher castes when compared with Dalits, they did not enjoy a superior status within the social domain of workers' society compared with the village society outside the plantations. This is the same in the graded caste hierarchy among the Dalits. While Pallar and Paraiyar castes are considered superior to Arunthathiyar castes within the caste hierarchy among Dalits, the higher Dalit caste status does not confer much social power because the Arunthathiyar does not acknowledge them. Such egalitarian practice is integral to the logic of the determination of social relations in the productive system of the plantations. For example, although the Dalit workforce belongs to different castes and sub-castes, they have to live together in the *layam* (meaning houses arranged in lines) and draw water from the same pipe.

However, within the regime of labour extraction and control, there existed forms of hierarchically placing human beings within the system based on various identity categories, mainly caste, gender and language. The caste system in its abstract form was a significant factor in bringing different caste groups into the plantation and creating the occupational order of the plantation hierarchy (Hollup 1994). Most of the managerial staff are from higher-caste Hindu communities or are affluent Syrian Christians and are mainly from the Malayalam-speaking majority in Kerala. The workers are primarily from Tamil-speaking Dalit communities (known as 'Scheduled' in the state nomenclature). This was evident particularly in the postcolonial phase when the caste, in its atrophied form, was very much present in the plantation class structure, with Brahmins, Nairs and Syrian Christians[9] at the top as the owners/managers;[10] most lower castes – such as Ezhavas/Nadars and Vellalas – and lower-class Christians in the middle as superintendents, field officers, clerks or supervisors; and Dalits such as Pallar, Paraiyar and Arunthathiyar and Dalit Christians at the very bottom as supervisors and wage workers.[11] To be sure, while caste position as such did not yield much power, the class order in the plantation was roughly consistent with the caste hierarchy (Jayawardena 1963), and the status differentiation between classes was also a status differentiation between castes.

The by-product of such employment of caste in plantation production is that the tea companies in the Peermade tea belt treated the plantation Tamil Dalits not only as a proletariat, as a factor of tea production, but also as lesser human beings of a different kind. While such classifications were part of commercialised tea production, they often exceeded their role within the plantation production system by reproducing multiple alienations of the workers. This also explains why different forms of labour extraction that often coexisted – such as slavery, serfdom, indentured and free – were based on racial identity, for example, in the Caribbean, as explained by Sidney Mintz (1978).

Caste consciousness has been central in mediating kinship and familial relations among the workers in the tea belt. However, the force of caste identity was transformed in the plantations compared with how caste mediated social relations in the workers' native villages in Tamil Nadu.[12] In Peermade, people of the same sub-caste greet each other with kinship terms meant for blood relatives, which is not usually done when referring to people of other castes/sub-castes. As Louis Dumont (1953) explained, the Dravidian kinship terminologies are centred around cross-cousin marriage relations, such as *Māmā/Athai* (meaning mother's brother/father's sister or the husband of father's sister/wife of mother's brother) or

Chithappa/Chithi (meaning father's younger brother or the husband of mother's younger sister/mother's younger sister or wife of father's younger brother). This act of reformulating caste identity outside the workplace is an example of the communalisation of caste, a process of attempting to differentiate oneself from others to enhance social status or prestige. As Chandra Jayawardena (1963) pointed out in the context of Indian labourers in British Guiana, a high caste can add to, and a lower caste can detract from, the prestige of a status achieved on other grounds. Therefore, the values of caste ritual status were symbolically engaged in affirming class position.[13] To be clear, the traditional values of identity categories such as caste still have force in the wider society, but they have been appropriated into the system of class relations in the plantations. This employment of identity categories in plantation production rationalised the class order. However, the economic crisis and the weakening of the plantation system reinvented and intensified the caste hierarchy among the plantation workers, as will be discussed in other chapters.

Graded patronage

Patronage in the Indian context is graded and is closely linked to the caste system and gender hierarchies, which could be traced historically, for example, through the *jajmani* system in India. In the plantations, patronage may be understood as *relational morality* (Piliavsky 2014), upon which the managerial staff and the workers' community are related to each other. Loyalty was important in the plantation order. Whenever the workers opposed the current regime, they glorified the past ones, including that of the whites. The workers often told me that the functioning of the plantations was well organised when the 'white men were around'. The whites were the invisible patrons for the plantations and a constant reference point for the ideal functioning of the plantation system and the patronage associated with it.

In the Peermade tea belt, the graded patronage is defined by the status difference between the layers of top-level managers, managerial staff, technical/mechanical staff, supervisors and the workers. The status differentiation is manifested in the graded patronage, where the patronage is distributed across various groups within the plantation production. The graded patronage in the Peermade tea belt is collective in nature as the workers are under the unequally distributed patronage of the whole managerial staff. This graded patronage is a major element in the generation of the relations required to transfigure the exploitative economy into a moral one. However, the patronage was more like an impersonal system in which a large number of people were involved as part of the sophisticated capitalist plantation system (Wolf 1982).

The graded hierarchy of caste is very much reflected in the graded patronage in the plantations. Top managerial staff had considerable prestige and symbolic power since they were in a position of absolute domination. They commanded the destinies of those below them in the insulated system of the plantations. In this insulated social world, the top managerial staff had been virtual lords of all they surveyed, and they were treated almost like nobility. The senior manager was called *Periya Durai* ('the master chief'), the assistant manager was *Chinna Durai* ('little chief'), the field officer was *Periya-ayya*, ('the big master'), the assistant field officer was *Kolunthayya* ('the field master') and the office superintendent was *Periyabisayya*, ('the master of the office'). All other office clerks and factory staff were referred to as *Ayya*, a Tamil word that means master/sir and denotes high admiration. The word *Ayya* also refers to father, pointing to patronage and domination, which facilitated this exploitative plantation system (Hollup 1994). What is more noteworthy is that the spouses of all the managerial staff were referred to as *Amma*, literally mother, which goes well with the patronage of the plantation system. Even the children of these staff were highly respected. The children of the staff often inherited their managerial staff positions. These 'inherited positions' helped the managerial staff to solidify their positions and to reproduce the plantation order. These hierarchical relations within the well-defined class order illustrate its marked continuity with its colonial past (Macfarlane and Macfarlane 2004). It also shows how the workers are made into subjects of the plantation regime that naturalises or objectivises their existence as tea workers (see Foucault 1982).

All the managerial staff, irrespective of their rank in the class order, received servants to do household work. They received butlers, gardeners and workers to take care of their cows. A servant was assigned to go around the staff houses to milk these cows. Whenever the water supply was obstructed, for example, due to an electrical problem, separate servants were assigned to fetch water from the common well. Since the regular jobs such as butler and gardener are considered 'skilled work' and the workers would earn a bit more money than the 'unskilled' workers, they would compete to win the managerial staff's patronage and secure those jobs.

Most of the facilities provided to the staff represented much more than just welfare provisions. They were primarily meant as a symbolic expression of superiority over the workers and thus facilitated the reproduction of hierarchy in the plantation. The staff's qualifications did not match their privileges: most of the managerial staff were either high school graduates or dropouts. Many of them managed to get the job because they were children of former staff. This may be a reason for their lower monthly salary compared with what is offered to outsiders with similar qualifications. Yet they enjoyed undue entitlements which their peer group outside could not even think of, such as servants and a spacious house with a large kitchen garden and compound fencing. The managerial staff might have received a lower salary than what was offered outside the plantations for similar qualifications, but the attraction of the plantation lay in the privilege of having many servants in a spacious house with its own compound. This paradox was explained to me by a former deputy manager of Hill Valley estate: 'it is not important to us whether the managerial staff feels respected and privileged in the plantation. But the workers should feel that all the managerial staff are important and need to be respected.' In the plantations, as Eric Wolf (1957, 140) observed, 'a considerable amount of labour time goes into the provision of services that may enable them (the managerial staff) to live in the style demanded by their social position'.

The workers seldom saw the manager and assistant managers. The latter rarely talked to the workers and often remained aloof. The field officer, supervisors and factory manager mediated the relationship between workers and the manager. They not only worked with the workers in the workplace, but they also maintained their relationships with the workers outside the workplace through their participation in marriage ceremonies and funeral rituals in workers' families. The relationships between field officers/factory managers and workers were often mediated by the supervisors, who also stayed in the workers' line but received certain additional facilities such as a private connection to the water supply. This informal relationship with a series of intermediaries mediates the formal relationship in the total institution of the plantation (see Goffman 1961). Such relationships also served the ritual function of ensuring that both classes knew their functions and social roles, which meant institutionalising them within the perfect hegemonic system of the plantation, with plantation management having absolute control over the system.

These informal relationships penetrated deeply into the workers' society. For example, all the cultural celebrations in the plantation were inaugurated by members of the plantation management. The invitation to inaugurate particular events was closely associated with the plantation hierarchy. For instance, the inauguration of small events such as the cricket tournament for children was done by supervisors, field officers or clerks on the plantation. But the more significant events, such as temple festivals and inter-estate workers' volleyball tournaments for the workers, were inaugurated by the manager of the plantation. When such major events were organised on the plantation, the manager was the one who often contributed the largest amount of money in meeting the expenses of the events. This was generally followed down the line in the occupational hierarchy, with the superintendent and the field officer/factory manager contributing money. This was also observed when the workers' children would stop at the managerial staff's houses for Christmas carols; they would always start at the manager's bungalow.

The managerial staff intervened in disputes around clearing welfare provisions for those under their patronage. This was very common with regard to most disputed welfare provisions such as medical leave and medical claims by the workers. Although the non-wage components were entitlements of all the workers as per the Plantations Labour Act of 1951, the managerial staff controlled access to the welfare provisions, and those who were under their patronage received better support than those who were not. Thus, the managerial staff exercised their control over the welfare provisions to produce paternal relations, differentiate the workforce and subvert class solidarity. However, I found no evidence of workers receiving direct material benefits from the managerial staff as part of the graded patronage. The only incident I am aware of involved excess fruit in the kitchen garden of the staff being given to the workers who were under the direct patronage of that particular staff.

The social power/status of the plantation management was also reproduced through their position as the 'leisure class' (Veblen 2007 [1899]) in the plantation. The symbolic exhibition of wealth and conspicuous consumption serve to retain the plantation hierarchy: as Mauss argued, 'material loss is a social gain' (Mauss 2011 [1925]; quoted in Martínez 2007). This is also where economic capital is translated into social and symbolic capital. The managers retained the colonial values that their British counterparts left behind, including late-night parties and elite (colonial) games such as tennis and badminton. The workers, meanwhile, played volleyball and kabaddi. The workers could not afford the infrastructural costs of the 'staff games', and the managerial staff actively discouraged the workers from learning them. I could not find anyone, even the servants in the colonial bungalows, who knew the rules. Some of the workers were present in the vicinity of the badminton and tennis courts to help organise these games. In contrast, the staff members came to the volleyball and kabaddi grounds of the workers only to inaugurate tournaments and distribute trophies. The hierarchical positioning and roles of the managerial staff and the workers in these grounds became a ritualistic display of class order. These grounds were also social spaces not only for the workers but also for their family members. The preferences, possibilities and everyday performances of the games produced a particular socio-cultural domination that is conducive to the reproduction of class order. Accordingly, the performance at the games produced socio-cultural capital that reiterated the distinctive aesthetics and tastes attributed to various classes in the plantations.

The occupational hierarchy was made intact through having job titles attached to names. This was a significant category of identity with which to be identified not only within but also outside the plantations. For example, if someone named John was a supervisor (*kankāni*), he would be referred to as 'John Kankāni' wherever he went in the tea belt. This was also applicable to other 'skilled' workers such as domestic workers in staff quarters being called butler (*potlār*), assistant in the medical dispensary (*marunthukārar*), mechanic in the factory, driver and so on. Whenever they paid their dues for temples, funerals or gifts in marriages or puberty rituals, their occupational identity was written along with their name. If the job title was left out in any such entries, the 'skilled worker' would take serious offence. This practice is in line with the references for the managerial staff as discussed earlier. Such practices led to both the workers and the managerial staff embodying and replicating the occupational hierarchy in the social order of the plantations.

Being a capitalist enclave away from the urban context, plantation frontiers offer a distinctive way to understand the reproduction of capitalist production relations. The workers' lives are confined within the plantations, where the factory and family merge on many occasions. This merging is what underpinned the holistic life experience of the workers where the plantation order (mis)appeared as the dominant social hierarchy. The way the 'economic' encompasses the 'social' in the plantation is evident in this 'coalesced life' and associated processes. The processes discussed here contributed to an intensified hierarchical differentiation of status in the plantations. It is only when the power relations (for example, occupational order) are transformed into status relations (for example, occupational hierarchy) that the exploitative production relations appear as a moral economy.

Spatialising hierarchy

The hierarchy was further reinforced by the plantation spatiality or the distribution of spaces and the imagination of these spaces by different classes in the plantation system. As Eric Wolf (1957, 138) rightly notes, in the plantations, 'the class structure finds expression not only in social terms but also in spatial relationships'. In the Peermade tea belt, the allocation of space for different groups of staff corresponded to their level in the class order of the plantations. The layout in the tea estates was confirmed to a basic spatial plan and is somewhat similar in its design throughout the belt. In most tea estates here, the manager's bungalow was located at some distance from the factory and workers' settlements, and the superintendents'/assistant managers' bungalows were nearby. These bungalows were fenced off from the surrounding tea fields and workers' lines. Workers and junior management staff had to obtain prior permission to enter the vicinity of these bungalows. This invisibility and fencing of managerial staff bungalows regulated the accessibility of workers to the manager and reinforced the condition of distance and distinctiveness of the manager and other higher-level staff. The spatial layout of the living accommodation thus stressed the separation between management and workers. However, the former were able to observe the workers' *layams* from the edges of their bungalow hills. This remote surveillance and the constant closer surveillance by the field officer was important for the class order. In a Foucauldian sense, the manager's bungalow and the field officer's quarters acted as major surveillance points within the plantation panopticon. The plantation panopticon, therefore, seems to have been made possible through a network of surveillance and control points distributed across the plantation management.

The managerial staff had separate gathering places such as badminton courts and guest houses close to the estate office and managers' bungalows. These spaces, which were usually fenced and exclusively meant for staff, were well maintained by the workers appointed for these purposes. Contrary to the private space allocated for the staff, the spaces intended for the workers, such as the plots around lines and volleyball grounds, were not fenced nor maintained properly. Workers' spaces were open and had no restrictions on entry. This public–private distinction in the spatiality or built environment in the plantation re-inculcates the idea of respective positions of different categories of people in the hierarchical production process. The peculiar design of plantation infrastructure enables it to act as an instrument of surveillance of the intimate spaces of the workers.

The plantation hierarchy was further imposed by structuring the domestic spaces and access to day-to-day necessities such as the water supply, which constantly served as a strong barrier between managerial staff and workers. Managerial staff were provided with well-furnished and fenced houses with private connections to the water supply. The residence provided for the manager of the plantation was usually a magnificent bungalow with a beautifully landscaped garden that echoed a colonial style. Almost all of them were built during colonial times and represent a Western architectural and aesthetic sense. There were at least three or four servants in the bungalow (selected from among the field and factory workers). Superintendents also had similar bungalows but with comparatively fewer servants, amenities and modifications. Clerks and other managerial staff lived in what was known as 'estate quarters', which were compounded individual houses with a private water supply and servants on certain occasions.

This was in contrast to workers whose domestic space and access to water were shared. They lived in barracks called *layam* divided into tenements, each with a tiny kitchen space, a single 10×12-foot room and an open veranda. On average, more than five members of a family lived in that single room. While the bungalows and staff quarters were made of

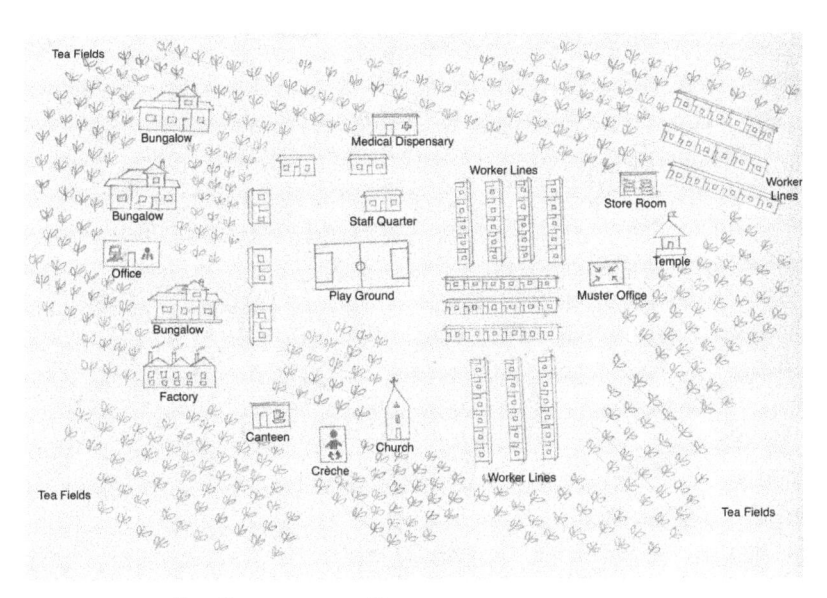

Figure 1.1: Hill Valley estate outline

cement and polished wood and stone, workers' lines were made of mud and stone, though new ones were constructed with cement. The workers' houses did not have any fences as they were organised in barracks. Some of their facilities were shared, for example, the common water pipe. Most of the facilities given to the staff were far superior to those of the workers, which underlines the power and status hierarchy of plantation society.

In the tea belt, strict territorial control had been a significant aspect of plantation spatiality. The workers could not enter many 'restricted areas' controlled by the staff, including the vicinity of staff clubs and their tennis court. The workers were allowed to enter the tea fields and the few cardamom fields only when they were working. The 'watchers' (security guards) sought explanations from the workers if they were found in the cardamom fields outside working hours. The workers and their family members were restricted from collecting firewood. If they were caught, they would be forced to take the wood on their head to the manager's office. In addition to this punishment, the workers would be suspended from work for a period of time. However, they would not be taken to the manager in the first place if they were under the patronage of the 'watcher' or the field officer. If they were taken to the manager, they could escape punishment if they were under that manager's patronage. The graded patronage helped to expand the life possibilities of the workers, although it also became an instrument of the reproduction of the plantation order at large. In contrast to the workers, the managerial staff assigned workers to collect firewood for their use. Unlike the workers, the staff did not have restrictions on their movement within the plantations. To be precise, the politics of allocation and accessibility to space in the plantations not only resulted in symbolic violence against the workers but also reinforced the embodiment of hierarchy.

Unions as the mediator

Four trade unions affiliated with various political parties were active in the tea belt: CITU of the Communist Party of India–Marxist, AITUC of the Communist Party of India, INTUC of the Indian National Congress and BMS of the Bharatiya Janata Party (BJP). It was the trade unions, rather than the political parties, that linked the workers with electoral politics in Kerala. The union leaders possessed tremendous influence over the plantation production and were the purveyors of politics in the plantation. They represented the workers in the Plantation Labour Committee (PLC – the wage board, a tripartite body comprising the state, tea companies and the unions) and often mediated the negotiations with the company regarding the bonus rate, working conditions and any other disputes that arose in plantation production. They also decided who should be promoted from temporary status to permanent. The unions appointed a few workers as conveners to mediate the relationship between the workers and the outside union leaders. The conveners' position was nominal with virtually no power. Their appointment only served to conceal the fact that the unions did more to represent the interests of the estate management than those of the workers. Underlying all this is the fact that the workers did not have their own representatives in the unions and consequently were relegated to marginal positions in plantation politics.

The union leaders in Kerala were not plantation workers. The union leadership was primarily made up of career politicians from non-Dalit Malayalam-speaking individuals from Ezhava and Syrian Christian groups. They have used the caste hierarchy, socio-cultural capital and networks to retain dominance in union leadership.[14] A hierarchical relation existed between the unions and the workers. Most of the workers addressed the union leaders as 'sir' (a widely used denotation to address someone of higher authority, in this context, in the plantation). A few workers, usually technical workers and supervisors associated with the left-wing trade unions, called them *Sakhāvu* (which in Malayalam means 'comrades'). Before the crisis, the workers paid monthly dues (*chanthā*) for the functioning of unions. However, all the unions sought donations from the tea companies as well.

Many workers opined that the unions were 'friends' of the plantation company and that the 'resistance' that the unions organised against the company from time to time, for example, for a hike in the bonus, was often a political gimmick planned by the leaders and the planters. There was a belief that the unions and the company were in cahoots, with the unions acting to deflect and mollify worker discontent concerning bonuses. This belief in an unholy alliance seemed to be confirmed when the elder brother of a union leader became an estate manager. In the neighbouring tea belt of Munnar, the union leaders (those affiliated both with Congress and with the Communist parties) lived in the quarters and bungalows owned by the planters. It was only when this was exposed in the media that the higher leadership in the respective unions ordered their officials to vacate these houses (*The Hindu*, 10 February 2010). The conveners in the tea belt were assigned easy or privileged tasks. They were thoroughly bought off and oriented to union and company interests.

While the union/party ideologies differ at the macro level, the workers treated them all as conservative when it comes to practice on the ground. Therefore, union membership was often passed on to the next generation: in other words, union membership was a matter of inheritance for the workers rather than a choice that the workers made based on a reflexive understanding of political ideology. At the same time, they have been known to change their union affiliation for personal reasons. For instance, if there is a conflict between two families affiliated with the same union, the union may prefer one family over the other. The family which was ignored by the union would move to another. This also happens when the unions fail to recommend someone for promotion from a temporary worker status to a permanent one. This makes the unions an undisputable authority in the plantation system that mediates the workers' relationship with the company as well as with the political parties. These processes also suggest that the unions were part and parcel of the system-maintaining process in the plantations. The unions, therefore, are integral to the moral economic relations of the plantations. They act as what James Ferguson has called an anti-politics machine, 'depoliticising and whisking' exploitative relations out of sight (Ferguson 1990, xv). At the same time, the subscription of such 'moral economic relations' varies for the workforce, and it is challenged when the workers think that there is a breach in the moral relations, as was evident in the recent strike by women workers in the Munnar tea belt (Raj 2019).

Nonetheless, the Tamil Dalits as a community have been reproduced within the plantations for over five generations and have continued to be despite the recent economic crisis and the weakening of the plantation system. In explaining the breach of the moral economy for the workers in the crisis context, this chapter merely points out that there is a complex set of mechanisms involved in the plantation production order that naturalise and legitimise the formal hierarchical relations of class in the plantations. It is also possible that the breach of moral relations by the state and the company is evoked more in a time of crisis. However, the same moral economic relations that smoothed the plantation order in its heyday became a cultural logic for the workers to assess their abandonment in a time of crisis. In the rest of the book, I unpack the structures of multifaceted violence and alienation the workers experience as they struggle for a decent living amid the crisis. The next chapter examines how the subsistence economy of workers during the crisis oscillated between the labour work inside and outside the plantation, merchants of the nodal town, moneylenders and, to a small extent, the self-help groups.

Notes

1. As an instrument of paternalistic discipline under capitalist production, welfare policies have received due attention in the literature on the reproduction of factories (Li 2017). Similarly, the use of kinship terminologies to generate a moral commitment to the capitalist workplace has also been a matter of discussion (De Neve 2008). These processes central to the conventional and dominant understanding of paternal capitalism are not discussed in this book.
2. I define occupational hierarchy as a status differentiation brought in by the occupational order. The order or stratification is related to power, while hierarchy is about status (Dumont 1980). This is also in line with Bourdieu's understanding of hierarchy as a unity in division (Bourdieu 1977, 165).
3. I use the term symbolic power in a similar way to Bourdieu. For Bourdieu, symbolic power emanates from the sources of symbolic capital such as prestige and honour that legitimate the hierarchical relations in society (Bourdieu 1977, 165). In other words, symbolic power is the power to consecrate, that is, the power to produce sacred (hierarchical) social divides and make the divide worth being recognised (Bourdieu and Wacquant 1992, 210 n.172). By keeping Bourdieu's insights in mind, I explore the practice of symbolic capital and how it facilitates the reproduction of the plantation order.
4. Spatial alienation was important for reproducing the plantation class structure. For instance, in the initial years of plantation development, Travancore state refused to grant land for cultivation in the immediate environs of the plantations. This facilitated the total isolation of the plantation from the rest of the world (Baak 1997, 121; see also Wolf 1957 for a similar argument in the Latin American context).
5. In his seminal work *Asylums*, sociologist Erving Goffman (1961) defines a total institution as a place of residence and work where many similarly situated individuals, cut off from the wider society for an appreciable period of time, together lead an enclosed, formally administered round of life. Goffman's analysis helps us elaborate upon the spatio-social isolation and insulated and rigid internal structure of plantations, as already pointed out by anthropologists working across plantation societies in different parts of the world (Wolf 1957; Thompson 1959; Smith 1967; Best 1968; Jain 1970; Beckford 1972). An important criticism against the 'insularity of plantation' argument is that the plantations were always porous. People always moved in and out, and the plantation belts fade into the larger society (Selvaratnam 1988; Jegathesan 2019). However, it is important to recognise that the plantation system is distinct, with its own class order and a unique network of allied apparatus that facilitated the plantation society, which is radically different from the caste-ridden native villages of these workers. Unlike in the villages, there is a blurred boundary between organisation and society in the plantations (Best 1968). Edgar Thompson (1959), for example, stressed the importance of examining the plantation as a social system and a political institution with its own moral order (similar to a school or a church). Thompson also emphasised the specificities of the plantation as an institution, mainly its relation to the land and territory in which it exists. Unlike school and church, the plantation is a 'settlement institution' which 'cannot exist without territorial assumptions' (Thompson 1959, 44). Sidney Mintz (1966) discusses the territorial assumptions of plantation development for a much larger region of the Caribbean, examining the region as a distinct 'sociocultural area' and pointing out how the plantation system had defined the socio-economic and political character of the plantation region. In addition to recognising the porousness of the plantations, one has to also pay attention to their uniqueness.
6. Alvin Gouldner (1954) presents an ethnographically engaging discussion on how various types of rigid bureaucratic practice in industrial settings tend to control the whole factory life. He observes that the nature of bureaucracy in industrial institutions plays a significant role in orienting production relations, even beyond the factories.
7. The factory manager was called a tea-maker during the colonial period. This term is still used in the plantations.
8. Office clerks are considered superior to supervisors because of the higher educational qualification required for the clerical position and also because they are recruited directly for the position, unlike supervisors who have usually been promoted out of skilled worker grades (such as watcher or assistant to the field officer) and sometimes even from among manual workers. There are many examples where the children of office clerks managed to achieve the same position. Such intergenerational inheritance also differentiates the status of office clerks and supervisors.

9   Although non-Hindus appear to be outside the Hindu caste hierarchy in its ritual implications, the caste system exists across various religions in India. Their caste position is often understood in relation to the Hindu caste groups. The Syrian Christians are conceived as Vaishya (merchant) caste in Kerala society since no merchant caste is present in Kerala's caste system. This informal accommodation of the Syrian Christians within Kerala's social hierarchy allowed them to engage in plantation business.

10 In the Peermade tea belt, prominent Syrian Christian plantation owners include A.V. George and family, who own the Ashly and Stack Brook estates; A.V. Thomas & Company, who own the Carady Goody, Vasupidungi and Pasuparai estates; the Palamadam family, a prominent Christian family based in Kottayam who owned the Periyar estate; MMJ Group of Companies, owned by a prominent Syrian Christian family from Pala, who own the Churakulam, Bonami, Vagamon and Kottamalai estates; and POABS group, whose chairman, P.A. Jacob, is a Syrian Christian, who own the Pasumalai, Manjumalai and Pambanar tea estates. The Kozhikanam, Thangamalai and Mount estates were owned by Ram Bahathur Takur (RBT) Company, a venture of a Brahmin family from Bihar; and the Koduakarnam, Ladrum, Glenmary and Woodlands estates are owned by Hope Plantations, an enterprise of a Bengali high-caste family. POABS and Bethel Plantations took over the estates of RBT and Hope Plantations, respectively. Bethel Plantations is owned by Thomas Mathew, another Syrian Christian.

11 Almost 70 per cent of the workforce in the plantations in Peermade belong to the Dalit community, with the remaining 30 per cent comprising workers belonging to non-Dalit Nadar/Vellala/Ezhava castes. This is not to say that all these minority communities can be found in every estate in the belt. However, at least a few members from one of these communities work in all the plantations. Most of these non-Dalit workers are scattered through supervisory and skilled (such as plumber and mechanic) occupations within the plantation system. These non-Dalit castes are nonetheless low-ranked castes in the traditional caste hierarchy, often referred to as Bahujan.

12 This situation parallels Clyde Mitchell's (1956) study of Kalela dance in the Zambian copper belt. Although the production system itself primarily determined the social relations in the copper belt, the social relationships outside the work situation were mainly influenced by differences in tribal membership.

13 The use of kinship terms for caste relations in the plantations is an aspect of situational selection of categories of identities, as discussed by Clyde Mitchell (1956) in the case of intertribal relations in the copper belt of Zambia.

14 This is in contrast to, for instance, what happened in the Tamil Nadu plantations, where the workers' discontent with the major trade union wings of the Indian National Congress and Communist parties (Viswanathan 1999) led to the growth of trade union wings of Dalit political parties.

2
Workers: stay on, move out

The crisis had radically reconfigured the rigid plantation production system, including its erstwhile class order, patronage and the phenomena of total institution. The plantations were no longer mere enclaves producing exotic tea for the international market. They had become a completely unsettled place. There have been eight cases of suicide and 12 deaths due to starvation and denial of medical care since the crisis in the tea industry gained momentum in the late 1990s. One was of a 14-year-old schoolgirl, Velankanni, from Pasumalai estate who hanged herself in 2003. She felt humiliated by the taunts of her school friends for wearing a torn school uniform that her parents had borrowed. When Velankanni committed suicide, the post-mortem revealed that there was no trace of food in her intestine (*The Hindu*, 28 September 2003). I met her father, Devasahayam, during my fieldwork. He was reluctant to talk to me initially as he thought I was a newspaper journalist, and he did not want to talk about the tragic death of his daughter. He agreed to have a short conversation when a mutual acquaintance arranged a meeting. He told me that Velankanni committed suicide due to shame over their deprivation. He could not manage to buy her things since he was suffering from health issues and was unable to do physically demanding work. Nonetheless, he had to work inside as well as outside the plantation from the very beginning of the crisis since his wife stayed at home as she could not find work. The six-member family had to survive on the father's income, and the deprivation resulted in the tragic death of Velankanni.

In 2012, a 15-year-old girl from the Ladrum tea estate was allegedly raped and murdered by a powerful politician and legislator in Tamil Nadu. Her father had been ill for a long time and her mother was the sole breadwinner until the tea crisis took her meagre income away from the family. The mother went outside the plantation to work, but still she could not meet the family's basic needs. This forced the parents to send the young girl to work as domestic help in the politician's house. The employment agents promised the girl and her parents that she would be sent to school and would only need to help with the household work during the evenings and weekends. A local court sentenced the politician and two of his aides to 10 years' imprisonment in December 2018. However, they were acquitted by a higher court in July 2020, citing the failure of the prosecution to prove the charges of rape, murder and conspiracy. The violence of the crisis is embedded in and transmuted into other forms of violence, including the rape and death of a plantation Dalit girl. The crisis in fact contributed to massive violence against the plantation workers and their families in the tea belt.

Stay on

In the abandoned plantations, the workers had to survive by collectively plucking and selling tea leaves in a system controlled and administered by trade unions. In the partially functioning plantations, where the factories were shut down and only plucking was done, they had to be content with weekly *chelavu kāsu* distributed by the plantation management. In both situations, their livelihood was maintained at the barest subsistence level. The cessation of even the meagre wage employment offered and the deferred payment of wages shattered the conditions of life. Thus, the temporary closure of the plantations (and consequent opening up of the hitherto closed institutions of the plantations to the outside world) forced plantation communities into a radical renegotiation and reorganisation of the terms of their existence.

There were variations in how the selling of tea leaves was organised in the tea belt. In Mulveli, which was locked out in 1999, a cooperative labour committee was formed to manage the plucking of the leaves and their sale in the local market and to monitor the distribution of the amount earned among the workers. The labour committee consisted of eight members representing trade unions, estate staff, supervisors and workers.[1] Under this new system, workers only worked three days a week, with four hours of daily work. These short working hours were the result of the poor yield due to lack of fertiliser and care for the tea bushes. The labour committee took the plucked leaves to the town and sold them to a wholesale merchant. The amount received was divided equally among the workers. According to Sivan, a 46-year-old male supervisor and a member of the labour committee, in 2010 the workers received approximately 70 rupees per day for three days per week,[2] which meant that a worker received around 840 rupees per month from the tea plucking. In most cases, both wife and husband engaged in plucking, and the couple received about 1,680 rupees.

In Pavaiakanam estate, however, plucking was done individually. The unions distributed tea bushes among the workers: each permanent worker (*varushathāl*) was allotted 1,500 tea bushes, and each temporary worker (*vārathāl*) had 500 bushes. But these bushes were aged and did not provide a reasonable yield. A permanent workers' family (with both husband and wife working) received approximately 2,000 rupees per month. The temporary workers' family received only one-third of the amount made by permanent workers (about 670 rupees) as the couple would have only 1,000 bushes. Sometimes, the workers mortgaged the bushes allotted to them to mobilise money for emergencies such as healthcare or marriage and to buy herbicides and fertilisers. While plucking was done individually, the workers who belonged to different unions were required to sell their leaves only to their union representatives at a price lower than the market rate.[3]

A union worker in the Thangamalai estate told me that the unions now sought new sources for financing their activities (including the income of the unions' full-time workers/leaders) as they no longer receive the monthly *chanthā* (payment) from their member workers since the crisis. Therefore, the unions get money from those who have the contract for the tea leaves plucked in the plantations. He added that this is a 'secret' everyone knows (*ūrarincha rahasiyam*). This was a major transformation for unions in the crisis context: they transformed from an intermediary/negotiating institution between management and workers into a managing authority that supervises and coordinates the cooperative setup as seen in various estates in the belt.

The men sought employment outside the plantations, mainly in the booming construction sector. Some of them were also employed as carriers of devotees in the Sabarimala Pilgrimage Centre. This earned them a monthly income of at least 3,000 to 4,000 rupees during the three-month ritual season every year. At the same time, the women sought work under the employment guarantee scheme and manual work such as picking peppers and harvesting cardamom in the immediate surrounding areas of the plantation. The migrant women sought work in the domestic industry as housemaids (*velaikāri*) and home nurses.[4] Many of them also moved to textile factories in the Tirupur region and fish processing units in Gujarat. Young men have also been recruited by home nursing agencies to care for people at nursing homes. Home nursing is a new buzzword in

Figure 2.1: A ruined tea factory in the Peermade tea belt

the plantation society as more and more girls and boys who are literate and have a high school education are recruited by home nursing agencies and sent to households all over southern India.

In the partially working plantations, the management reduced the working days to three to four days a week. The workers were not paid their wages regularly. Under this system, a family managed to get around 2,400 rupees every month. Since it was nearly impossible to survive on the income from tea plucking under the new setup, the men from the abandoned as well as from the partially working plantations sought work in cardamom/tea gardens of small-scale planters on the outskirts of their respective estates, on days that they were not working on the plantations. This outside work was paid at the daily rate of around 150 rupees. But the outside work was not guaranteed. The workers could only find work for about 10 days a month, which means men could increase the household income by only 1,500 rupees.

The retired workers engaged in the Indian government's Mahatma Gandhi National Rural Employment Guarantee Scheme (MGNREGS) aimed at securing the livelihoods of people in rural areas by guaranteeing 100 days of wage employment in a financial year to a rural household whose adult members volunteered to do unskilled manual work (National Rural Employment Act 2005). This scheme provided the worker with roughly 1,000 rupees monthly. But the payment was often kept pending due to the bureaucratic formalities in the government offices. I came across many workers whose pay had been delayed because the clerk responsible for registering the payment voucher was allegedly on leave.

While not all the plantation families benefited from the scheme, it was a significant and the only source of income for most of the workers engaged in the scheme. This is especially so in the case of older people where both husband and wife worked under this scheme and earned a monthly income of 2,000 rupees. In the case of young women who were temporary workers, their income from the scheme was an addition to the money earned by their spouses from work outside the plantation.

Some of the families supplemented their income by raising cattle and chickens. Of the 385 families in Hill Valley, 81 (21 per cent) had chickens and 96 (24 per cent) had cattle at their houses. A very few in the plantation occupied small pieces of land called *Puthuvēli* (meaning 'new fence') in the remote hilly terrain outside the fringes of the plantation that they used for small-scale tea, cardamom and jackfruit cultivation. The average income through cultivation varied from 600 to 1,000 rupees depending on the size of the plot and the productivity of the tea plants. But this helped only a very few since these plots were occupied by estate supervisors and a few workers at the top of the social leadership. The land was often rocky and the yield was poor. Most of the occupants did not have the land deeds (*Pattā*), which means the government could reclaim the land from the occupiers. This also means that the land cannot be used as collateral for securing loans from banks. To be sure, the previous description of different situations of the subsistence economy of those who still depend entirely on the plantation reveals that a worker's family, on average consisting of five members, managed to make around 2,500 to 4,000 rupees in the 2009–10 period, which was a meagre income for a plantation household to survive on in rural Kerala.[5]

For more significant expenses, the workers relied on collateral-free loans from the state or nearby banks via their self-help groups (*sangham*). These groups were established as part of the micro-credit revolution in South Asia. Nonetheless, the activities of these groups in the plantations intensified only after the crisis. The loans were meant for financing minor income-generating activities such as small-scale cattle farms. However, such loans were spent on healthcare, children's education, marriage ceremonies (particularly to pay dowries) or to pay off the debt owed to moneylenders at a very high interest rate. As the hospitals in the plantations had been closed down during the crisis, the workers were forced to spend large amounts of money on healthcare. The government hospitals in the Peermade region were neither as well equipped nor as efficient as government hospitals in other regions in the district. This may be because most people in the region (mainly the tea workers) primarily relied on the hospitals run by the plantations before the crisis. That is to say that the crisis had put more pressure on the government hospital, which was already constrained by limited resources. As the workers were forced to approach private hospitals, anything beyond an ordinary illness would financially burden the workers for a lengthy period and sometimes forever.

While the micro-credit movement is primarily aimed at poverty reduction, it contributed very little to the subsistence economy in the tea estates. As Jonathan Pattenden (2010, 498) points out regarding a similar case in South India, this enforcement of the debt cycle upon the rural poor in effect makes the self-help groups a proxy moneylender. In a cycle of debt, the workers had to borrow from moneylenders at a higher interest rate to pay back the loan borrowed through their self-help groups. This high interest rate traps the workers into a debt cycle and further perpetuates it. I observed an interaction between Shanmugam, a 45-year-old man in Greenland estate, and a moneylender. The moneylender agreed to pay him 1,000 rupees, at an interest rate of 10 per cent per month, on the agreement that Shanmugam would pay back the whole amount in two months. The entire interest amount for the payback period is taken from the lent amount. In other words, Shanmugam received only 800 rupees. So in effect, the interest rate is 12.5 per cent per month, not 10 per cent. When the moneylender left, Shanmugam told me that he needed the money to send to his two children studying in Cumbum, a small town in Tamil Nadu close to Kerala's border. The moneylender lent him 1,000 rupees because previously he had successfully paid back 600 rupees plus the interest. He was happy that he had been able to gain the trust of the moneylender because now it would be easier for him to borrow more money from him and to convince him to lend money to his friends. This persistent indebtedness and consequent impoverishment show that the debt bondage that brought the tea workers' ancestors to the plantation (Lal 1993) continues to haunt them and binds them within their social reproduction as an underclass/outcast community, though the nature of the debt bondage differs. Thus, the subsistence economy of workers in the midst of the crisis oscillates between labour work inside and outside plantations, moneylenders and, to a small extent, the self-help groups.

At the same time, it is not only local moneylenders who entrap the poor but also the larger financial companies who enfold them into their network of debt, as recently argued by Sohini Kar (2018). I would add that the neoliberal logic of financial networks not only enfolds the poor workers but also rationalises the debt as well as the crisis. In the crisis context, self-help groups also function as instruments of depoliticisation of the workforce. This is because, in the new development rationality of the micro-credit system, the responsibility for securing economic opportunity lies with the individuals and not with the state, as argued by Katherine Rankin (2001) in the context of Nepal.

In the midst of debt and crisis, the workers often depended on credit from grocery stores in the nodal towns. It was important for the workers to build a relationship with these stores in order to make use of the credit facility. A worker would be introduced to a grocery merchant by one of their co-workers who had been a loyal customer and had a good relationship with the merchant. The merchant would agree to provide groceries on credit after an informal assurance from the new customer-worker that he would remain a loyal and regular customer. In this way, the workers establish a relationship with the merchants in their respective nodal towns. Some of the managerial staff in the tea belt also had grocery and garment shops in the town. The workers from the tea estates owned by the same company were allowed to buy necessities on credit, which would then be deducted from their wages back in the tea estate. In one of the nodal towns, a garment shop run by the tea company offered clothes to its workers on credit, which was then deducted directly from the monthly payment of their wages.

I came across many discussions between workers about which of the grocery merchants in the town were more compassionate and friendly in dealing with the tea workers. Here compassion refers to the extent to which the seller trusts the workers in their repayment capacity vis-à-vis the credit limit for the tea workers in the various grocery stores. However, the relationship between sellers and workers became tense whenever the latter failed to repay the credit instalment when the sellers or their representatives visited the estate lines to collect the credit amounts every Saturday (the day of *chelavu kāsu*). Shouting at the workers who had defaulted in public, particularly in front of their houses, was a strategy employed by the sellers to humiliate the workers to force them to repay their dues. Such incidents further damaged the relationship between sellers and workers. Nonetheless, their mutual dependence was inevitable since the business in the town was, by and large, dependent on the tea workers. This also means that the business in the nodal towns was affected during the crisis. This transformation in the relationship between the sellers and the workers also indicates the weakening of ancillary institutions that developed around the plantation system.

Move out

Around 100 families from the Peermade tea belt migrated to the manufacturing and industrial heartland of the Tirupur-Coimbatore region between the late 1990s and 2014, where they were employed as mainly semi-skilled casual labour. Other families who left the plantations moved back to their ancestral villages in Tamil Nadu. I spent some time in both areas. In Tirupur, I interviewed 34 families working mainly in the textile and garment industry to understand their circumstances. Tirupur is a garment township located 30 miles from Coimbatore, an important industrial settlement known as the 'Manchester of South India'. The owners of the mills and the stitching units are mostly from the dominant Gounder (Kongu Vellalar) and Naicker (Kammas) caste communities. In addition to Kallar and Gounder workers, there is a significant Dalit population among the workforce from the Paraiyar and Arunthathiyar castes. The plantation Dalits represent a small proportion of those working in the textile industry. Among the 30,000 workers in the dyeing units (*Hindu Business Line* 2011), they account for about 400.[6]

Most of the Tamil Dalits from plantations that I met were engaged in skilled and semi-skilled work in garment-related industrial units.[7] There were three kinds of production units in which the Tamil Dalits worked: dyeing (semi-skilled), stitching (semi-skilled) and marketing in larger firms (semi-skilled). Out of 34 Tamil Dalit men I interviewed, three worked in the dyeing units as machine operators, 26 worked as tailors in stitching units and five worked in marketing departments of Chennai Silks, a large firm that exports clothes to the Gulf, Europe and North America. Some of them were married. Among the women, a few were housewives, and some worked as salespeople in shops. Some of them worked as tailors along with their husbands. While the majority of the plantation Dalits worked as labourers in dyeing units, the three machine operators were interviewed because they were from the neighbouring estates of Hill Valley and were accessible.

In 2014, machine operators in dyeing units were paid a daily wage of 600 rupees. The marketing executives were paid a monthly wage that varied between 8,000 and 14,000 rupees depending on experience. Tailors were paid on a piece-rate basis depending on how many pieces they stitched together,[8] and daily wages based on this work varied between 275 and 750 rupees. When working a 12-hour day (8 am to 8 pm), a tailor could bring in 700 to 750 rupees. This was possible when the small stitching units received contracts from large firms with direct connections with the buyer abroad. During the off season, tailors worked 8-hour days (9 am to 5 pm) and earned between 275 and 400 rupees. Despite earning better wages in Tirupur, the workers experienced a new kind of exploitation here. Regular employment in small stitching units was based on workers consenting to stay and work overnight to meet deadlines from the larger firms. Dalit workers in the knitwear units often had to work through the night while taking only short naps. It is perhaps no surprise that the suicide rate among migrant workers in Tirupur was high. In 2011, a fact-finding team of university students from Delhi found that more than 800 workers in the Tirupur garment industry had committed suicide between 2008 and 2011 (Sanhati 2011).

The dyeing units, where people work 10 hours per day (8 am to 6 pm), have different problems. They are notorious sources of pollution, and dyeing and bleaching units cause serious health hazards for long-serving workers. The dyeing units were shut down on the grounds of pollution in 2011 after the intervention of the Chennai High Court. Many large units managed to reopen while the small units remained closed. The closures have meant that many plantation Dalits have moved to stitching units in Tirupur or the machinery manufacturing industries in Coimbatore. As such, driven by one crisis (in the plantations), entering into another crisis (the dyeing industry) and pushed again elsewhere (to the stitching units), the plantation Dalits have become part of India's 'footloose' informal labour (Breman 1996) that oscillates between different occupations in different industrial townships in search of less precarious jobs.

I identified three young women aged 19, 23 and 26 who had moved to Tirupur from the Hill Valley estate working under an illegal 'sumangali scheme'. The girls would receive food and lodging from the company, and their wages would be paid only at the end of the contract term, which ranged from 18 months to four years, or they would be paid periodically to the girls' parents. The contract is supposed to end before the girl is married, and the wages that have been withheld are meant to pay for her dowry. Such marriage schemes are a form of (outlawed) bonded labour. Under both the contract and the sumangali system, wages for work done are withheld to control and discipline the workers. Tirupur's dependence on and maintenance of this precarious casual or bonded labour force is not at all hidden from the popular and academic discourses (see Carswell and De Neve 2014). While there is no scarcity of labour laws applicable to the Tirupur textile and garment industries, they are rarely implemented. Many workers I interviewed had not even heard of a 'labour officer'. A supervisor who had seen the labour inspector visiting his stitching unit told me that 'the laws are made not for the workers, but for the labour officers to extract money from the employers'.

Working outside the plantations in the garment units of Tirupur enabled a certain degree of upward economic mobility for plantation Dalits, who earned more money than those who stayed behind. However, there were disadvantages of having to move out of the plantation economy. Firstly, these new forms of work are neither secured nor guaranteed, in the way plantation work once was. Secondly, whereas the plantations had provided some form of housing, families who moved outside the plantations had to pay rent and often had facilities poorer than those in the plantations; many lived in the slums and ghettoes of the cities they moved to. Finally, people who work outside are also subject to a type of caste discrimination that they do not face in the plantations.

A few workers made failed attempts to obtain employment outside India, which often resulted in deeper financial debt. For instance, at the peak of the crisis in 1999, around 50 workers lost their savings to a fake agent who promised to take them to Malaysia to work on rubber plantations. They also borrowed large sums from moneylenders in the tea belt. As they migrated out of the plantations to repay their debts and support their families in crisis, access to livelihood options became scarce and scary, especially in the dam-dispute context. This uprooting is an excruciating process in the way it is imagined and experienced by the workers and their families.

Economic versus social mobility

To understand the patterns of migration and diversification of livelihoods within households since the crisis and the relative advantages and disadvantages of work outside the plantations, I undertook 10 detailed household case histories of families who had been living next to each other in 1980 in the Hill Valley estate (see Table 2.1).

These brief life histories indicate the severe impact of the crisis on the ability of plantation workers to stay on the plantations across generations. This is the case both for sons, many of whom were unable to become permanent workers in their 'home plantation', and for daughters, who normally will marry within the plantation sector although outside the 'home plantation' but who now often move out of the plantation economy with their new households. In all six of the families who retained the plantation connection (Houses 2, 3, 4, 5, 6 and 7), it was elder siblings who stayed back because they secured employment on the plantations. The younger ones had to leave. In addition, although a daughter of

Table 2.1: Ten case histories of tea worker households, Hill Valley estate, Kerala

1. (Pallar): Jacob (1948) = Yesamma (1950). Children: Prema (f) 1969; John (m) 1971; Arul Mary (f) 1975.
Prema married a photographer in a neighbouring estate and works as a tea plucker. Arul Mary married a relative of Prema's husband in the same estate. Arul Mary stitches clothes for women and children. John left for Coimbatore in 1996 after the crisis. Yesamma lives with John. Jacob died in 1998. **Persons still on plantations: 2 of 5.**
2. (Paraiyar): Sunderraj (1950) = Thayamma (1952). Children: Selvam (m) 1971; Ilaiyaraja (m) 1974; Kumari (f) 1975; Divya (f) 1983.
Kumari married a relative in Chennai. Kumari studied to grade 8 and worked as a salesperson in a textile shop in Chennai. Divya studied to grade 10. She is unmarried and lives with the family of Ilaiyaraja. Ilaiayaraja moved to Chennai with his parents. Selvam stayed back as a permanent worker. Sunderraj and Thayamma died in 2006 and 2010. **Persons still on plantations: 1 of 6.**
3. (Nadar): Varghese (1952) = Selvi (1952). Varghese's parents: Prakasam Nadar (m) 1932; Susaiyamma (f) 1935. Children: Francis (f) 1974; Stella (f) 1977; Makson (m) 1979; Nikson (m) 1984.
Selvi died in 2014 at the estate. Varghese lives with his son Makson who stayed on the estate but worked outside. His wife is a tea plucker and has been a permanent worker since 2012. Nikson is a schoolteacher in a private school in Munnar. Francis married a Pallar caste man, a permanent worker, who lived on the plantation. Stella is married, lives with her husband in Mysore, and is a general nurse. **Persons still on plantations: 3 of 6.**
4. (Paraiyar): Periya Pandian (1946) = Lekshmi (1948). Pandian's father Sudalai (m) 1925. Children: Karuppasamy (m) 1960; Valli (f) 1966; Sundaram (m) 1970; Suresh (m) 1980; Robin (m) 1984.
Sudalai died in 1992. Karuppasamy stayed back in Hill Valley. Valli married a permanent worker in a neighbouring estate and is a permanent tea plucker there. The rest of the household moved to their native village in Tamil Nadu in 1998. Suresh is now a tailor in Tirupur, Robin is an assistant to a mason in his native village, and Sundaram worked in a dyeing unit in Tirupur but returned to his native village. **Persons still on plantations: 2 of 8.**

5. (Paraiyar): Gomas (1948) = Muthumma (1951). Children: Sekhar (m) 1969; Kamalam (f) 1970; Lekshmi (f) 1972; Parvathy (f) 1975; Elango (m) 1977; Thangaraj (m) 1980.

Sekhar is a permanent worker in Hill Valley. Muthamma has lived with Sekhar since her retirement. Gomas passed away in 2008. Kamalam and Lekshmi married men from Koodalur, Tamil Nadu. Parvathy married her cousin in Hill Valley, so she stayed back. Elango moved to another town with his wife. Thangaraj is a manual labourer in a neighbouring tea estate, and his wife runs a roadside tea shop in the estate. **Persons still on plantations: 5 of 8.**

6. (Arunthathiyar): Arumainayagam (1932) = Sornam (1935). Children: Rasaiyya (m) 1952; Malaiyarasi (f) 1953; Ganesan (m) 1957. Malaiyarasi's children: Muniyandi (m) 1973; Pazhani (m) 1977; Thanam (f) 1977.

Arumainayagam and Sornam died in 1998 and 2001 respectively. Rasaiyya and Ganesan are permanent workers and live in Hill Valley. Malaiyarasi retired from Hill Valley as a tea plucker in 2006. Her daughter is married to a barber in Kumily, a plantation town. Both Muniyandi and Pazhani moved to Tamil Nadu with their wives. **Persons still on plantations: 3 of 8.**

7. (Paraiyar): Chinna Pandian (1946) = Vellaiyamma (1952). Children: Murugaiah (m) 1968; Samuthiram (f) 1969; Ravi (m) 1970; Ghanam (f) 1972; Sasikumar (m) 1974.

After retirement, Chinna Pandian moved to his native village in Tamil Nadu and died in 2004. Vellaiyamma and her son Sasikumar live in their native village in Tamil Nadu. Samuthiram and Ghanam married men from their native village in Tamil Nadu and lived in villages there. Ravi and Murugaiah stayed in Hill Valley. Murugaiah is a permanent worker. Ravi was a temporary worker and since the crisis has worked in a stone quarry outside the plantation. Ravi's wife became a permanent worker in 2012, and they continue to live in the same house where Ravi's parents lived in Hill Valley. **Persons still on plantations: 2 of 7.**

8. (Paraiyar): Sudalai (1946) = Lekshmi (1949). Child: Madasamy (m) 1968.

Sudalai and Lekshmi died in 1998 and 2001 respectively. Madasamy was a permanent worker but left the plantation and returned to his ancestral village in 2004 when his wife deserted him. **Persons still on plantations: none.**

9. (Paraiyar): Chinna Sudalai (1948) = Parvathy (1950). Children: Saraswathi (f) 1968; Vellasamy (m) 1970. Chinna Sudalai is the younger brother of Sudalai. Chinna Sudalai died in 2007. Parvathy and her son Vellasamy (temporary worker in the estate) moved to their ancestral village in Tirunelveli district in Tamil Nadu. Saraswathi married a manual labourer in Koodalur village near Cumbum valley, Tamil Nadu. She died in 2008 in mysterious circumstances. **Persons still on plantations: none.**
10. (Paraiyar): Velliyappan (1951) = Masanam (1954). Children: Selvi (f) 1970; Mallika (f) 1974; Murugesan (m) 1976. Velliyappan died in 2008 in Hill Valley. Masanam then moved to Tamil Nadu to live with a relative. Murugesan lives outside the plantation with his family. He is an assistant to a mason. Mallika and Selvi married men from Tamil Nadu. Both of them work as agricultural labourers in their village in Tamil Nadu. **Persons still on plantations: none**

Note: Houses are all from Line 2 of Hill Valley estate. The table traces the families from 1980. The years listed are the year of birth of each family member. For those born before 1950, this is the year registered for plantation work, but this may be imprecise. f = female, m = male.

House 1 only moved to a neighbouring plantation when she married, her mother left the plantations altogether and moved to Coimbatore to live with her son. This may at least in part relate to the stigma attached to parents living with their daughters as opposed to their sons.

Out of the 10 families, three families (Houses 1, 2 and 4), from which many family members left the plantations in the years of the crisis between 1995 and 1998, are considered in greater detail to understand their vulnerability and mobility. The first of the three families is that of Sundaram (House 4). Sundaram, 46 years old, was a temporary worker in the Hill Valley estate when the crisis hit the tea industry. In 1997, when he was 27 years old, he moved out of the plantation with his wife Kokila, his parents and his youngest brothers Suresh and Robin. He has four siblings – one elder brother, two younger brothers and one sister. The elder brother Karuppasamy is a carpenter on the Hill Valley estate. One younger brother works in Tirupur's textile industry as a tailor. Another brother is a manual labourer in construction in his native village Nagaram in Tamil Nadu. His sister is married to a permanent worker on a nearby tea estate. Sundaram dropped out of school when he was nine to take care of his younger siblings. He began working as a servant for a Syrian

Christian family in a valley town when he was 13. The Syrian Christian family 'recruited' Sundaram through a friend who was a field officer on the Hill Valley estate. It was common to recruit plantation workers' children as servants for relatives of the managerial staff. Sundaram returned to the plantation after five years as a temporary worker. He worked in the tea factory for eight years. As the company did not promote him to a permanent position, allegedly due to the economic crisis, Sundaram moved to Nagaram, his native village in Tirunelveli district of southern Tamil Nadu. He told me that he moved because he realised that he did not have a future on the plantation. Sundaram's story is similar to those of many youths who were temporary workers during the crisis.

Back in Tamil Nadu, he managed to obtain a ration card and rented a hut for 500 rupees per month. Having been employed as a manual labourer on the plantation, Sundaram could not manage to become a semi-skilled worker such as a driver or mechanic. He became an assistant to a mason in his native village, earning a daily wage of 350 rupees. Sundaram also went to southern Kerala whenever he could not find work near his village. The wage was higher in Kerala (500 rupees). Sundaram said that although wages were higher in Kerala, so was the cost of living. He managed, however, to save money by sleeping at construction sites and subsisting on rice soups which he cooked in a kerosene stove he carried with him. For a brief period, he worked in the dyeing units of the textile factories of Tirupur. This paid better. When I asked him about the health hazards of the dyeing units, Sundaram responded: 'At the end of the day, what I care about is how much I could save for my family. I do not care about my health.' He was paid 650 rupees for working nine to 10 hours a day. Although daily manual labourers should not work more than eight hours, he had to work a bit more to keep his job secure. He lost his job after the government temporarily shut down the dyeing units because of the pollution.

Sundaram was vulnerable to the debt trap since his income was central to the survival of his household as his wife did not do any paid labour. Sundaram told me that he wanted his wife to concentrate on taking care of the children's education and not bother about bringing in income for the family. His father could not work due to poor health. His mother found work under the MGNREG scheme. His mother's income was a much-needed addition to the family, but most of her money was spent on 'tonics and pills'. Sundaram, however, managed to save more money than his brother Karuppasamy, who stayed back in the plantation, as his wage was much higher than the plantation wages. However, as is evident from the narrative above, Sundaram lived a precarious life as a migrant casual labourer relying on various odd jobs, in contrast to the secure job his elder brother had on the plantation. According to Sundaram, the price 'to see some money' was not having a secure job in the plantation.

Another price he paid was facing overt caste discrimination. Sundaram observed that for Dalits, their future lies in the towns. He wanted to move his family to the city not only for economic reasons and for his children's education but also because he faced severe caste discrimination back in the village. He told me that upper-caste tea shops there discourage Dalits from entering by creating 'unnecessary troubles' such as providing tea in dirty cups and asking for exact change (the exact cost of tea and snacks). Even if the tea shops had plenty of coins and smaller denominations, they would demand that Dalits pay the exact amount. Sundaram was disappointed that he could not move his family to a town.

Sundaram could not tolerate explicit discrimination. He had enjoyed relatively egalitarian relations in the plantations, where caste identity is overshadowed by the class order of the plantation production relations. The unbearable discrimination led him to join the Dalit Panthers (VCK – Viduthalai Chiruthai Katchi). Through VCK, he became a community leader for the Paraiyar Dalits. He was entrusted with the responsibility of resolving family feuds and conflicts within the group. In one of our meetings, he told me that he did not know much about B.R. Ambedkar, a great social reformer and the father of the Indian constitution who fought vehemently against the caste system and untouchability. There is indeed no statue of Ambedkar nor any socio-political organisation in the Hill Valley estate dedicated to the cause of Dalits as there are in many other parts of the country. He came to recognise 'Ambedkar's sacrifice', as he puts it, only after moving to Tamil Nadu. The experience of caste discrimination away from the plantation in turn led to a greater consciousness of caste identity and a Dalit movement among the Tamil-Dalit plantation workforce. Whenever someone such as Sundaram visited the plantations, they were eager to talk about the role of caste in Tamil villages and how divisive caste is there, unlike in the plantation where, according to Sundaram, people from different castes live like siblings. However, the Dalit consciousness in the plantation often resulted in group formation on the basis of sub-caste identity, as in Sundaram's case. Sundaram talked about the unity of Dalits, but he was still part of VCK, which has been identified with the Paraiyar community in Tamil Nadu.

While Sundaram wanted to move his family to a big city, Ilaiyaraja (House 2) succeeded in moving his family to Chennai. In 1997, at the age of 40, Ilaiyaraja left for Chennai with his parents and younger sister. He chose Chennai mainly because his ancestors came from a village located around 40 kilometres from this city. Ilaiyaraja used to be a temporary worker, and the economic crisis led to a loss of guaranteed work on the plantation. Ilaiyaraja's elder brother, Selvam, remained at the estate as he was a permanent worker. Ilaiyaraja had studied up to grade 10. His high school education helped him obtain a job as a marketing agent for a cement company in Chennai. He was paid 7,000 rupees a month. His father passed away in 2008 and his mother did not work. His wife, Jayalakshmi, worked as a salesperson in a textile shop in Chennai and earned 6,500 rupees per month. So, the total income of Ilaiyaraja and Jayalakshmi was 13,500 rupees per month.

However, for Ilaiyaraja, this income was not enough to survive as 'lower middle class' in a major city, as he needed to pay 5,800 rupees in rent and 270 rupees for electricity and water supply per month, monthly school fees of 700 rupees each for two of his children, his mother's medical expenses and a loan amount of 1,200 rupees for his motorcycle. The rest was spent on food. He saved a maximum of 1,000 rupees every month. Ilaiyaraja could have chosen to stay at the family house in the native village to save money, but instead he rented accommodation in another location to mask his caste identity. He told me that he did not want his children to feel the inferiority of being identified with the 'S.C. colony', or what is popularly called *'parai chēri'*, a derogatory term used for the Dalit colonies in Tamil Nadu.

Another family that moved out of the plantation is that of John (House 1), a 46-year-old Dalit Christian of the Pallar caste. John had also been a temporary worker, and like Sundaram and Ilaiyaraja, he lost his job. John went to Coimbatore with his parents in 1997. He has two elder sisters and one younger sister, all of whom married into workers' families in tea estates in the Peermade tea belt. In Coimbatore, John became an assistant to a plumber named Murugan who had moved out of the plantations in the late 1980s. After one year of training, John became an independent plumber in 1998 and is now a popular plumber in the area. According to him, he was busy and did not need to beg for work. He made around 15,000 rupees per month and supported his entire family; his father had died three years earlier, his mother was too old to work and his wife could not find 'suitable' (non-manual labour) work. He has a son and a daughter, aged 14 and 12 respectively. Both were studying in a Christian management school. Despite John's success, he said he had to lie about his caste (or he had to pretend to be a person of higher caste) to become friends with the upper-caste small business owners in the industrial town of Coimbatore. It is these petty capitalists who provide work for John.

As mentioned, Karuppasamy and Selvam, the elder brothers of Sundaram and Ilaiyaraja, stayed on at the plantations. Karuppasamy inherited his father's status as a permanent manual worker. His wife, Maria, is also a permanent worker, and she inherited the work from her mother. Both Selvam and his wife are also permanent workers. The flip side is that Karuppasamy and Selvam earn less than half as much as their younger siblings outside the plantations. Selvam told me that the lack of money is a serious problem for 'major spending' such as hospital expenses, children's education, weddings and ritualised gift exchanges. They both said they had considered leaving the plantations on many occasions but did not want to go back to their native villages. The relative protection from caste discrimination needs to be regarded as a positive effect of being in the plantation despite the lower income. At the same time, three ex-temporary workers, Sundaram, Ilaiyaraja and John, have one thing in common in their otherwise different trajectories outside the plantations: they now all experience *overt* caste discrimination, whereas the caste discrimination they faced in the plantations was of a more structural, much less overt, kind.

The case of plantation Tamil Dalits in Tirupur is even more distressing. The fear of caste discrimination is so severe that most Tamil Dalits from the Kerala plantations in Tirupur hide their caste identity; I did not encounter anyone who disclosed it. Workers told me that revealing their Dalit identity would affect their ability to secure a skilled or semi-skilled job. A senior finance manager of a large firm told me that nepotism is a major factor when it comes to appointments and that Dalits would not be considered even for clerical positions.

I came across other Dalits from Tamil Nadu villages who concealed their caste identity in Coimbatore and Tirupur. But it is more difficult for them. The plantation Tamils can take advantage of the fact that the Tamil high castes have little knowledge of Kerala's caste hierarchy and practices. The plantation Dalits claim to belong to higher castes from Kerala (for example, to be Christian Nadars). They hide the details of their ancestral villages and their relatives in Tamil Nadu to limit the chance of getting caught. Those who conceal their caste have a better chance of getting a job or a house to rent than those who cannot or will not hide it. I met six families who managed to find housing in streets dominated by upper-caste people simply because they lied about their caste. I also met with 17 families who had returned to their ancestral villages in the Tirunelveli district of Tamil Nadu. They shared stories of 'cultural shock' as they were confronted with caste insults and violence of a kind they had not experienced in the plantations. They had to use the public water tap and purchase their groceries at the state-run ration shop (PDS) at separate times from the higher-caste villagers, and they faced caste segregation in the use of separate temples and burial grounds from those of the higher castes.

The plantation workers' search for new means of subsistence in the unorganised sectors shows that they are becoming part of a larger pool of the Dalit community who form most of the labour force in the unorganised and informal sectors. As Thorat and Attewell (2010) observe, this migrant Dalit labour force in the informal economy is a de-unionised and marginalised population who have been uprooted from their land to work elsewhere. Accordingly, as the plantation workers merge with these migrant communities, as in the case of the Tirupur textile industry, they end up as an alienated workforce, as a continuation of their ancestors, who were in a similar situation in the early years of plantation development. Indian capitalism has historically relied on an unorganised workforce and their exploitation by major and small business owners, which results in the absolute poverty of the workforce (Harriss-White and Gooptu 2001). It is in this situation that plantation Tamils finds themselves as they integrate into the unorganised labour force dominated by Dalits.

Although Tamil Dalit workers migrated as indentured labourers in the colonial period, they won a modicum of security and protection in their low-paid manual labour jobs in the tea industry over the decades. As shown in this chapter, with the crisis, as the plantations came under new regimes of control, labour rights were slashed, vacancies were not filled, temporary workers replaced permanent ones and the plantation Tamils became part of the casual seasonal migrant labour force in other parts of the country. The crisis in the global tea economy ushered in by neoliberal reforms led to the casualisation of the workforce in the tea plantations. The crisis forced the workers to become 'footloose' labourers, for they move from one place to another in search of a livelihood and a dignified life. Their struggle for livelihood and their experience of caste discrimination discussed in this chapter is further elucidated in the next with more ethnographic discussion of the retirees in the crisis context.

Notes

1 The labour committee changes every month, whereas the union representatives are retained. One of my informants told me that there is a competition to get into the committee as the members share the unofficial dividend received from the contractor (the wholesale tea leaf merchant, who buys the leaves at a lower rate due to his association with the labour committee). It was also alleged that the committee sold the leaves at below the market price because of their unholy alliance with the contractor. Accordingly, the workers do not receive the amount to which they are entitled. While I heard the same allegation from a few other informants, this could also be a new structure of suspicion in the crisis context. The increasing insecurity creates tension within the workers' society, leading to an atmosphere of deep mistrust between the workers.
2 During my fieldwork in 2010, the average exchange rate was 45 rupees to USD 1.

3 For instance, when the market rate for 1 kg of green leaves was 10 rupees in the local market, the workers had to sell it for 7 rupees to the trade union's designated intermediary.
4 'Housemaids' refer to women employed in housework such as cooking, cleaning, laundry and so forth. This is similar to its usage in English. Home nurse refers to those engaged in nursing or taking care of people due to illness, disability or old age. Most of the women who work as housemaids are illiterate and in most cases are over 40 years old. Home nurses are usually literate and younger (between 18 and 30 years).
5 To quote Jean Drèze (quoted in Morris 2010): 'For a family of five to have reasonably good nutrition, nothing like meat or fish or any such thing, but just one egg per person per day, one banana, some dhal, some vegetables, a reasonably balanced diet – it would cost more than Rs.200 ($4.4; £3) per family per day.' So while a family needs at least 6,000 rupees for basic survival, the workers' family earns roughly half of that, which is 3,000 rupees.
6 While there was no difference in the terms and conditions of work between other workers and plantation Dalits, the plantation Tamils had fewer choices in moving to another stitching or dyeing unit. This is due to the lack of networks and functional literacy that other groups accumulated over years of association with the units. Furthermore, the plantation Tamils preferred to find job opportunities through their 'plantation network' between the 100 families, for they were sceptical of contractors in general.
7 More than 3,000 small textile and garment manufacturing units rely on contract work from larger companies (http://www.knitcma.com/KNITcMA_HtmX/Vision.htm).
8 The tailors are specialised in stitching different parts of cloth. For example, in the case of a shirt, one tailor will stitch the sleeves, one will stitch the neck and another will stitch the rest.

3
Retirees: failed attempts to stay on

The agony of grief

The crisis in the tea plantations shattered the dreams of the retirees who, after 40 years of work, were entitled to an end-of-employment pay-out or gratuity (*service kāsu*).[1] Such was not forthcoming due to the crisis, and payment was deferred for those who retired in or after 2000. The deferral of retirement benefits was a blow to many workers' aspirations such as buying a house plot, arranging marriage for their children or seeking medical treatment that they had been delaying. For the retirees, receiving the pay-out was the only means to retain respect, sustain kinship relations and engage with everyday sociality in the plantations. The pay-out was vital to be able to fight the alienation resulting from being a Dalit-Tamil-underclass retiree in the plantations.

    The retirees expressed a particular understanding of the crisis in the plantations, having been engaged in plantation work over the long term; they had seen the progression of the plantation economy through various stages and had formed their expectations accordingly. Many of the retirees I encountered had more than 40 years of experience in plantation work, and the crisis had a particular poignancy for them. The misfortune is that the workers who retired from 2000 to 2010 also suffered severely during the early years of postcolonial state formation, when labour laws were rudimentary and infrastructural facilities for workers were strictly limited. For instance, the company allocated half of a tenement (*pāthivīdu*) to each worker, not a full tenement (*muzhuvīdu*) as is the case now. Temporary workers only received the veranda of a full tenement. The promise of the pay-out was the only thing that sustained many of them throughout the hard years of plantation life. The deferral of the payment on which their dreams depended has caused disappointment and bitterness.

These workers have over time created their own social and cultural world in the plantations, which provided them a sense of control and order in their lives despite scarcity and hardship. The creation of a unified and partly isolated plantation community gradually encouraged the workers to cease considering themselves displaced from Tamil Nadu as a consequence of the indenture system. Returning to their native villages would mean re-engaging with caste discriminations from which their ancestors had attempted to escape. Despite the crisis, most workers did not want to consider the prospect of returning to their villages. They very much wanted to remain in the plantation since it had become their home; it was a place where they had developed a sense of kinship, where many of their children were born, educated and worked, and where many of their parents had died and been buried. But for many the ability to stay depended on the continuation of the plantation system and on receiving the deferred payouts. The economic crisis and the subsequent lockout of the plantations dashed their hopes of clinging on to plantation life and its community.

In order to hold on to the plantation, they needed to have their own place to live after retirement. The retirees adopted many strategies to secure a place within the plantation belt. Some attempted to buy small plots of surrounding land, but a common strategy was to secure a permanent position for their children in the plantation so that the existing tenement they had occupied in the plantation could be retained. Many had built small outbuildings to the tenement or had planted fruit trees, thus attaching themselves to the buildings where major social occasions had occurred. In a few cases, the strategy was to try to gain permission to continue living in their children's tenement house, promising to contribute from their pension. The stigma associated with parents living in their daughters' households constrained the retirees' options for accommodation. In accordance with customary understandings, staying with a daughter's family means the parents also rely on the daughter's family even if their daughter is working and contributing towards the income of the family into which she has married. However, staying with a son-in-law's family is more acceptable if they are not totally dependent and are able to independently contribute to the household income. For instance, the parents could stay with their daughter if they had any inheritable property, which includes the gratuity amount and the provident fund. In a few other cases, circumstances that allowed the parents to stay with their daughter's family include an agreement between the daughter and her husband regarding her parents' needs and her dominance in making decisions in her family's affairs.

By disrupting this moral economy of exchange within domestic relationships, the crisis further alienated many retirees from the communities they had in effect created. This is expressed in the perception of a lack of respect and recognition as a function of the deferment of their retirement benefits and their ability to redeploy those benefits as gifts and obligations among relatives. A major reason for this loss of respect and recognition is that the retirees were no longer treated as active members of the workers' society. I have seen workers arrange marriages for their children when they were still permanent workers because fewer people would want to attend functions in the retirees' homes. This concern was very evident whenever workers discussed and gossiped about such occasions. These issues also come to the fore when workers engage in quarrels and make comments related to the retirement of other workers. For instance, people often say, 'You can't dance for so long', which means the other person can't hang around the plantation for much longer. Many retirees told me that such insults led them to think of immolating themselves in front of the company office in protest.

As Penny Vera-Sanso's (2007) study shows, the socio-economic policies formulated to improve the life situation of 'weaker sections of society' often fail to recognise the needs of the ageing population. Their neglect by the state means that, for the elderly, the maintenance of respect and status in plantation society depends on retirement benefits, which enable them to suspend the cultural forces that produce the lowly status of retirees. The pay-out for the retirees was often crucial for their ability to sustain the social and economic obligations of the elderly to kin. Children's reliance on transfers from their parents and grandparents is widely noted in South Asian studies (for example, Vera-Sanso 2006, 2007). But elderly individuals' loss of autonomy and of the individualised ethos that had become part of modern plantation life also upset them. Many did not want to be a burden or indebted to their children and saw a moral dignity in economic independence.

On the Hill Valley estate, 121 workers retired in the period 2000–11. Of these, 47 had passed away by the time I started fieldwork in 2011. The relatives of most of the deceased told me their last wish had been to receive their gratuity before they died. This theme of 'longing for gratuity' dominated the funerals of deceased retirees. I attended three such funerals during my fieldwork. Of those retirees who were alive, 34 had moved back to their native villages or to industrial centres in Tamil Nadu to secure their livelihood. Those who continued living on the plantation (40 retirees) largely relied on the MGNREGS. These retirees were distressed by the ongoing deferral of gratuity payments. This contributed to existing hardships such as poverty and poor health. Many of the older generation characterised their situation as 'still waiting to be buried' (*mannukulle pokāma kidakken*). Most retirees I talked to frequently returned in various ways to the topic of death. Although initially I underestimated its significance, assuming it was a natural topic of conversation for older people whose health had been ruined by 40 years of plantation work, I soon realised that the intensity of their talk about the futility of life and death was closely related to the crisis and the deferred payments. There was a strong sense that life had cheated them and that their life was now a tragic story. Certain aesthetics of pain and suffering were used to formulate their biographies and highlight their sorrow.

While the retirees in general had lost hope of receiving a gratuity, a few opted for small-scale trade, where they would buy tea in bulk from the company and sell it outside the tea belt, specifically in hotels. The company encouraged this option, since the price of the tea for the retirees was closer to the market rate (80 rupees per kg), when the market rate was just five rupees higher than the factory price. Those who had not chosen this strategy told me there is no point in getting a gratuity in bits and pieces in the form of tea, for they always considered it their life savings. This lump sum amount holds out the promise of being able to purchase a house or a plot of land. Furthermore, the purchase of tea was risky since they did not have the social network, the cultural capital or the functional ability to sell the tea. Those who opted to buy tea in bulk often complained about the futility of this arrangement, as they had to give it to others at a discount to resell on their behalf, which brought its own complications.

Adding to the distress is the fact that many plantation workers were not involved in pension schemes. Pension schemes for retirees from the provident fund require workers to initially deposit 30,000 rupees to be eligible for the monthly pension, which varies from 700 to 1,000 rupees depending on years of service. The pension scheme was implemented only in 1972. Most Hill Valley estate retirees do not have pensions since they did not have the money to pay the initial amount. While paying the initial amount and getting into the pension scheme was indeed economically beneficial, even workers who could manage to pay the initial amount did not opt in out of suspicion over the scheme. Sevvatha, one of my informants, told me these things are 'not practical' and that we need to have educated children to get good advice (*padicha pullanga vēnum*). The lack of a pension makes the retirees much more vulnerable since the pension scheme, despite the amount being so small, is the only scheme that provides financial security to the retirees.

The crisis affected the workers unequally and this accentuated the stigma felt by those who did not have sources of support other than their gratuity. This would include especially those who did not have sons who could meet the expenses of their retired parents. For example, many of those employed in the MGNREGS were considered the most affected and were sometimes despised by others because of the popular assumption in the plantation that only those who did not have any other options for livelihood would seek work under the scheme. The shame of state support implied a lack of autonomy and kinship.

The workers had the opportunity to file a case against the pay-out deferral. Yesuraj, a retired worker, received a favourable verdict. The court also ordered the company to pay 10 per cent annual interest for the period the gratuity was deferred. While this 10 per cent is applicable to all the workers, each retiree must file a separate case to receive this verdict and these payments. Workers found it difficult to meet the court expenses and most of them refrained from pursuing this option. Further, there were always rumours the company was going to sell a few of its estates to pay the gratuity, causing the workers to wait a few more months before taking any action. Invariably, the gossip and rumours convinced the workers to wait to take action, and many continued to wait. The ethnographic discussion of the retirees as they attempted to resist alienation shows multiple aspects of the crisis: from the experience of caste discrimination in the village of social origin, to the strategies they devised to overcome their alienation in the context of the deferred pay-out.

Between the devil and the deep blue sea

The experience of Saraswathi, a retired worker in her early sixties, illustrates the alienation of retirees, for she had to face the worst experiences of untouchability for being a Dalit woman. Caste processes have changed historically over time, but in many places those changes have not brought any significant weakening of caste discriminations. Caste has worked its way into different modern contexts. Saraswathi's situation suggests that in some cases moving to their villages of social origin was not a viable option for retirees as the intense practice of caste in Tamil villages discriminated against the Dalits.

In 2005, a year before her official retirement, Saraswathi took voluntary retirement and left with her son, Selvam, for her native village of Kallupatti in southern Tamil Nadu. Saraswathi went from experiencing the hardships of plantation society to an unfolding tragedy that approaches the dark themes of 1970s Tamil movies such as *Aval Oru Thodarkathai* (*She Is a Never-ending Story*), which depicts the poverty and agony caused by unexpected tragedies in working-class families.[2] Saraswathi's husband, Kalimuthu, passed away in 1998 as a result of binge drinking. Devi, Saraswathi's daughter (her elder child), passed away a year after Devi's husband, Manikkam, was killed in an accident while loading wood in a truck. Saraswathi accused Devi's in-laws of sorcery (*sei-vinai*) that she believed had killed her daughter. While these tragic events happened in 2006 and 2007, respectively, Devi's son committed suicide in 2009, allegedly due to ill treatment by Devi's in-laws with whom he was staying in Kudalur village in Theni district of southern Tamil Nadu. In addition to this pain and agony, what made Saraswathi, in her own words, 'close to a dead person' (*jadamā vāzhuren*) was Selvam's excessive drinking after his wife had two abortions and possibly because he was distressed by the early demise of his only sister, her husband and their son. He also believed (similarly to many workers who lamented tragedy in their family) that sorcery by Devi's in-laws had ruined the family.

In 2006, Saraswathi, along with Selvam and his wife, left Kallupatti for Kudalur to stay with Devi after Manikkam died. Saraswathi and Selvam's presence and support were important for Devi, since her in-laws accused her of being a bad omen and causing their son's death, and they often fought with her. In Kudalur, Saraswathi rented a hut for 500 rupees per month. Saraswathi and Devi undertook extremely low-wage manual labour in nearby agricultural land (*kāttu vēlai*), while Selvam commuted to different locations for work in the construction industry as a helper (*kaiyāl*) for a mason (*mesthrie*). Selvam's wife suffered from various health issues and did not work. Their routine was severely impacted by Devi's sudden death around eight months after Saraswathi arrived in Kudalur. After Devi's death, Saraswathi and Selvam returned to Kallupatti where they lived in a relative's small mud house and undertook work similar to what they had done in Kudalur – Saraswathi for *kāttu vēlai* in agricultural land (particularly weeding) and Selvam as a *kaiyāl* in the construction industry.

However, the distress in their personal lives was fuelled by caste discrimination in Kallupatti. In the village, 'untouchable' Dalits did not have the right to sit inside the teashop or to drink tea from a glass cup (*kuppi*). Dalits had to stand outside the teashop and drink from either a coconut shell or a steel cup depending on what was available. Since Saraswathi and family were not used to these explicit everyday forms of untouchability rooted in the ritual aspects of the caste system, the feelings of caste humiliation they experienced in Kallupatti were more intense than they were for those Dalits who were originally born and reared in the village. This is because, as mentioned earlier, they were relatively shielded from explicit caste discrimination on the plantation. This means Saraswathi had grown up enjoying the relatively egalitarian social relations made possible on the plantations, where the higher castes had little power compared with their counterparts in Tamil Nadu. Accordingly, the economic crisis and the consequent deferral of retirement benefits forced plantation Tamil Dalits to migrate back into the caste atrocities from which they had originally attempted to escape when they had first migrated to the plantations.

Saraswathi asked me not to tell other workers about the discrimination and forms of untouchability her family experienced in her native village. Although many workers would be sympathetic to her miseries, a few might taunt her for leaving and for her lack of foresight. As I will discuss in Chapter 6, in the context of the crisis, the workers differentiated themselves economically and socially. Saraswathi feared that someone would use her situation to assert their own superior capacities to control life's chances and cope with the crisis. Saraswathi told me she had not cheated or hurt anyone (*yārukkum oru dhrōhamum seyyalai*) in a way that would warrant being so badly treated by the goddess Mariamman. She considers herself, in this regard, morally upright, as many others in the plantations testified. She used to help many people. For instance, she told me (and many of her former neighbours confirmed) that whenever women from the neighbouring tenements needed rice, kerosene, sugar or any other necessary commodities, she was never hesitant to share, and she was never concerned over whether they would return it. In her own words, she never told them 'no' (*illannu sollamātten*).

I talked to Saraswathi whenever she came to the plantation to check if the retirees would be getting their gratuity soon. One day, she was very upset after the estate manager told her that a significant amount from her gratuity would be deducted towards her electricity bill since she had failed to cancel her tenement's electricity connection when she moved out. She was unaware the connection had to be cancelled or that she would be charged even if she was not using the electricity. The workers' tenements in the Hill Valley estate were electrified only in 2001, and the older generations of workers, such as Saraswathi, are still unaware of the bureaucratic requirements involved in electricity connections. This made her so sad that she described her alienated situation in thoughtful words, beginning with a proverb: 'My life is like a beggar's life (*Pichakāran pozhappu*), this land (the plantation) let us neither live nor die. If I get the gratuity, I would ask my son to move out of the village and close my eyes (would not mind to die then).'[3] While these analogies to a beggar's life paint a grim picture of plantation life, they are not exaggerations, particularly given the centrality of the retirement benefit to their livelihood. The ingenuity and creativity of many Dalit (plantation) women is demonstrated in their presentation of their life situation in poetic terms, where they often draw analogies from myth but also from contemporary Tamil films (Daniel 1996; Ram 2007; Jegathesan 2019). Indeed, many popular films re-localise or re-embody the narratives of myth, and both myth and film in turn become allegories that are re-localised and re-embodied in the personal poetic narratives of Tamil women, who are sensitive to the poetics of tragedy.

While Saraswathi indeed believed in the power of sorcery and blamed her daughter's in-laws for her death, other workers saw Saraswathi's belief as a strategy to cope with the shame of her and her family's inability to save her daughter and grandson. The aesthetics of tragedy here is one of alienation, of loneliness – an alienation from the social world but also from the protective care of the gods and, what is more, of Mariamman. It is the poetic paradox of this situation that draws out Saraswathi's deep sense of injustice. In short, Saraswathi was trapped between the devil and the deep blue sea. She was unable to return to the plantation since she could not find an alternative place to live or retain the tenement in the Hill Valley estate. However, staying in her village of origin would mean she and her family would be exposed to the vicious caste practices from which her ancestors had escaped.

Saraswathi's story elucidates the effect that caste had on those who returned to their Tamil villages, just as it did on the plantation youth who were forced to hide their caste identity in the urban context as explained in the next chapter. Crisis and the deferred pay-out exposed the workers to stigmatised forms of their identity. The deferred pay-out drove Saraswathi and her family to relocate to Tamil Nadu, where they experienced intensive forms of caste discrimination. As Saskia Sassen (2014) puts it succinctly, these workers, who were once central to the development of capitalism, are increasingly expelled from the global economy as soon as they cease being of value as workers and customers. As Sassen further points out, their expulsion is not anomalous but is integral to the deepening of capitalist relations. In other words, the expulsion is the result not of the crisis of capitalist economy but of its bolstering (see also Harvey 2010). A close observation of how the retirees experience their alienated life amid the crisis shows that the alienation produced by the deferred pay-out and by their exposure to stigmatised forms of their identity are closely interlinked.

Failed attempts to stay on

While Saraswathi's situation exposes the tragedy of alienation of those who attempt to escape plantation life, the story of Shanmugham and Saroja, a retired couple, elucidates the retirees' struggle to cling to the plantation society and their attempt to resist being alienated further and exposed to the caste atrocities in their village of origin. Shanmugham was born on the Hill Valley estate in the early 1940s but moved to his native village of Irukkanthurai in southern Tamil Nadu when he was 10 years old. In Irukkanthurai, he had to work as a bonded labourer (*Pannaiyāl*) for a landlord (*Pannaiyār*) for five rupees per month to repay the amount his father had borrowed from the landlord to arrange his elder sister's marriage. He told me the landlord's henchmen forcefully took him from his hiding place, which he recalled was full of giant milkweeds. His father was forced to assent to Shanmugham's bonded labour since there was no other way to pay off the debt. Shanmugham was in bonded labour – or, in his own words, he 'took the hoe [*manvetti*] in his hand' – by the age of 12. He escaped to the plantation after two years of bonded servitude, where he joined two of his elder brothers who were already working on the Hill Valley estate. He secured permanent work on the plantation and at the age of 18 he was married. Tragically, Shanmugham's first wife passed away after nine years of marriage, leaving Shanmugham with their two small children (a boy and a girl). Shanmugham was married again in 1966 to Saroja, who was then living with her parents in a neighbouring tea estate. The couple had two daughters, Selvi and Mary.

One of Shanmugham's elder brothers took care of the first two children as Shanmugham moved to a separate house after his second marriage. In 1995, Shanmugham arranged Selvi's marriage by cashing out a life insurance savings account. He later arranged Mary's marriage with the gratuity he received after retiring in 1996. Shanmugham and Saroja, however, were able to retain their house on the plantation since Saroja was still a permanent labourer. Shanmugham told me he led a decent life even after his retirement; he was able to have his *kanji* (literally rice gruel but colloquially food in general) without much difficulty. However, the couple's life situation was drastically changed when the tea company shut down part of its operation in response to the crisis, resulting in reduced workdays and deferred wages. Saroja retired in 2002 and was not given her gratuity. As a result, both she and Shanmugham had to seek work outside the plantation, and they registered under the MGNREGS. When they were not able to get work under the scheme, Saroja looked for work as a tea plucker or pepper picker in *puthuvēli*; Shanmugham found some work in the cardamom fields or else the cultivation of vegetables, also in *puthuvēli*.

While Shanmugham insisted that he managed to find money to buy rice, he nonetheless said he worried ceaselessly, especially about having 'a roof over their heads'. He often complained he did not even have a hut in which to rest his head at night (*thalai sāikka kudisaiillai*) and his eyes often filled with tears, as he did not have enough money to rent a place. Saroja often intervened with self-critique: 'We have rented our brains' (*Puthiye kadam koduthuttēn*). By this, Saroja meant they should have planned better for their future and bought a small piece of land or a house for security after retirement. In other words, they did not use their brains. Saroja's expression is common in India, where there has been a dramatic rise in the cost of living – and especially in prices for land and gold – as a result of neoliberal policies. The hike in land price has added to the crisis for the plantation workers, as plots around the plantations are virtually unaffordable. The difficulties are exacerbated for Shanmugham and Saroja for cultural reasons connected to the question of respect. The couple felt they could not stay with their daughters because of the social humiliation involved. Shanmugham could not approach his son for support, or exert the obligation due to a father, because his brother had taken over the role of rearing his son. His son does not regard him as his proper father. However, Shanmugham's son-in-law agreed to help him rent a house as long as Shanmugham shared a significant amount of his wife's pension pay-out with his elder daughter.

In mid-November 2011, I was sitting near the crèche-turned-church when Shanmugham came rushing in the direction of the closed factory. When I asked why he was rushing, Shanmugham smiled and said he would tell me upon his return. Half an hour he returned with a grim expression. He had gone to meet the estate manager, who had stopped at the factory for a routine equipment check. Shanmugham had tried to negotiate a special deal: he would not make an immediate claim on Saroja's pension pay-out if the manager would let them rent a plantation tenement for a few years. The manager had refused his request, saying it would be illegal and he had no authority to do so. Shanmugham told me to keep quiet about his secret meeting with the manager, although he did not really care if I told others on the estate because he knew many workers were making similar attempts. Conversations with other retirees confirmed that many were trying to keep their accommodation on the plantation. This incident also underlines the increased alienation

Shanmugham had experienced as a result of the crisis. Shanmugham and Saroja's alienated situation shows that the deferred pay-out had created great uncertainty, which had serious implications for their sociality and kinship relations. The retirees' plight gives a potent sense of the alienation they are experiencing that has ramifications throughout the community they head. The pay-out would have given them a chance to fully establish themselves in a new horizon of possibility – to buy land and to overcome an alienated condition of dependency. These hopes were dashed. The deferment has forced the plantation workers at the end of their days back into a world of alienation that they had hoped to leave behind.

While Shanmugham and Saroja struggled to retain their tenement, other retirees have occasionally requested small advances from their gratuity, citing medical reasons or a child's marriage ceremony. While the deferred gratuity may range from 50,000 to 90,000 rupees, the advance the workers requested to meet their proposed expenses ranged only from 5,000 to 10,000 rupees, or around 10 per cent of the total. A few received the requested amount, but most were denied because 'the company did not have enough money'. This forced them to rely on their children for money, which was a blow to their attempt to regain autonomy and respect in the plantation society. Complicating the situation, the retirees' children often encouraged their parents to apply for an amount so as to meet large expenses such as their own children's education. The failure to obtain an advance created animosity within the family, threatening the retirees' attempts to cling to the plantation life by living with their children. In other words, the failure to obtain the advance resulted in further alienation. The following discussion of Subbaiyya and Parvathi explicates the foregoing concerns of the retirees.

In search of respect

Parvathi and her husband, Subbaiyya, were permanent workers on the Hill Valley estate and retired from service in 2004 and 2000, respectively. While Subbaiyya was born and reared on the Hill Valley estate, Parvathi was brought up on the neighbouring Puthumalai estate. They married in 1964, and Parvathi moved to the Hill Valley estate, to which she could transfer her permanent worker status because the two estates were owned by the same company. The couple have two sons and two daughters. A daughter and a son were living with their families on the same estate, and Parvathi was staying with the son. The other daughter is married to Parvathi's elder brother's son (*marumakan*), and they live on the

Puthumalai estate. The other son works as a medical sales representative in Chennai.

Subbaiyya worked in the tea factory for the entire 40 years of his working life. The exposure to tea dust caused him serious respiratory problems,[4] and he often had to be hospitalised. He told me the plantation manager had given him only 5,000 rupees as an advance from his gratuity. He has had to rely on his sons for money for treatment two or three times. Subbaiyya told his sons he would repay the expenditure when he received his gratuity. However, his sons were also affected by the crisis and were unable to grant Subbaiyya's request. Therefore, Subbaiyya had to skip going to the hospital. When I asked why he did not insist his sons take him to the hospital, he said he hated begging (*pichaiedukkavirupamillai*). He felt his dignity and self-esteem did not allow him to make repeated requests to his sons. Further, he told me he knew his sons did not have money and they had their own families to look after. He told me that he was suffering because of working in the factories, and he had not received money to treat an illness had been caused by factory work. Strangely, he was smiling when he told me this, but I know from other workers that Subbaiyya often became irate when the plantation manager denied his requests for advance payment.

Subbaiyya was often at the forefront of protests organised against the deferral of gratuity payments. He once told me the money he was demanding had been generated by him suffocating in factory tea dust (*podikullaninnuvēlai sencha kāsu*). He was afraid he might die without seeing it (*inthakāsapākkakoduthuvaikkathu pōle*). He added that his dead body should not be carried to the cemetery until the company had paid his wife the money. If his dead body were to be carried away, it would not burn out of grief. He often repeated this comment whenever the chance arose. He made a similar statement when a local TV channel reporting on one such protest interviewed him. This statement became popular in the everyday conversation of plantation workers after Subbaiyya's death in 2011. He used to work all 26 workdays in a month. Many people remember seeing him in the khaki uniform he wore on the way to the factory and how the dust covered his face as he walked back from the factory to his house. He was remembered as a family man who seldom went to teashops. In the plantation society, refraining from going to a teashop implies that one is a responsible man who puts the important and everyday needs of his family ahead of his own needs in terms of finances and pleasures. Unfortunately, Subbaiyya passed away without seeing his gratuity. He died in despair.

Indeed, deferred gratuity has become a source of alienation and despair for many retirees who were waiting for death and sought to give something back or to leave a memorialising gift that would show that their work had meant something, had delivered something, even if it was small and humble. It is in these small, humble gifts that the poor Dalits sought their dignity and autonomy; this is what redeemed work and the sacrifice of work, making it a moral project. The problematisation of their gratuity payments led many to feel soiled – that their sacrifice had been futile and that they could not redeem themselves and regain their dignity before death – for this was also a question of a good death, of preparing oneself morally for death, and one did so through reconciling gifts, obligations and debts with family. It is here that the existential pain of poverty is felt, that the hidden injuries of caste and class coalesce.

After Subbaiyya's death, Parvathi complained to many people that the grief of a deferred pay-out had 'killed' him. I visited Parvathi when another informant told me he had often seen her visiting the manager's office demanding both Subbaiyya's and her own pay-outs. Her distress over the pay-out deferral had caused her turmoil just as it had her husband. In a long conversation, Parvathi described the difficulty and embarrassment she had experienced while visiting the manager's office. Most often, the manager would not be in the office. Sometimes, the other staff would tell her the manager might come back in an hour or two. She would wait again but often would not meet the manager even then. If the manager happened to be present, he would send his personal assistant to inform Parvathi she would be contacted later and did not need to wait on the office veranda.

In fact, what made her angry was that she was demanding the money for which she had toiled (*uzhaithakāsu*) for 40 years, breaking her back as a tea plucker in the sloppy hills. She told me that neither she nor any other worker should need to bow her head before someone and wait like a dog (*nāimāthirinikkanum*) while demanding her own hard-earned money. She asked me ironically whether she was asking for a share of the ancestral property of the management staff. She was still angry as she described the incident, although she previously received an advance of 10,000 rupees due to her 'repeated walk' to the office, which is 4 kilometres away from the Hill Valley estate. The pay-out becomes a condensed metaphor of the injustices of existence, of the inability to redeem and control one's circumstances, a total alienation despite all the work.

A few weeks after my conversation with Parvathi, she moved out of her son's house because of what she considered ill treatment by her daughter-in-law. She went to the Puthumalai estate to live with her daughter. I went to Puthumalai to understand the reasons for the shift. She told me she was tired of being insulted by her daughter-in-law – that no one, including her own son, recognised her as a human being (*manusiya yārum mathikkaruthilla*) after her retirement. In the middle of our conversation, Parvathi's daughter left the room to make tea for me. Parvathi used the opportunity to tell me that her daughter's husband, Manikkam, wanted to know if Parvathi would transfer the gratuity to him. But she did not want to promise him the money, since it was the only hope (in her words, 'hold') to keep her alive. Parvathi told me Manikkam no longer spoke to her because she had not promised him the gratuity. She thought she would go back to her son only when she received the gratuity. This is because, as she put it, everyone needed only money and no one wanted to talk to someone who did not have money – even her own children. There is a sense in which old people use the promises of gratuity to secure their existence in their old age, and the management of these promises becomes increasingly difficult for them, especially with in-laws. As I was preparing to leave after the tea and conversation, Parvathi told me that since her husband passed away, it was her turn to 'go into the soil'.

The retirees' alienation is explicit in their complaints that they were not getting the respect and recognition they used to receive in the plantation society. The respect Parvathi demanded in the plantation community at large is specifically expressed in her visit to the manager's office. She associated the lack of respect and recognition with the deferred gratuity – a sign that the economic crisis had alienated them from the plantation life to the extent that they were forced to imagine death as the only way out. By negating the retirement benefits, the plantation company negated the possibility for a dignified existence for retired workers. The workers have a personal existential relation with the plantation system in a way that the collapse of the plantation system also meant the collapse of the workers' livelihood, social life and sense of autonomy and dignity in the world.

The alienated being

It is evident throughout the chapter that retirees reflect on the crisis as more than just a difficult time in their own lives. Rather, the crisis and the consequent gratuity deferral forced the retirees to rethink the futility of human life itself. Most of the conversations I had with the retirees had 'death' as the dominating theme. I noticed certain aesthetics of death, a certain tragic narrative that captured for them the depths of alienated existence in suffering and sacrifice. The crisis evoked a strong sense of the futility of human life, of the injustice of not being able to access the financial reward earned and dreamed about whenever women had to climb a steep hill with heavy baskets of tea leaves in the monsoon rain, and the men had to suffocate in the factory's dust. They had suffered low wages, and they contented and mollified themselves with the thought that a small treasure was waiting at the end, not just for them but also for their families: something would be left for their children that would memorialise their existence and redeem it. The deferred gratuity shattered their hopes and the meaning of life. It is through the imagination of death and through invoking such a theme to dominate everyday conversation that the retired workers attempt to resist their condition of being alienated.

Meaninglessness, powerlessness and social isolation are considered major attributes of alienation (Seeman 1959). These are evident in the narratives of everyday life of the retirees. The retirees felt they lacked control over their life situation and that life became meaningless when their gratuity was deferred. They were isolated from wider social relations in the workers' settlement, and their 'powerlessness' is evident in their narrative about the futility of life and in the moments when they blame themselves for their life situation. The denial of the self – a major feature of alienation – is evident in all three stories discussed in this chapter. Most of my informants were critical not only of the whole situation they were in but also of themselves. The intensity of alienation is evident when Saroja laments renting out her brain, when Saraswathi says she is 'close to a dead person' and that her life is like that of a beggar and when Parvathi complains that no one treats her like a human being. Alienation seems to be the only phenomenon through which the retirees express and experience their life. As Marx observes, 'alienation from the self means that the worker does not affirm himself but denies himself, does not feel content but unhappy' (1959 [1844], 73). At the same time, this denial of self is significant not only with regard to the lack of control experienced due to economic exploitation as workers or retirees, but also due to the casteist postcolonial stigmatisation of their identity as women and men of the Tamil Dalit minority.

In summary, the workers in general and the retirees in particular were alienated on multiple counts during the crisis: they were alienated from their labour, plantation life, kinship relations, family and from their own being. In the context of an abandoned plantation, they were located neither in nor outside of it. It is the perfect liminal phase of being betwixt and between, neither here nor there (Turner 1967, 1969). The next chapter further explores the situated dimensions of alienation, discrimination and prejudice against Tamil youth in a dispute context, which adds insult to the injury of the crisis. Some of the youth were potential tea workers who had to change their strategies due to the crisis. The ethnographic accounts describe attempts by youths to follow new life trajectories outside the world of the plantations, a world that still exercises limiting effect. These involve, on the one hand, the continuing constraints of Dalit identity and, on the other hand, the great difficulty in establishing the terms of their new life beyond the existence of the plantations through purchasing their own 'soil' for the permanent settlement of their families and kin. They explicitly reveal these youths' alienated position within as well as outside the plantations with special reference to the impact of the economic crisis.

Notes

1 The retirement benefits include two key components: the gratuity and the provident fund. The gratuity is calculated by multiplying half of the last three months' salary by the number of years of labour. The workers need at least 180 days of work to qualify for the gratuity. A person retires on completing 40 years of labour or reaching 58 years of age, whichever comes first. The provident fund is a combination of employer and employee contributions, each of 12 per cent of the worker's daily wage.
2 This movie became an analogy to refer to the bleak conditions in plantation society when the workers associated their life situations with various characters in the movie.
3 Saraswathi's statement portrays the plantation as an institution responsible for both the life and the death of the workers. This parallels the lives of tin miners in Bolivia, as June Nash (1979) explains it in her book *We Eat the Mines, and the Mines Eat Us*. The miners depend on the mines for a living but eventually suffer from lung disease and thus lose out to the mines.
4 Medical studies have shown that long-term work in tea factories causes serious respiratory and other health hazards (Jayawardana and Udupihille 1997).

4
Youth: hidden injuries of caste

With the collapse and reconfiguration of the plantation economy, the possibility of youth falling back on plantation employment evaporated. This increased the anxiety of the youth because of the social and cultural expectations placed on them to provide for their parents and kin. Their search for new employment and education opportunities outside the plantations increased their awareness of their position as an underclass and of their status as members of the Tamil-speaking Dalits. This further motivated them to secure circumstances, especially land and houses, which would enable them to combat the sense of alienation that the plantation crisis had, in a sense, further stimulated. I clarify that the migration of the plantation youth for education and employment outside the tea belt is a phenomenon that occurs independently of the crisis but that has achieved a greater urgency because of the crisis.

Tamil Dalit youth in the plantations increasingly sought work outside the plantations – in urban areas of Kerala, in the manufacturing and garment sectors in Coimbatore and Tirupur in Tamil Nadu and some even in their ancestral villages in Tamil Nadu. While they often earned more money in the new work sites than on the plantations, they were also subjected to new forms of insecurities facing the mass of workers who make up India's informal economy. However, while their structural position on the plantations was based on their historical class, gender and caste position, it was only when they left the plantations that they faced explicit caste discrimination to such an extent that almost everyone who went to work in Tirupur tried to hide their caste.

Three cases are presented here to illustrate the difficulties that plantation youth encountered while establishing new life trajectories. These cases are representative of the different kinds of problems and challenges associated with the common strategies adopted by youth.

A common strategy among the plantation youth is to seek further education, usually in Thiruvananthapuram, despite having little money and facing difficulty in finding accommodation (Case 1). Some of the youth return to Tamil Nadu and re-encounter the caste discrimination that their forebears once escaped (Case 2). Others try to stay on the plantations but struggle to buy a plot of land due to rising land prices (Case 3). What I describe in these cases is representative of many Dalit youth in Kerala (and India in general). But I consider that the plantation background and Dalit status of the youth whose struggles are recounted here give a greater intensity to their experiences.

The struggle for lodging

Around 70 per cent of the plantation youth who wish to pursue higher education in Kerala move to the capital city of Thiruvananthapuram. Those who wish to pursue higher studies in Tamil Nadu mostly move to cities near their family's village of origin, with Tiruchirappalli and Nagercoil being the most popular destinations. My focus on the plantation youth in Thiruvananthapuram is important because this group is highly literate and upwardly mobile compared with those who sought manual and semi-skilled work. The educated youth's mobility is a comfort to their relatives in the plantation who have been affected by the crisis and who must look to them for cash assistance for events such as marriages and, often, merely for subsistence. The prospects of upward social mobility of the educated youth are, however, restricted by the social discrimination they experience in the wider society.

The migrant plantation youth can be said to have a cognitive map of functions and opportunities presented by various townships in Kerala, and this informs their choice of the place of migration. For example, Tamil youth consider Kottayam as an important medical training and treatment centre, Mundakayam as a place for finding labour-intensive jobs and so on. Thiruvananthapuram is regarded by them as the most important centre for educational opportunity. This is primarily because of the presence of free student hostels in an environment where there are many government-run liberal arts colleges. Many of the colleges in Thiruvananthapuram offer the option to study Tamil as a subject for undergraduate and graduate degrees, and also as a legitimate subject subsidiary to others. Moreover, the city is close to the southern districts of Tamil Nadu.

In 2012, 52 of the 130 residents in the Model Hostel for Boys in Thiruvananthapuram were Tamil students, 23 of whom were from the

Peermade tea belt.[1] Students from the plantation belt also stayed in the Kerala University Hostel for Boys. Of the 90 students in this hostel, 28 were Tamil boys, 15 of whom were from the Peermade tea belt. These students were enrolled in one of the four government colleges or in one of the two industrial training institutes (ITIs) in Thiruvananthapuram. There was a substantial increase in the number of students from tea plantations residing in the two hostels in 2012 compared with 2002–3 (when there were only 29 students from the tea plantations). However, the enrolment of students between 2012 and 2020 was stagnant, perhaps indicating the long-term effects of the economic crisis in the tea plantations. In 2012, 13 female students from the Peermade tea belt stayed in the Model Hostel for Girls and another seven stayed in a private hostel in the city.

On completion of their courses, about 10–15 per cent of the boys remained in Thiruvananthapuram while the others went elsewhere for employment. Some of them took up sales jobs (selling credit cards, mobile SIM cards or insurance products). A few others managed to get teaching jobs or were employed as translators (this is, however, an exception rather than the rule). Most of the students were seen to take up either blue-collar work or jobs in the food service industry (as cooks, waiters and so on). Among the girls, two stayed back in the city as they had married Tamil boys. Others returned to the tea belt and mostly worked as schoolteachers or coordinators of self-help groups; one worked as a clerk with a local government office.

The case presented in this section gives a qualitative account of the experiences of three educated Dalit plantation youth seeking education and a place of residence in an urban environment (Thiruvananthapuram). Muthukrishnan, Manohar and Nithin, who were friends in the plantations, had to overcome their background as Dalit plantation youth to achieve their desire for further education. They encountered situations on a daily basis which reasserted their devalued status as Dalits. Here, I present their background in brief before giving an account their experiences in the urban world that informs them of their Dalit status – a realisation produced in the larger outside world of the city which was not apparent in their life in the plantations, especially before the crisis.

Muthukrishnan was not competent in English or Malayalam (the languages in which the course examinations were taken). He was educated in the Tamil language in the plantation. This was common among the plantation youth, and as with many others, he failed to pass his exams. He decided to try to gain the necessary language competencies to pass his examinations. To gain the requisite language skills, however, he first had to secure an income and accommodation. He found work as an assistant at a roadside food stall with the help of a friend from the plantations. He worked from 6 pm to midnight and received 100 rupees per day, amounting to 3,000 rupees per month (he supplemented this income with other casual work such as selling mobile SIM cards). This income was well short of what was needed to live in the city, even frugally, and he had to resort to cheap housing. His friends Manohar and Nithin also faced substantial financial constraints. They also took up a number of casual jobs to meet their living expenses.

Manohar's educational situation was similar to that of Muthukrishnan, and he also was not competent in English or Malayalam.[2] He failed his exams at college and in the meantime had to find some means of earning an income so that he could re-appear the exams. He found a job as a waiter in a club. Nithin had a lot in common with Muthukrishnan and Manohar. He studied for a bachelor's degree in geography in a government college located close to the campus of the University of Kerala. He failed in two courses and had to pass them to graduate. While Muthukrishnan and Manohar took up manual labour jobs, Nithin was hesitant to engage in manual labour and was determined to find a white-collar job. Manohar and Muthukrishnan teased Nithin for not taking up *menial* jobs as they did and instead 'going for grapes beyond reach' (*kidaikkātha munthiri*). After a month's search, Nithin found a job as a marketing agent with a mobile service provider. His task was to find customers who were either government servants or had permanent jobs at private firms. He would earn 4,000 rupees per month if he could find 75 customers in a month. Muthukrishnan, Manohar and Nithin were all keen to succeed. Whenever they got an opportunity, the three friends would engage in conversations with each other to improve their English and pass their exams.

Muthukrishnan, Manohar and Nithin searched for cheap housing to stay in. During the course of their search, they all resided illegally in one of the government-run hostels and escaped to the plantations whenever they feared being discovered. They generally entered the hostel late at night and left early in the morning. They also feared that their friends would be expelled as a punishment if they were found to be in violation of hostel rules. Nithin described their current situation as 'the life of dog' (*nāy pozhappu*). There were few alternatives to renting. Each of them was prepared to pay a little more than 1,000 rupees from their monthly earnings. Their families back in the plantations were also demanding help at this time, which limited their expenditure. The situation was grim because most landlords demanded two months' rent in advance and an additional security deposit of 20,000 rupees which was practically impossible for them to provide. The three of them expressed their plight through sarcastic jokes they frequently shared. Muthukrishnan commented that their only possibility was a haunted house, as portrayed in Tamil/Malayalam movies. They hired a local broker to help them in their search for housing. He informed them of a place in the heart of the city, and when they arrived there to meet the agent and the owner of the house, they realised that it was located in a Dalit colony or neighbourhood.[3]

This settlement is notorious for thugs – a stereotype of the underclass Dalit population.[4] The three friends were urged by the broker to rent the house and they decided to do so. I questioned them about this information. The broker had recognised that the three youth were Dalits. The broker told them forthrightly that the settlement was appropriate for them. They were effectively trapped in the Dalit category to which their parlous situation owes a great deal. It was during their search for accommodation that they became acutely conscious of their identity as Dalits.

The rented house was on the south-eastern edge of the settlement, facing a main road in the city that connected the railway and bus stations with various highways to cities to the north. The house was the ancestral property of a 35-year-old Nair man who had served as a soldier in the Indian Army. The army job was not a well-remunerated one and renting out the house was a major source of supplementary income for him. He also did not want to live in the house because of its location. So the picture is clear: plantation youth who searched for cheap accommodation ended up in a settlement of people belonging to their own community (which offered them some social and political security because there is a degree of solidarity among different Dalit communities across India).

The plantation youth, as college students, were socially connected to some extent to other caste or class groups in the city. These social links are abruptly broken, however, once the youths leave college, and relations with their plantation kin and other acquaintances among Dalits are strengthened. Outside college, they recognise more intensely the diminished respect they receive from the wider society. It could be argued that the once the plantation youth leave college and the student hostel, where they maintained a relatively secure identity as a student under the closed institutional structure of the state, they confront negative evaluations of themselves, constraining them within their own immediate linguistic, ethnic and racial milieu.

Housing is a major means by which the marginalised are positioned and grouped by those outside into self-reproducing ghettoes, creating communities of poverty, squalor and disorder. At the same time, for those inside, housing is a means of providing a sense of community, intimacy, care, reciprocity and self-politicising. The stigma associated with being a Dalit pushes them into shared domains of residence and sociality that confirm, in the city, their general state of alienation in society as a whole.

I stayed in the house rented by the three friends. I asked them how they felt living in a colony stigmatised for allegedly being filled with thugs. The three of them looked at each other, hesitant to answer. Then Manohar smilingly broke the nervous silence and said that the colony was ideal for them for many reasons, one of them being that the landlord did not keep a close eye on the house. This gave them the freedom to support other youth who, like them, were compelled to risk living unlawfully in hostels. Nithin interrupted with the comment that the house was a 'refugee camp' almost from the very first day they rented it. He added that it was a place where plantation workers could stay when they came to the city for medical care.[5]

This house (and similar houses occupied by other plantation youth) also functions as a temporary hostel, where relatives and neighbours stay when they begin their college education as it takes a few months to gain admission to the college hostel. Furthermore, the parents of many students (particularly female students) who come to the city for their children's college admission stay in such houses for a day or two. A facility of this kind is hardly a possibility in the mainstream middle-class or upper-middle-class settlements, where independent houses or the upstairs of houses are usually monitored and the number of guests who can be accommodated is limited.

The importance of the house as a low-cost source of accommodation for plantation workers who visited the city for various purposes was evident during my own stay there. Whenever I visited the three friends, I had to share the space with someone from the plantation who had come to the city for medical treatment or college admission. The longest stay during my presence in the house was by Manohar's father's younger brother (*chithappa*) and his wife (*chithi*). They had come to the city to seek medical treatment for their daughter, who was diagnosed with congenital heart disease. While Manohar's *chithi* stayed in the hospital with her daughter, Manohar and his *chithappa* prepared food for them and delivered it to the hospital because they could not afford the food in the hospital canteens or nearby restaurants. Manohar's *chithappa* told me that their initial plan was to go to Theni Medical College in Tamil Nadu but they decided to go to Thiruvananthapuram Medical College instead when Manohar offered to help them.

The general situation of the three friends – their plight and that of many of their relatives and friends from the plantations – was dramatically illustrated in a tragicomic incident. When I was staying in the house, many jokes would be made about the difficulties they confronted in their urban life. One such sad but funny incident regarding an early encounter with a group of young men in his neighbourhood was narrated by Muthukrishnan. One evening, while Muthukrishnan was alone in the house, two men who appeared to be around 35 years of age knocked at the door. They introduced themselves as neighbours and told Muthukrishnan that they wanted to meet the newcomers to the colony – the plantation youth. As the conversation progressed, the local residents enquired about the whereabouts of other residents of the house. Muthukrishnan answered a battery of questions but was unnerved as he suspected the men were local thugs – such was the reputation of the area. Finally, the two men demanded 200 rupees from Muthukrishnan, promising to repay the money soon. Muthukrishnan did not believe them. Moreover he had no money to spare because of the demands of his parents in the plantation who were out of work. His father also needed medical treatment for a thyroid disorder. Muthukrishnan had no other option but to engage in the following performance.

Muthukrishnan smiled and extended his hands as if in prayer and uttered in broken Malayalam, 'My dear Brother, I do not have any money. Why don't you come inside and search for two hundred rupees. Really, I do not have any money' (*Ente chetta, enteduthu onnumilla. vene nokkikko. Ente roomil onnumilla*). He appeared so pathetic that the men accosting him broke out in guffaws. They were sympathetic and ashamed all at once. They said, 'his poverty was undoubtedly genuine'. The men then assured Muthukrishnan that they would never again demand money from him or any other residents of the house. They went on to say that they were very embarrassed and would rather commit suicide than demand money from him again. How could they confront an impoverished man such as Muthukrishnan!

Everyone present in the house laughed when Muthukrishnan narrated this story. Our amusement stemmed not only from Muthukrishnan's theatricality but also from the dark truth the story revealed. It was in many ways a dramatisation of the everyday experience, and indeed a parody of Muthukrishnan's and his friends' actual situation. The fact that his situation provoked sympathy from the local toughs also shows that everyone in the neighbourhood was in the same cruel situation. As Donna Goldstein (2003, 12) observes in her captivating ethnography of the poor in Rio de Janeiro's favela, the aesthetic of laughter is closely tied to the materiality of the poor's misery. It is the 'laughter out of place' that psychologically sustains the poor (Goldstein 2003, 101).

Broadly, the attainment of higher education does not seem to have a marked effect on the upward social mobility of Dalits (Mosse 2010; Jeffrey et al. 2004). Following Bourdieu (1986) on how cultural capital affects educational success, it may be said that the negative social capital that Dalits possess as Dalits works against them.[6] The negative social capital is evident in their failure to get jobs in the labour market relative to their educational attainment, and this, in turn, influences their high dropout rates from educational institutions. Their relative poverty and the pressures on them to meet obligations at home in the plantation belt (as an effect of the crisis) also have a deleterious impact on their ambitions. In this complicated web of causes, the reproduction of inequality and existing hierarchy amid the crisis is carried out through cultural alienation and stereotyping, which render these groups vulnerable. This, in turn, leads them to reconstitute communities and practices that, for some, reproduce conditions of their own marginalisation. The intensity of cultural alienation is more acute in the cities in Tamil Nadu, where a large number of plantation youth seek work. The situation of Gokul and others elucidates further how the youth deal with negative images of their caste.

Hidden injuries of caste

Gokul's parents lived on the estate and his younger brother worked as a technical assistant in a well-known electronics firm in Kochi. Gokul studied up to grade 10 at the high school in Peermade. In 2002, he moved to Chennai to seek new opportunities as the crisis continued to affect life on the plantation. Gokul found a job as a salesperson in the bag section of the biggest retail shop in Chennai. I visited Gokul in May 2011. As I interacted with Gokul on the pretext of being a customer in the shop, I tried to understand the nature of the social relations Gokul was enmeshed in. The shop was in an eight-storey building and had more than 200 employees. The shop was owned by a man belonging to the non-Dalit intermediary Nadar caste who employed men and women belonging to his caste in key positions. In fact, most of the employees in this retail shop were from the Nadar caste of southern Tamil Nadu. Gokul's friend, who had helped him get the job, suggested that he hide his caste because Dalits were often referred to derogatorily, even in casual conversations in workplaces. Gokul disguised his caste and introduced himself as a Christian. He refused to answer questions that would reveal his caste identity. The owner and key managerial staff at the shop may have thought that Gokul belonged to their caste (a significant percentage of Kerala Nadars are Christians).

Gokul stated that the owner and other staff in the shop often spoke highly of their caste and used degrading racial slurs against lower castes in his presence, assuming that Gokul shared their opinions. For instance, whenever two workers quarrelled, they would refer to each other as son of *Parayar* or *Arunthathiyar* (*chakkiliya paya makan* or *para paya makan*), meaning the other person's real father is an 'outcaste'. These references are, of course, demeaning and dehumanising for the Dalits who hear them. Gokul narrated many such instances in which the workers made fun of Dalit sub-castes. Gokul could not challenge such references because most of the workers belonged to upper castes, and he had to retain his job to send money to his jobless parents on the plantation. Gokul's conversation indicated that he often remained silent or even smiled when the workers made derogatory references to his (Dalit) sub-caste when they quarrelled or cracked jokes. Gokul told me that it was not difficult for him to get along with his co-workers. The only condition was that the co-workers should not find out about Gokul's caste identity. His projection of an alternative identity to hide his Dalit identity, as I understood from observing and talking to him, was necessary for him to avoid 'certain unnecessary experiences in the workplace'. Gokul had seen many of his friends being taunted for being Dalits. Gokul added that there were many Dalits among the workers who disguised their caste in order to keep their jobs in the retail shop.

Michael, another plantation youth, migrated to Coimbatore to work as a driver in a stone quarry. He, too, disguised his caste. Gokul and Michael were both from Dalit families that had converted to Christianity. These Christians were often treated as inferior to the Syrian Christians of Kerala, who claim to be 'original/early' Christians, as well as to be Brahmin converts to Christianity. In Coimbatore, Michael was part of a church group, where he identified himself with the dominant upper-caste group in the church. He was introduced to the church by an upper-caste supervisor in the stone quarry. Impressed by Michael's conduct, a family in the church wanted him to marry their daughter. This put him in a difficult position because the family would enquire more about his family in Kerala through their kinship network. If they were to find out the truth about his caste, it would create problems for him not only in the church but also in his workplace. Michael fled to another location before the family discovered the truth about his caste identity. Michael told me that two years before this incident, he, along with a group of Dalit boys, shared the cost of an ambulance to take the corpse of a fellow Dalit to the tea belt. They did not want their relatives to come to Coimbatore as that would have exposed their caste identity. The fact that the Dalit youth from the tea belt were ready to pay a large amount of money for the ambulance shows the intensity of categorical oppression they were experiencing as migrants.

The urban migration of plantation youth can be seen as a way to escape the crisis. Anonymity and ignorance concerning the society in Kerala (and other distant parts of India) help to shield the Dalit youth from prejudices which are likely to hurt them. As Gokul's story illustrates, using another identity as a mask (as a way to 'pass') echoes the situation of Blacks in colonial-racial contexts as discussed by Frantz Fanon (1967) in *Black Skin, White Masks*. It is the radical denial of oneself (self-alienation) that is affected by the structures of domination and oppression. Dalits must become 'other' to themselves to make their way through the system. This is even more true for Dalits from the plantations in the context of the crisis.[7] The masking and becoming 'other' also bring forth a radically different mode and politics of experiencing identity. Although they sometimes treat themselves as fraudulent performers, the helpless act of masking one's self results from domination that is embodied in the experience of being a fraudulent performer. At the same time, this performance and the ensuing experiences generate a sense of anti-caste consciousness that enables them to understand the structural dimensions of their marginality. Masking their identity in this context is also a negation of caste – an intense political act, just as 'coming out' as a Dalit is in other contexts.

The struggle for a house plot

Before the crisis, the plantation workers were not ashamed of not owning housing plots. It was mainly the supervisors, the managerial staff and their relatives who owned land outside the plantations. The workers' landlessness did not serve to stigmatise them because the class structure of the plantation production system defined who could (and who would) own land. As such, the landlessness of the workers was a naturalised condition. The situation, however, changed in the early 1990s after the crisis, when the workers had to seek alternative housing to accommodate their families. In the changed circumstances, the responsibility of finding a place to live fell largely on the shoulders of the plantation youth. I have heard the older and retired workers repeatedly stating that they raised their children when the plantations were functioning well and that now it is time for the youth to find a way out of the current difficulties. In other words, it was the moral duty of the youth to take over the needs of the family, including buying land.

For landless plantation workers anywhere in the world, a housing plot is a symbol of success, a new indication of social differentiation and stratification and a social display of wealth (Martínez 2007). But only a few plantation workers in the tea belt had the necessary resources to buy a housing plot during the crisis. In a way, landlessness is a hidden injury for the workers (Sennett and Cobb 1972). The Kerala urban middle class had been buying land in the plantation region – land that the plantation youth and workers (including retirees) wanted to secure for themselves as a stake in the world in which they had entered and discovered new possibilities for escaping their history and memories of abjection. The interest of the urban middle class in land in the region had inflated the cost of even the smallest parcels of land well beyond the reach of the plantation workers and their families. At the same time, the increasing real estate prices in the tea belt was part of a larger trend of rising prices of land across Kerala's neoliberal economy. The increasing privatisation and commodification of land resulted in the urban middle class and elite across Kerala dispossessing the marginal communities in the highlands, including the indigenous communities in northern Kerala (Steur 2017). In the Peermade tea belt, the real estate boom became a context for the reproduction of the parlous condition of the workers, a social reduction in part along the class–caste social divide of the outside world.

The ethnographic discussion of two youths' attempts to amass the necessary resources to establish what they call their 'own soil' (*sontha mannu*) in the plantation belt tells us about this social reduction. Vinay, who is 19 years of age, went to school only up to grade 8. His father was a sweeper and his mother was a temporary worker in the Hill Valley estate. After grade 4, his mother's elder sister (*periyamma*) took him with her to Cumbum, a border town in southern Tamil Nadu. In May 2009, when Vinay was in grade 9, he left for Tirupur along with two of his cousins because his *periyamma* wanted him to take care of her pigs and cows in his spare time. His cousins left Tirupur after two months, but Vinay stayed with a friend's uncle on the tea estate. He worked as an assistant to this man, who was a cook in a hostel for girls working in various textile factories in Tirupur. Despite many requests from his family to return home to the plantations, Vinay stayed on for another 18 months. On hearing that his father was seriously ill, he decided to return home. The news of his father's illness was a lie. However, Vinay had no regrets because his employer had reduced his pay from 3,000 to 2,000 rupees per month. The employer thought that Vinay would not go back to the plantations because of the shortage of work there. This is a clear example of the exploitative situations that Dalits very often face. The sum of money that Vinay was forced to live on meant he had no chance to purchase a plot to build a house.

On returning to the plantations, Vinay worked as a room boy in a hotel in Cumbum. He was paid 100 rupees a day and, additionally, tips. He would visit the plantations for two days of every month. During these times I would find him sitting near the crèche with Mani, a local real estate agent sought out by plantation workers who wanted to buy small housing plots (of three to five cents).[8] I often saw Vinay buying cigarettes for Mani. Their friendship seemed unlikely to me because Mani, who was over 30 years of age, was much older than Vinay and outside the age group of his usual friends. When I asked Vinay about his friendship, he told me that he was interested in Mani's knowledge of the market and his connections outside the plantations. Mani owned a half-acre of land on the outskirts of the plantation and this made him important to anyone interested in buying housing plots. Mani's property was ideally situated immediately outside the plantation boundaries and close to the satellite towns. Another property was available, but it was relatively far away.

Vinay felt that his friendship with Mani would facilitate him getting a worthwhile plot once he had saved enough cash because Mani had both knowledge and connections. Saving cash, however, proved elusive. Vinay predicted that it would take him four more years to save the necessary cash. But things were not moving forward when I left the field. Vinay thought that his father might be in line for an interest-free loan (of one lakh rupees) from the government but that did not come through. However, he managed to get work as an assistant mason at a nearby construction site and sent his brother, Kannan, to work in the textile factories in Tirupur. As of December 2020, no plot had been bought.

Sudhir, unlike Vinay, had saved enough cash to buy a plot. Sudhir was 28 years old in 2015 and was working as an assistant to a chartered accountant in Chennai. He had saved 30,000 rupees after three years of work and urged his father, Balakrishnan, to look for housing plots. Coincidentally, Balakrishnan's name appeared on the list of beneficiaries of a government grant-in-aid scheme, designed to help Dalits buy a housing plot and build a house. This was added to Sudhir's savings and, along with the pawning of his mother's gold chain, he finally had sufficient cash to buy a small plot. Balakrishnan approached a few people who he thought might have connections with others who planned to sell their land. Mani, the middleman, was also approached. I often saw

Balakrishnan visiting various private small holdings in *puthuvēli*, at the outskirts of the plantations, in search of suitable housing plots. Finally, he found a real estate agent, Anoop, a Syrian Christian, who owned two acres of land and a tea shop in the midst of *puthuvēli* area. Anoop was ideally situated for his business and his tea shop was a key brokerage point. He became very friendly with Balakrishnan and was to show him a 35-cent plot. The negotiations began. However, the price was so high that, instead of five cents, Balakrishnan had money only to buy three cents. Balakrishnan enquired whether he could buy three cents of land rather than the whole 35 cents, but Anoop refused to negotiate over so little – even five cents was too little. Balakrishnan told him that he would come back to discuss the price again after two days.

Balakrishnan, accompanied by his sister's son Suresh, who was also Anoop's friend, returned to negotiate further, and it was Suresh who took control of the negotiations. Suresh used his friendship to convince Anoop to persuade the landowner to sell three cents of land. Anoop demanded 30,000 rupees for each cent and made it clear that that was the lowest the owner of the plot would go. He also added that being Suresh's friend, he was offering a straight deal. Balakrishnan was stunned by the price because he expected to pay at the most 20,000 rupees for each cent of land. He offered a price of 23,000 rupees for each cent but Anoop was not interested. After a few minutes of silence, Suresh told Anoop that he would think about the price and get back to him within a few days.

As Suresh and Balakrishnan left the tea shop, Anoop murmured to me that he did not need to lower the price because the valley people (the upper-middle-class/upper-class people) buy land without negotiations and that they know it is cheaper than land elsewhere. Anoop's comments reflected the difficulties the plantation workers faced because of land inflation brought about by the expansion of the urban middle class and elite into the area. Soon after this I met Balakrishnan, who told me that he would wait for Anoop to lower his asking price because Balakrishnan was sure that no one would pay the amount Anoop demanded for the plot. However, the plot was sold after a week to a person from Kanjirappally, a town in the valley. Balakrishnan was disappointed and Sudhir, when he visited the plantations later, expressed his anger and stated that 'outsiders should be barred from buying land in the high lands'. Sudhir's statement echoes a common opinion among the plantation youth that they have been cheated by the land dealers, the wealthy valley people and the plantation companies in the context of the crisis.

The dilemma of the youth

While on the one hand these youth had to try to earn enough money to buy three cents of land and meet the medical expenses of parents or close kin, on the other hand they had to engage with the stigma and marginality associated with their identities. Thus the plantation youth were caught between a materially deprived and a socio-culturally estranged position, which are interlinked processes. However, as in the case of Gokul, a perception of self-worth is important for the realisation of self-worth. They play with their identities in order to create the image of self-worth in their urban lives. While this attempt to create self-worth had some success, notwithstanding its paradox, their quest for money to buy a plot of land as small as three cents was becoming increasingly challenging.

The dependency of Vinay and Sudhir on Anoop and Mani illustrates new forms of alienation affecting the plantation youth in the context of the crisis. Some people, such as Mani, are functionally literate about the processes involved in buying land in the new neoliberal circumstances such as inflation of land value. The general functional illiteracy of plantation workers in the context of the crisis results in their being easily cheated by those with experience in the real estate business as well as by building contractors. Furthermore, the forms of trust within the plantation society could be easily converted into forms of exploitation when the market economy and associated commodification intensified. Therefore, the major forces in the plight of plantation workers are not only their functional illiteracy and negligible savings but also the historical circumstances that created such conditions. The economic crisis nonetheless intensified and exposed the vulnerabilities generated over decades by the capitalist system of production in the plantations, which was furthered by the categorical oppression associated with caste, gender and ethnicity.

The commodification of land follows, as a function of the crisis, from the atomisation of plantation society and the fractionalisation of social relations. It is further exacerbated by the attraction of relatively wealthy outsiders to the region and the increasing financialisaton of the real estate market. In contemporary India, land is replacing gold as the source of family wealth, and it is the wealth of women that is partly transformed into land or serves as a deposit for land. However, during the crisis, it was the migration of the youth that potentially provided income that was invested back into land. As discussed earlier in the chapter, migration exposes the youth to negative values associated with Dalits and

Tamils. These matters were less relevant in the plantations, where they did not have to mask their caste. However, in the world outside the plantations, caste influenced their patterns of settlement in urban areas and became vital in structuring their social relations. The urban migration of youth can be seen as a step towards upward social mobility. However, the very process of such migration and settlement was a factor in reasserting a stigmatised identity that was a major factor in thwarting their ambitions of social advancement.

In Thiruvananthapuram, Dalit identity became defined and problematised in the search for housing. The plantation youth had little choice but to rent housing in a Dalit colony. They were effectively trapped in their categorisation as Dalits. Caste continued to be a crucial factor in their urban experience – in a deeply stigmatised sense. This was not in the ritualised-relational sense of caste as seen in villages, but it was nonetheless thoroughly demeaning. What is more, the difficulties encountered by plantation youth in the city required them to participate in the engagement of their categorical identity as Dalits in order to gain a foothold in the city. In doing so, they colluded in processes of their own urban marginalisation and re-subordination.[9] Dalits are socially and culturally directed into settlements occupied by other Dalits as a function of their caste degradation by other higher or in-castes. The struggle for the realisation of self-worth to overcome a sense of failure was explicit among the plantation youth. Outside the plantations, the Tamil Dalits found semi-skilled work as drivers and mechanics, but they did not secure higher positions such as clerks. They also did not receive local self-government nominated assignments, such as contractual clerks, contractual drivers for hospitals, peons and sweepers in offices of local governments.[10] Unlike other caste groups, they did not have the required networks and lacked the functional literacy necessary to assert themselves in the labour market.

More importantly, their identity as Tamil Dalits was stigmatised within Kerala society. A popular belief in Kerala is that while Tamil Dalits are better at hard, manual labour than Malayalis, the Malayalis are better at jobs involving mental expertise, and such stereotypes affect the way Tamils are employed in the labour market. The Malayali Dalits are located in between Tamil Dalits and upper-caste Malayalis in the categorical relations as many Malayali Dalits perceive Tamil Dalits to be below them in hierarchical relations of ethnicity. Incidents of Tamil Dalits leaving work because of discrimination and humiliation are not uncommon. Makenthiran, a 21-year-old who worked as a concrete specialist for a construction contractor in the valley town of Erumeli in Kerala, faced abuse by his Malayali co-workers with whom he shared a room in Kanjirappally. One evening after work, everyone got drunk and repeatedly referred to Makenthiran as '*Pāndi*', a caste and racial slur in Kerala that refers to Tamils and portrays them as 'uncivilised'. The term can be applied to all Tamils but is specifically used to refer to Tamil Dalits (Raj 2020). Makenthiran was provoked by the continuous abuse and reacted by engaging in a nasty fight with one of his co-workers. While others intervened and stopped the fight, all the Malayali workers began to maintain a 'safe distance' (as Makenthiran calls it) from him. This caused Makenthiran psychological distress and he decided to return to the plantations.

The hidden injuries of caste suffered by Dalits are antithetical to modernisation narratives, such as Gandhian utopianism, socialist universalism and modern capitalism, that proclaim the weakening of the caste system in neoliberal Indian society (Mosse 2020). Such narratives, which are also dominant in the modern sociology of caste (for example, Béteille 2012), proclaim that its force (in a traditionalist village sense) is significantly weakened in processes of modernisation, urbanisation and migration to cities.[11] However, such arguments overlook the fact that, for Dalits, economic mobility is not often accompanied by social mobility. Jonathan Parry (2020) provides an extensive discussion on the relationship between caste and class in economic enclaves in India. Parry (2020, 24), inspired by Béteille and others, argues that that the grip of caste as an encompassing ideological framework has been weakening. However, Parry (2020, 25) observes that 'the deepest social cleavage in the ex-villages-cum-labour-colonies that fringe the BSP Township is between Satnamis, the largest "untouchable" caste in the local hierarchy, and the so-called "Hindu" castes'. It is therefore clear that modernisation narratives of caste are possible only when Dalits are kept outside the analysis. Such narratives treat Dalits as outliers to this general proposition and also do not see the potency of caste to reformulate itself in dynamic conditions. By failing to recognise the significant role of caste, these narratives, in fact, erase the everyday struggles of Dalits for a non-stigmatised life worth living.

The situation of Dalit plantation youth, as discussed in this chapter, challenges the narratives often associated with modernisation theories (and the rationale underlying them), which argue that urban migration will lead to shifts in social and economic status and opportunities. The case of plantation youth suggests that caste finds a way into categories of urban identity, just as tribal identity finds a way into the urban copper belt in a different register than in rural social relations (Mitchell 1956). In order to understand this shift in caste identity, one needs to pay close attention to its situated dimensions and the ways in which it reproduces itself in various contexts. The alienating effects of categories of identity in a dispute situation placed within the larger context of the economic crisis calls for a phenomenology of economic crisis as distinctively experienced by the larger crowd of 'footloose' workers across the world.

Notes

1. Model hostels are exclusively meant for Dalit students and are funded by the scheduled caste welfare department.
2. After completing grade 10 in the government high school in Vandiperiyar, Manohar moved to a Christian management school in Rayappanpetti in southern Tamil Nadu for his higher secondary school education (two years of pre-collegiate education). He told me (and this was certified by his friends) that, while at school, he was studious and committed to getting a decent job. But when he entered an undergraduate course in Thiruvananthapuram, he struggled in his studies, mainly because the languages of instruction were Malayalam and English. He failed in the English course. The Tamil youth had difficulty understanding Malayalam when English course tutors communicated the meaning of prose and poems in Malayalam. There was a common saying among the students of the model hostel that 'passing the English course means to have the bachelor's degree in your hand'.
3. 'Colony' is a term commonly used in Kerala to indicate urban enclaves predominantly occupied by Dalits. The youth told me they felt as if they were back in Tamil Nadu because the colony was internally organised like a Dalit settlement in Tamil Nadu. For example, I was told by a Tamil youth that it was in this colony that the very first association of fans of Tamil film actors was formed in Kerala. Large flex boards with pictures of fans beneath large posters portraying Tamil movie stars are hung in this settlement, as in Tamil villages.
4. I must make it clear that I do not subscribe to this opinion. I authoritatively write about the 'popular' imagination because I lived in Thiruvananthapuram city for four years. The college I attended was located less than a mile from this colony.
5. Although the nearest major hospital to both plantation belts in Idukki district (Munnar and Peermade) is Kottayam Medical College, many go to Thiruvananthapuram for major medical treatments because the plantation workers often have extended kin who are students in the city to help them.
6. Pierre Bourdieu's (1977, 1986; Bourdieu and Wacquant 1992) conceptualisation of various forms of capital is useful in understanding the alienation of the plantation Tamils that is evident in the case of the plantation Dalit youth discussed here. Bourdieu classifies different forms of capital – economic, social, cultural and symbolic – with respect to their nature and functions. They are interlinked and can be converted from one form of capital to another. For Bourdieu, various forms of capital acquire meaning only when they are convertible. The reproduction of the plantation Tamils within their underclass/outcaste/linguistic minority condition could be explained by referring to having or not having such forms of capital.
7. The Dalit plantation youth might be reproducing the hierarchy of caste by impersonating the upper castes. However, this cannot be understood as an aspect of Srinivas's (1952) Sanskritisation. In Srinivas's theory, the lower caste emulates the values of the upper caste but not necessarily by hiding their lower-caste status. In the case of the plantation youth, the idea is not to achieve higher social status but to survive and not to get beaten up or be humiliated.
8. A 'cent' is a unit of measurement used in India. One cent is equal to $1/100$ acre (435.6 square feet or 48.4 square yards). The state regulations require one to possess a minimum of three cents of land in order to qualify for financial assistance from the state of Kerala to build a house. Kerala still offers financial assistance for buying three cents of land as well as for building a house through housing projects. However, it is very difficult to buy three cents of land with the money offered by the state, and the amount allocated to build a house is too little. While the cheaper, as well as a viable option, is to build a roof of metal sheets or clay tiles, the government regulations require that the roof should be concreted with cement. This regulation sometimes

results in tragedy. In the Pettamalai estate, for example, a house under construction collapsed because cheap hollow bricks were used for the construction while the roofing was done with concrete. The hollow bricks could not withstand the weight of the concrete roof. The collapse of the house resulted in the death of a mason and his assistant.
9 Caste as a category for urban settlement and social interaction is thoroughly distinct from the nature of caste relations in rural villages. Hence the anthropological analysis of caste needs to be mindful of the transformative nature of caste as a dimension of what Mitchell (1956) discussed as the logic of situations.
10 The contractual posts are not covered by affirmative action.
11 Such modernisation approaches to caste are also evident in studies critical of Louis Dumont's analysis of caste (for example, Appadurai 1986). One of the major criticisms of Dumont is that he underestimates the importance of social change in colonial and postcolonial India and thus the weakening of the caste system. The situation of plantation youth in the city, in turn, stressed the operation of caste as an important category of social relationships in the urban context, which is no less important than its operation in villages is India, although it is distinct from it.

5
'Dam'ned in dispute

The revival of a dispute between the states of Tamil Nadu and Kerala over the control and safety of the Mullaperiyar Dam exacerbated the suffering of Tamil workers affected by the economic crisis. As mentioned in Chapter 1, Malayalam – the official language of Kerala state – is spoken by the majority. Tamils constitute the major linguistic minority, and the plantation workers include the larger share of this Tamil minority. The rediscovery of Malayali nationalism (Kerala nationalism), defined in opposition to Tamils or Tamil Nadu nationalism, has had damaging consequences for the plantation Tamils.[1] The dispute became a decisive juncture at which the prejudice which was relatively submerged was brought to the surface. The ethnic stereotyping of lower-class/outcaste Tamils captured by the slur of *Pāndi* was used more often than before.[2] Accordingly, the dam dispute became a significant factor in the economic crisis. While the economic crisis affected the workers' livelihood, the dispute over the dam alienated them even further in terms of their socio-cultural life because of the increasing antagonism against Tamils.

The category of Tamil identity, which was less significant in the plantation production system, emerged as an important category of identity in the structuring of social relations as a consequence of the crisis (Mitchell 1956; Barth 1969; Kapferer 1995). Similarly, the 'traditional' principles of caste hierarchy, as I have argued, were partly suspended in the industrial class context of the tea estates. But now, with the transformation in the socio-economic and political order of the tea estates, the workers and their families were thrown into greater dependence on a socio-economic field dominated by their Tamil-Dalit stigmatised identity. In this field, the Tamil-Dalit identity had a diminished social and economic status. This new socio-political field locates the plantation workers as an underclass that equates, if differently, with the stigma born of their 'outcaste' status in their villages of origin in Tamil Nadu. In this context, they were subject to values rooted in the historical formation of the category – Tamil Dalit – which reinvigorated dimensions of their lowly position as formed in the conditions of caste hierarchy.

As shown in this chapter, the vulnerability of being located at the bottom of the caste hierarchy and the bottom of the class structure is magnified by the presence of anti-Tamil prejudice – a factor that also affects others in Kerala, if far less so. Other Tamil group ethnicities in Kerala, such as Iyers, Vellalas and Tamil Muslims,[3] are relatively integrated within the generalised identity of Keraliyar. However, this is not so with the Tamil Dalits of the plantations whose Tamil identity is strongly marked because of their origin as indentured labourers (which gives them virtually permanent status as migrants) and their outcaste Dalit identity. Thus, hostility towards the Tamil minority in Kerala, in the main, is directed towards the estate communities, who were *treated* as 'migrants' from Tamil Nadu. Accordingly, the dam conflict added insult to injury by further alienating the plantation Tamils from control over their life situation.[4]

The rift between the two states also resulted in an indifferent attitude towards the Malayali-speaking linguistic minority in Tamil Nadu. But what is notable in the Kerala case is the subtle nature of the violence and the increase in discrimination against plantation Tamils following the dispute over the dam. The majority of Tamils in Kerala are working-class Dalits who depend on the plantation economy, unlike the Malayali minority in Tamil Nadu, who are engaged primarily in small businesses and middle-class, white-collar jobs, and who constitute less than 1 per cent of the total population (National Census 2011).

The dispute

The Mullaperiyar Dam was constructed to irrigate the arid southern region of the erstwhile Madras Presidency of the British Empire. The dam was built at the confluence of two rivers, the Mullayar and Periyar; hence, the dam came to be known as Mullaperiyar (as it is known in Malayalam) or Mullaiperiyar (in Tamil). The dam was created by diverting the west-flowing Periyar river towards the east; in other words, the river was redirected away from Kerala towards Tamil Nadu. Although the river flowed through and was under the control of the princely state of Travancore (which now forms the central and southern regions of the state of Kerala), the British forced Travancore state to approve the construction of the dam. The dam's construction began in 1887 and was completed in 1895 under the direction of John Pennycuick, a British engineer.[5]

The agreement between the colonial government of the Madras Presidency and the princely state of Travancore was based on unfair terms and conditions since the lease was signed for an unrealistic period of 999 years with little monetary return to Travancore state. The dam was also entirely placed under the control of the Madras Presidency, and Travancore state had no rights over it. The dam came under the control of the state of Tamil Nadu after Indian independence. With the formation of Kerala state in 1956 and its incorporation of Travancore, the dam became a hot issue. The new Kerala government questioned the validity of the agreement signed during the colonial period and demanded ownership and control over the dam. It claimed that the river originates and flows within the territorial limits of Kerala. Nonetheless, repeated agreements have been signed between Tamil Nadu and Kerala whereby Tamil Nadu has maintained control over the dam.

The dispute between the states has been reignited by Kerala's concern over the strength and safety of the dam, causing Kerala to call for a new dam to be built. This demand gained momentum in 1979 when Machchhu Dam in the state of Gujarat collapsed, resulting in the death of more than 2,000 people. Newspaper reports in Kerala raised suspicions of similar damage to the Mullaperiyar Dam. Demands for a new dam were reactivated between 2000 and 2001 following two earthquakes in the dam's vicinity (Madhusoodhanan and Sreeja 2010). Since 2001, a series of demonstrations and protests have been organised by the Mullaperiyar Agitation Council (Mullaperiyar Samara Samithi) with the support of local factions of various political parties. Between 2001 and 2011, the legal battle between Kerala and Tamil Nadu also kept the issue alive. The protest movement in Kerala was intensified and received media coverage whenever the supreme court held a hearing on the issue. This struggle, known as the 'Mullaperiyar agitation', intensified in October 2011 when the monsoon rains caused an increase in the water level of the dam, followed by a series of mild earthquakes in Idukki district throughout 2011.

The protest

By October 2011, the Mullaperiyar Agitation Council had intensified its protests with a hunger strike in Chappathu, a small town located a few miles downstream of the dam. Within a week, the council received wider support from all the major political parties in the region. The struggle took a new turn when a prominent politician from the region who happened to be the Minister for Water Resources took over leadership of the protest and joined in a hunger strike in Thiruvananthapuram, the capital city of Kerala state. November witnessed an escalation of the protests, with various Kerala-based political parties and caste organisations participating in rolling hunger strikes with different groups striking at prearranged times. Protests included enactments of dam collapse through street plays, picketing of government offices, calls to boycott commodities produced in Tamil Nadu and an online campaign to support the agitation. A massive letter-writing campaign was organised all over Kerala addressed to the Prime Minister of India demanding his intervention.

On 8 December 2011, the Left Democratic Front in Kerala organised a state-wide human chain protest. The human chain ran for 150 miles from the satellite (plantation) town of Vandiperiyar to Kochi on the coast, which symbolically represented the area that could be affected by the collapse of the dam. The idea of the chain was to express a collective pledge that a new dam would be constructed. Movie stars and clergy from the various Christian denominations were also present at multiple points along the human chain to express solidarity for constructing a new dam. Fear of the dam's collapse was further intensified by the widespread screening of a film about the dam shown in cinemas throughout Kerala. Documentaries and short animated films on the dam's potential collapse were widely circulated. A popular documentary concerning the dam was titled *Muzhangunna Maranamani* (*Death Bell Rings*). By the third week of November, the Ministers' Cabinet in Kerala demanded that the dam's water level be reduced to 120 feet from 136 feet.

The protests organised in the tea belt were careful not to employ anti-Tamil expressions since they wanted to make sure they had the support of local Tamils. The Left Democratic Front party leaders who spoke in the human chain protest also stressed and reiterated that the Tamils in the tea belt would also suffer if the dam collapsed. Some well-known faces from the local factions of the party were given prominence in the human chain in an effort to win local Tamil support. The political parties and the Mullaperiyar Agitation Council were successful to a certain extent in winning the support of the plantation Tamils, mainly as a function of the trade unions. The workers from the Green Valley estate participated in the human chain under instruction from their union leadership.

On the other side of the border, Tamil Nadu responded by arguing that the dam is strong and there is no likelihood of it collapsing. The Chief Minister of Tamil Nadu alleged that the ongoing demonstrations in Kerala were politically motivated and that politicians in Kerala had generated undue panic among the people of Kerala for narrow political gain. Documentaries on the allegedly weakened dam were banned in Tamil Nadu. The state of Tamil Nadu also produced a documentary that portrayed the dam's construction as strong and beyond scientific reproach. The political rhetoric of the time was dominated by a discourse that portrayed Tamils as victims of ethnic prejudice against the Tamil/Dravidian race. No serious protests occurred in Tamil Nadu when they first broke out in Kerala. However, massive demonstrations started in Tamil Nadu when the demonstrations in Kerala turned violent and attempts were made to occupy the dam site. This infuriated the farmers and agricultural labourers living in the bordering villages of Tamil Nadu, who organised counter-protests challenging Kerala's demands for a new dam. On 5 December 2011, road and rail links between the two states were blocked by various Tamil political parties, intensifying the conflict.

The last two months of 2011 saw attacks against Malayali and Tamil inter-state travellers. Incidents were reported of stones being thrown at vehicles. A major reference point for identifying the minority was the registration numbers of the vehicles that crossed state boundaries. The attackers were looking for the vehicle numbers of the opposing state (TN for Tamil Nadu and KL for Kerala). Other travellers were stopped and prevented from continuing on their way for several hours. Many Malayali-owned shops

Figure 5.1: Protest in a plantation town in the Peermade tea belt

in different parts of Tamil Nadu, as well as Tamil-owned shops in Kerala, were damaged by agitators.[6]

The border crossings between the two states were closed by the police from both states after a violent clash on 12 December 2011. The children of the plantation workers studying in Tamil Nadu could not travel home for the Christmas holidays. Many remained in their hostels or in relatives' houses. In one instance, two children were unable to cross the border into the Chokkamalai estate to attend their mother's funeral. Eventually, they were taken by a Tamil Nadu police vehicle to the Kerala border, from where the Kerala police took them to the funeral. The children were only able to make the journey across the border because some youths, including myself, sought help from the higher police officials and the politicians of the border region. However, other Tamil Dalits who had sought work in Tamil Nadu due to the economic crisis had to travel through other border crossing points, which took them an additional six hours. Such incidents point to the fact that those who were chiefly inconvenienced by the protests were the Tamil plantation communities.

Being Dalits, being liminal

The Tamil community in the Peermade tea belt were the primary victims of the dispute. They were soft targets for abuse whenever they travelled into the Malayali-dominated valleys, especially at the peak of the protests. Some were beaten in the towns where they worked. During the protests, gangs of Malayali youth went searching for Tamils arriving on buses in the valley towns. One Tamil estate worker who narrowly escaped being beaten told me: 'We Tamils had better learn to speak good Malayalam for self-protection. If we speak Malayalam fluently, we could escape in the disguise of Malayali identity. We should take care to give them Malayali-sounding names.' He made this comment with a bit of sarcasm as he could speak Malayalam relatively well and therefore had escaped the attack. Some Tamil women and men working in the small cardamom and tea plantations in the Udumbancholai region were beaten and chased over the border into the Tamil Nadu town of Cumbum. Tamils who owned agricultural land in the nearby areas were also terrorised and told not to return. Migrant workers from Tamil Nadu who came to Kerala to work in the construction industry in the valley towns were also beaten.

Even Tamil plantation youths in government service as lower divisional clerks or office assistants were harassed and publicly ridiculed. I know of one case where a clerk was slapped in the face in the heat of an argument over the dam, and another was repeatedly provoked by being insultingly addressed as *Pāndi*. I heard of another incident in which a plantation family was forced from an auto-rickshaw by the driver taunting them with the ethnic insult *Pāndi*. Generally, during and as a result of the protests, Tamils in the region felt humiliated and dehumanised.

Accordingly, the physical assaults against Tamils were often accompanied by acts of humiliation, such as chasing them out of their estate houses or lands and calling out the ethnic slur *Pāndi*. These humiliations have serious repercussions, impacting Tamils' dignity and self-worth. This is reflected in the comment of an informant who was chased away from his one-acre plot of land in a village near Cumbumettu. I met with him to learn the details of the attack against him at the satellite town of Vandiperiyar in January 2013. He told me that it would have hurt him (relatively) less if those Malayalis who had chased him from his land had slapped him in the face rather than chasing him away because the act of running away like a coward was indeed humiliating. Such processes of humiliation are as significant as physical assaults since the act of humiliation has a more profound impact on the social construction of the identity of Tamils and, therefore, on the place of the Tamil minority in Kerala. In other words, the humiliating acts were inferior-*ising* in nature and displayed the hidden racist stereotypes and prejudices against Tamils in Kerala society.

Not only did the plantation workers have to face humiliating assaults and threats in Kerala, but also their Tamil-Malayali-influenced accents provoked a similar reaction in Tamil Nadu. One person from the plantation community told me that he was repeatedly questioned and intimidated for having a Malayalam accent as he travelled to the border town of Cumbum in Tamil Nadu. At a roadside shop, he requested tea using the Malayalam '*chāya*' rather than the preferred Tamil usage 'tea'. Tamils in the tea shop suspected he was from Kerala, and he narrowly escaped a beating. As the dam dispute made clear, plantation Tamils are in a liminal position for *not being authentic Tamils in Tamil Nadu* and for *being authentic Tamils in Kerala*.

I now discuss a case of explicit ethnic prejudice and stereotyping in the context of the dam conflict. I underline two analytic points in my description of the event. Firstly, despite the egalitarian tone of the state rhetoric in Kerala (Jeffrey 1992), the event reveals that the formal bureaucratic order of the state is oriented so as to disadvantage Tamils and, more specifically, the Dalit plantation communities. Secondly, I emphasise the subtlety of bureaucratic and disciplinary practice and how this functions in the continuing alienation and subordination of the populations of the tea plantations. The discussion has a broader bearing on the fact that Tamils and Dalits are disproportionately the subjects of negative state disciplinary practice. Over 60 per cent of persons in the region of the plantations are Tamil Dalits (Census 2011).

The subtle nature and the intensification of discrimination against Tamils are revealed by describing how the Tamils were harshly punished for minor offences and by exploring the nature of their experience as they passed through the police station and court proceedings and finally ended up in jail. The plantation Tamils were more vulnerable to subtle forms of discrimination since they did not possess the material resources or have the political support to counter the discrimination they experienced in the dispute context. The plantation Tamils were not familiar with the bureaucratic practices of Kerala state, such as how to handle a police case and who needs to be contacted to mobilise support against mistreatment in the police station. The operation of their class, caste, gender and linguistic identity reproduces the tea workers as being in the most vulnerable position in society.

A brawl and a blow

A group of plantation youth were celebrating New Year in the Green Valley estate on 1 January 2012. Around noon that day, one member of the group, Pratheesh, received a call from the wife of his elder brother Martin telling him that Martin had been severely beaten by a group of Malayali youth. She asked Pratheesh to come to the neighbouring estate (the Ponmalai estate) as soon as possible to take Martin to the hospital. Pratheesh was 28 years old and unmarried, and he owned and had been driving a jeep that shuttled plantation workers from the estate to the town. The jeep was purchased from a used vehicle shop by pledging gold in a private bank, as collateral for a loan.

Martin had moved to the Ponmalai estate to live in his in-laws' house after his marriage. Martin had to move to his in-laws' house because his wife was the only child of the house and had to remain at home to take care of her parents. Pratheesh, along with two of his close friends, Christopher and Muthuraj, Pratheesh's younger brother Robin, and Robin's friend Murali ('Pratheesh and the others' hereafter) rushed to the Ponmalai estate to take his brother to the hospital.[7]

While drunk at the New Year celebrations, Martin had made some statements in support of Tamil Nadu over the Mullaperiyar issue. The Malayali youth in the Ponmalai estate, who were also neighbours of

Martin, made demeaning anti-Tamil comments in response. Words very soon became blows, and Martin and his wife were attacked. Pratheesh, Robin and their companions reached the estate and discovered Martin in a bloodied state. The Malayali gang attacked Pratheesh and the others, beating them up. Other Tamil relatives of Pratheesh summoned the police, but they did nothing (only two policemen came), so other Tamil youths intervened, driving off the attackers. These Tamil youths came from elsewhere on the estate but only intervened when they learned that the fight was over the issue of the Mullaperiyar Dam. When the other Tamils intervened and ended the clashes, the police told Pratheesh and the others that they would accompany them to the hospital as they had bruises all over their bodies. Pratheesh and the others initially refused to leave with the police and demanded the arrest of the Malayali youths. The police promised them that the Malayali youths would be arrested with the assistance of more police. Pratheesh and the others then agreed to go to the hospital, believing that the police would arrest those who had beaten them up.

Instead of taking Pratheesh and the others to the hospital, the police took them to the police station and made them wait until the police sub-inspector arrived. Pratheesh and the others made no protest because they were frightened. They were soon to learn that the mother of a Malayali youth injured in the fight, who herself had become involved in the fracas, had registered a complaint with the police of 'attempted murder'. While this charge was levelled at Pratheesh and his companions, no charge was brought against the Malayali youths who had started the brawl and inflicted the injuries that had motivated the intervention of other Tamil youths on the estate. My subsequent enquiries revealed that the mother (Malathi) of one of the Malayali youths had herself been injured accidentally, either by a misdirected blow from her son or by a blow (again accidental) from the head of one of the Tamil youths (probably Robin). But the general opinion (among those connected to the Tamil youths) was that in all probability, the charge brought against the Tamils was to counter the accusation made by Martin's wife (who was admitted to a private hospital) to the police.

It was very clear that Pratheesh and the others had been beaten up by the Malayali youths and were the victims. That the Malayali youths were not charged indicates a discriminatory bias. To press the police to charge the Malayali youths as well, Martin and his wife went to the hospital on the advice of Kannan, a graduate from the Green Valley estate. In his mid-30s, Kannan was working as a clerk in a private insurance company in Vandiperiyar town. The Tamil youths relied on Kannan's advice in what turned out to be a fruitless attempt to escape police charges since Martin was also arrested later.

I learned about the fight right after the police took Pratheesh and the others to the police station. I witnessed the event from the moment of their arrest through the court proceedings leading to a three-week custodial sentence. I asked a police duty officer about the seriousness of the charge. Thinking that I was a Malayali (I am fluent in Malayalam), he stated that these *Pāndis* got into trouble because they fought with the *locals*,[8] indicating that the Tamils are outsiders, in effect foreigners. While waiting for the police sub-inspector to arrive, I gained permission from the duty officer to talk with Pratheesh and the others. All of them bore the marks of their beating, with wounds all over their bodies and swollen faces. They pressed up against the cell door and whispered (so that the police duty officer would not hear) their story to me. Their main concern was not that they needed hospital treatment (which they did) but about the risk of being kept in police detention since they feared more beatings and the dishonour that a police case would bring for their families. The plantation society in the Peermade tea belt has a significantly lower crime rate than other parts of Kerala. The plantation workers did not experience the intervention or presence of police in their day-to-day life on the plantations. Therefore the registration of a criminal offence and the intervention of police are intimidating for plantation Tamils, and criminality is also against the moral code that has evolved in the plantation society. Furthermore, they were worried about their relative isolation in such a situation, being thoroughly conscious that they did not have an effective social and political network in the Malayali-controlled state police and judicial system.

The ward member's husband (a union convener of a right-wing party) visited Pratheesh and the others.[9] He visited them because Muthuraj's father was affiliated with his union, just as Pratheesh's father was affiliated with the right-wing party's union whose convener the ward member's husband was. He assured Pratheesh's father that no charges would be brought. However, his visit was largely a courtesy since he did not help them as he promised. Hence the local politician's visit was proved to be just an aspect of vote bank politics. What was more the pity was that the local politician and those who accompanied him had dinner in the police canteen and Pratheesh's father had to pay for it. While the ward member's husband and those accompanying him were having dinner, a local union leader visited Pratheesh and the others. While the union affiliations of the two families should have provided the socio-political network necessary to get Pratheesh and the others out without charge, the network was rendered ineffective because of the local antagonism to Tamils and because the network that they activated is in effect controlled by Malayalis from the dominant classes antipathetic to Tamil interests. That the union leaders played at helping them revealed the fact that ultimately power is in the hands of Malayalis, whose concerns are at variance with those whom the unionists represent. The subtlety of the forces against Pratheesh and the others was being expressed.

A few of Pratheesh's relatives from the estate came to the police station and we stood as a group in the entrance of the station until the sub-inspector arrived at approximately 8 pm. The sub-inspector invited the ward member's husband and the union leader into his office to discuss the issue. Before going into his office, the sub-inspector turned to the group standing in the entrance and shouted that we should leave the grounds of the police station. What was notable in the moment was that the sub-inspector referred to the group as *kōmālikal* (jokers), which was sarcastic and insulting to those who were eagerly wondering whether Pratheesh and the others would be freed or not. These kinds of insults always had to be tolerated by the workers.[10] However, Pratheesh's father was permitted to wait in the corridor because of the 'privilege' of being the father of a potential miscreant. The discussion between the sub-inspector, the ward member's husband and the local union leader lasted 10 minutes. After the meeting, the ward member's husband and the union leader came out of the station compound to inform us that the police would not make a decision until the following day after checking with the woman who had been admitted to the government hospital. The police argued that the woman had a head injury. It might be noted here that Martin and his wife (the Tamil victims) were not admitted to the government hospital, with the police asserting that their injuries were relatively minor.

Kannan suspected that Martin and his wife may not have been admitted to the government hospital because the union leaders might have intervened secretly to prevent Martin from being hospitalised so that he would have no pretext for bringing a counter charge. The union leaders have influence in the government hospital through the hospital staff who were union members. Later, on the advice of Kannan, Martin and his wife went to a private hospital. Kannan's suspicions concerning the bias of the ward member's husband and the union leader were apparently borne out by the fact that the information they gave to Pratheesh was false. The police charged Pratheesh and the others with attempted murder, and they were remanded in jail without trial for 15 days at the magistrate's hearing. This was to facilitate further 'questioning' of the accused. It was at the discretion of the judge to decide if the accused needed to be sent to judicial custody or not. Unfortunately, the judge decided to send them to jail under judicial custody. I was present at the magistrate's hearing of the charge. When Pratheesh and the others heard the verdict, their faces turned grim, and Murali, the youngest of the five, began to cry. They were taken from the court premises to the jail located a few hundred metres from the court.

I followed the jeep that took them from the court to the jail and got a chance to talk to them for five minutes while they were waiting for the gate to open. Murali told me that he was very scared because the jail looked like a fortress. The other four – Pratheesh, Robin, Muthuraj and Christopher – were also frightened and close to tears. Murali came closer to me and asked if his father had said anything about the issue. Murali's father was so angry with him that he did not come to see him either in court or later in jail. I consoled Muthuraj (Pratheesh's friend) and told him to hope for the best; Muthuraj told me that what worried him most was not the hardship of being in jail for 15 days but the kind of image that would create about him back at the plantation. He was worried that he would be considered a villain when he returned there. Murali, once again, started to cry as they were taken inside the jail.

As they had been remanded in custody, they had to find a lawyer to apply for bail. The expense of finding a lawyer was high. Furthermore, they needed to find someone who owned land that could be pledged (as a bond) in the court for the bail. Since there were five boys, they needed someone who owned more than two acres of land. As most plantation families are landless, Pratheesh's father had difficulty finding someone who owned land. Finally, he managed to find Raghu, who owns two acres of land on the hilltop near Pambanar, to pledge the land to get bail for the five youths. The families of these five youths had to find money to pay security (at least 25,000 rupees, as Pratheesh's father communicated to me) to Raghu to cover the risk he was taking by pledging his land. The families also had to find money to pay the court fee and the advocate fee of 6,000 rupees per person. This large amount fell to Pratheesh's family to pay since Pratheesh had asked the others to go with him to the Ponmalai estate. However, Pratheesh's family could not come up with the amount needed to get bail for all five. So Muthuraj and the others had to rely on their parents and families to come up with the money for bail. The amount was so high that it would put these families into debt for at least another year until they could repay the debt they had to incur to get bail. Understandably, Muthuraj's elder brothers and family were upset.

The defence lawyer was recommended by the union leader who had participated in the discussion with the sub-inspector along with the ward member's husband. The union leader did not visit Pratheesh to offer any further 'assistance'. When I enquired about it later, the owner of a tea shop near the police station told me that the union leader simply wanted a cut from the lawyer and that he had no interest in the case. The union leader wanted to have the case registered so that the accused (Pratheesh and the others) would approach a lawyer through him. The union leader acted as the lawyer's broker, which Pratheesh and the others were not aware of. Pratheesh and the others did not have the social networks (or social capital) to find a lawyer, which the union leader used in his favour. I had the impression that the union leader, who was also a local politician, genuinely wanted to help the Tamil youths. But I was proved wrong.

Pratheesh's father went to the lawyer connected to the leader because he thought there would be a reduction in the lawyer's fee. Pratheesh's father later told me that no reduction in the fee was made, although he tried in vain to negotiate with the lawyer's office assistant who handles the fees. Kannan also told me that union leaders commonly function as brokers for lawyers in the tea belt since union leaders come to know about fights and other issues in which the police intervene. The net result was that the union leader failed to help the Tamil youths and facilitated the negative outcome in his 'representation' of them. It should be noted that the political parties and unions often intervene to arrive at mutually agreed and amicable settlements. But this is usually only possible if the parties are from the same community. This was not so in this case, and the balance of favour went markedly against the Tamil youths.

Five days after the fight, Martin was arrested and sent to jail for 14 days of judicial custody, allegedly for participating in the fight. That seemed ironic since no case was registered against those who assaulted Martin. Martin told me that the case was not registered against the assailants due to political support for them in the region. He was arrested while he was being treated in hospital. There was no protest from any political party or group against such a patently unfair action by the police. Martin had been in a serious road accident a year before the incident, and metal plates had been inserted into one of his legs. This metal plate was displaced by three inches during the fight, causing him severe pain. However, when the police arrested Martin and had him subjected to a medical examination, the doctor who examined Martin declared that he was not suffering from any injuries and could be arrested. Martin suspected that the doctor made his recommendation on the request of the police. After three days, the police had to take Martin back to the same hospital because he was crying all night due to the severe pain in his leg. The same doctor who had given the clearance certificate to take Martin to prison earlier realised this time the seriousness of Martin's poor health condition and asked the police to take Martin to another hospital. Martin suspected that the doctor changed his opinion this time to prevent any accusations of negligence and fraudulent actions.[11]

The police took Martin to a hospital in Kanjirappally. A CT scan done at the hospital showed that the metal plate was indeed displaced. Thus, the doctor who initially had cleared Martin to be taken to jail had done so either at the request of the police – as Martin claimed – or because he did not take Martin's condition seriously. In either case, Martin was not considered someone who deserved to be treated as a proper member of Indian society. In other words, the doctor may have assumed that he would not be challenged or prosecuted for his negligible treatment of Martin because Martin is a Tamil Dalit, and no political or social groups would come to his rescue. At the same time, his decision to agree to the request from the police would have provided him with more friends in the police department. Ironically, the extension of the doctor's social capital was a consequence of Martin's lack of social capital. When I spoke with Martin later in jail, he expressed a firm understanding of the forces behind his plight. He remarked that he was mistreated because plantation Tamils are 'orphans' whose pathetic condition is not challenged by anyone (*kēkka nāthiyillatha anāthai*). This metaphor of 'orphans' (*anāthai*) is widely used by plantation workers to refer to their parlous and alienated situation. The experience of being an 'orphan' echoes their ostracisation and lack of social support, which also demonstrates the depth of their alienation.

Unfortunately, Martin had to spend 16 days in jail before he was released to receive proper medical treatment. Pratheesh and his friends were released on bail four days before Martin. I visited them in Green Valley upon their release. Martin, who was deeply wounded by the incident both physically and emotionally, left for a relative's house in Kanyakumari in Tamil Nadu in search of a job as a driver. Pratheesh and the others remained in the Green Valley estate for a week before Robin and Murali left for their workplace (a stone crusher unit) far away in Coimbatore. Throughout the week after their return, relatives and neighbours visited the youths and their families, expressing solidarity with them in their situation of hardship – a common response within the plantation communities. I also paid a courtesy visit to express a mutuality of concern. Pratheesh told me that most of the temporary prisoners were Tamils and that they were being held in custody for petty street fights, bearing similarities to the case of Pratheesh and the others. Muthuraj, meanwhile, sarcastically observed that 'the Tamils are courageous people. This is because most of the Tamils were imprisoned for engaging in street fights. That is, fighting others is a courageous act. But the others were imprisoned on cases of sexual assault and robbery, which were not courageous at all.' I sensed aspects of hidden resistance (Scott 1985) in Muthuraj's comment. But Pratheesh intervened and said to Muthuraj: 'Will you shut up, Muthu? You got beaten, and you are talking about courage?' Pratheesh could not enjoy Muthuraj's joke as he was depressed by the whole incident. While Christopher (Pratheesh's friend) was glorifying their time in jail and trying to extract what he termed 'mileage' from being in jail and being a celebrity among the community of plantation youth, Pratheesh and the others' attitudes towards life had drastically changed. Murali and Pratheesh stopped drinking completely, although their drinking had only been occasional even before their jail term. Neither Pratheesh nor any of his accomplices had any history of criminality, and they were not familiar with the local modalities of police cases and subsequent detainment in jail. Therefore, they were terrified by their situation. I visited them many times in January and found them in a depressed mood as they were not granted bail for 21 days.

These reactions can also be understood with reference to moral life in plantation society. 'Going to jail' is considered a serious stigma because it indicates a failure of discipline and of the calculated beliefs in progress that are considered to be born under the capitalist mode of plantation production. The young men felt ashamed of being called criminals because they had absorbed this particular moral order about how their life should be improved. Gossip in the community supports such attitudes, and the talk of those who came to give support to Pratheesh and the others indicated such sentiments. This gossip worried Martin, and this is one of the reasons why he left the tea belt. I telephoned Martin to check on his new life situation in Tamil Nadu. Martin told me that he had developed a sense of guilt about sending his brothers and his friends to jail. While Pratheesh and the others expressed awareness that they had been victims of Malayali prejudice, such an opinion was not yet firmly established in the community as a whole. Indeed, the Peermade tea estates were less aligned in opposition to Malayali nationalism than those in the other tea belts such as Munnar, where there was a confirmed history of opposition to the Malayali ideology and a strong affirmation of Tamil identity.

Martin's fight with the Malayali youths on the estate does not seem to have been purely the result of his Tamil nationalism. As part of the New Year celebrations, he was drunk (as were the Malayali youths). However, the altercation between them broke out over the fairness of Tamil Nadu's and Kerala's positions on the dam. He was severely beaten *because* he brought up a sensitive issue in which the Malayalis were emotionally hurt, and the tension over the issue was at its peak when the fight took place. Pratheesh and the others told me that after they beat up Martin, the Malayali youths were shouting at them to go 'outside' the Kerala border to Tamil Nadu to fetch water. This conversation was confirmed by those who witnessed the fight. Furthermore, I should clarify that not all the events that led to the arrest and confinement of the Tamil youths could be ascribed to discriminatory practices in the context of the dam dispute. However, this is a major underpinning aspect that led to the event. The related factors are recommendations from the local political leaders supporting the Malayali youths who clashed with Pratheesh and the others. But the helplessness of the youths is located in the circumstances under which the case was registered against them and their confinement, which went unchallenged by the political parties in the region. That is to say, the Tamil youths' marginalisation from all kinds of powerful groups and networks makes them easy prey for institutional disciplining even though the original reason for them ending up in jail has nothing to do with criminal offences.

Stereotypes and alienation

As mentioned at the beginning of the chapter, the dam dispute is an event whose potency was a factor expressing some of the forces affecting the lives of the plantation workers and increasing the disadvantageous effects of the economic crisis. One of the general effects of neoliberalism and the processes of globalisation is the generation of a climate of social and economic insecurity combined with marked inflation. It was not just the plantation workers who were plunged into crisis; so were diverse elements of the populations in Kerala and Tamil Nadu. As has been widely described, there was a retraction in the intervention in socio-economic processes by the state. In this context, caste associations began to play a stronger role. To some extent, this may be tied to the growth of what can be referred to as religious nationalism – a feature of right-wing processes in Kerala and other Indian states. But despite this, the conflict over the dam further empowered caste associations. In effect, the conflict was instrumental in changing the overall context, which increasingly made Dalit populations the subject of hostility – both in Kerala and in Tamil Nadu.

It is evident here that the plantation Tamils were placed in a liminal position that further compounded their subjective awareness (for example, Martin's use of the term 'orphan' to refer to the estate Tamils) of a structurally objective alienated condition. Dimensions of the case I have discussed underline the powerless situation of the estate Tamils born of their hitherto isolation, which contributed to their political naivetey and, in effect, functional illiteracy. Having little connection with mainstream Kerala society (and impeded from having such by the organisational structure of the unions, for example), Pratheesh, Martin and the others had little experience of how things operated and were easily duped. Perhaps this could not have been avoided because they did not, as Bourdieu would have noted, have the necessary social and cultural capital, nor did they have the necessary education or linguistic skills. Being impoverished, they could not even operate within the ongoing networks of routine corruption. Their very underclass status contributed to their reproduction in this situation, which intensified their suffering at the hands of dominant processes. Thus their Tamil identity overlapped with their underclass and outcaste identity in the dispute context.

The fortunes of Pratheesh and his companions were affected by the rise of bigotry and prejudice in the context of the dam dispute and were, in a way, motivated by it. The price of bail was far above what they could afford from their savings. The durability of the effect of the financial burden was relatively significant for the families of the plantation youth. The financial debt they incurred as a result of the case was worsened by the seizure of Pratheesh's jeep for one month, which forced them to borrow additional money to pay the monthly premium on the loan for the jeep. If Pratheesh's family had owned land and had enough savings to pay the bail-related expenses, they would have been less affected by the whole incident. This situation is captured by a statement Muthuraj made during my fieldwork update in June 2012: 'The police case annoys me whenever I pay the interest for the loan from the moneylender.'

As Bruce Kapferer (1995, 56) summarises Clyde Mitchell's (1956) point in *The Kalela Dance*, 'categorical relations flow from the ideological and institutional orders of the bureaucratic state'. Estate workers in Kerala are victims of the Tamil category, which has inferior and stigmatised value in relation to the dominant category of Malayali. The arrest of the Tamil youths in the context of the dam dispute is connected to the categorical relations in which Tamil identity is contrasted with the dominant Malayali identity and in accordance with which state institutions privilege the Malayali identity. While political support varies from one case to another, it was clear that the Malayali-led political parties and trade unions would support the Malayali youth in any conflict with Tamil youth. Accordingly, the clash between the youths also revealed the relative power relations that these youths would be able to maintain with the unions. As discussed earlier, Pratheesh and his allies were in no way close to having control of the post-dispute circumstances, which is in contrast to the Malayali youths who could ascertain a privileged position in relation to the minority Tamils. Due to the difference in the power relations, the Tamil youths were scared to question their confinement in the police station. They were unaware of the bureaucratic processes involved in the police and judicial system (an aspect of their 'functional illiteracy') that worked against them.

The event resulted in Pratheesh and the others becoming more openly conscious of their Tamil identity. Their conversation came to reflect an increasing awareness of the marginality of their situation based on their Tamil identity. They noticed that those who assaulted them also belonged to the plantation working class, with the only difference being that Pratheesh and the others belonged to the Tamil minority, and they were not able to get the support of any political parties or union leaders. This lack of support needs to be noted particularly because Pratheesh's family and their extended kinship, on both of his parents' sides, are members of the union attached to the ruling political party. At the same time, Murali's family were affiliated to the union attached to the communist party, which has a stronger voice in negotiating local disputes in the Peermade region. Furthermore, the conflict between the youths started over the dam conflict between Tamil Nadu and Kerala, where the difference between the two states was assumed to be rooted in the language they speak. As mentioned at the beginning of the chapter, linguistic nationalism dominated other primordial sentiments in the conflict context. That is to say, categorical relations depend on different situations (Mitchell 1956; Kapferer 1995).

Then again, the youths had not been conscious that their caste and class identities were elements in their oppression. As mentioned earlier, the Tamil identity becomes problematic in Kerala mainly when it is correlated to the Dalit-underclass identity. The implication of their underclass position being responsible for their unfair confinement is clear from the fact that, because they are landless, they were forced to pay a large sum of money to someone who would agree to put up land as bail for the youth. The youths had to pay a considerable sum of money to this person to compensate for the risk entailed. Furthermore, because they were from the insulated world of the plantations and had a consequent lack of networks and contacts, the youths could not hire a lawyer. This lack of networks points to their 'outcaste' position, alienated from socio-political power structures. The significance of these encounters is all the greater because it indicates how attitudes in the wider social field disadvantage the plantation youth, especially where, as a function of the estate crisis, the plantation workers and the youth must depend on it more and more.

This chapter thus has explicated the resurgence of subtle forms of discrimination and the criminalisation of the plantation youth in the context of the dispute. It has also explained how things moved from insult to injury regarding the ongoing miseries suffered by the Tamils, which were essentially a legacy of the economic crisis. The dispute over the dam contributed significantly to the shift of the social field of the plantation Tamils from the total institution situation of plantations to the outside society, where categorical relations were refigured and redefined. The dispute also transformed Tamil workers, who had previously been loyal to the unions, but now identify more as Dalits. This transformation was reflected in the recent events of the jailing of the youths. While this chapter indicates how solidarity among the Tamil plantation community emerges out of conflict situation, the next chapter discusses how the plantation workers were divided socially in the context of the crisis.

Notes

1. See Ramaswamy (1997) for an interesting discussion of Tamil nationalism rooted in linguistic sentiment.
2. The origin of the word *Pāndi* is associated with the legendary Pandiyan dynasty that ruled Tamil-speaking regions in 600 BCE. Still, the modern use of the term conveys derogatory forms of ethnic prejudice and marginalisation.
3. Different waves of migration of Tamils to Kerala have occurred throughout the modern period. The Tamil Iyers settled around Palaghat and Travancore regions; the former became a major land-owning community, whereas the latter group migrated as the higher officials in the bureaucracy of the Travancore princely state. The land-owning higher caste of Vellalas and Tamil Muslims from the Madurai region migrated to the valleys of the high ranges of central Kerala. Another group of migrants are the Tamil Dalits, who were brought to central and southern Kerala as manual scavengers in the first half of the twentieth century. This migration continued in the postcolonial period. While Kerala was declared a 'scavenger-free state' in the early 1980s, the descendants of these migrants were incorporated into comparable occupations, often as cleaners/sweepers. The plight of these Dalits is detailed in a famous Malayalam novel, *Thottiyude Makan* (*Scavenger's Son*), by Thakazhi Sivasankara Pillai.
4. There are Tamil families living in the rubber plantations in Mundakayam valley, but they are identified as Malayalis rather than Tamils. This could be because the Tamils are better incorporated into the Malayali culture within the Malayali worker-dominated rubber plantations. This is in contrast to the tea plantations, where the majority of the workers are Tamils.
5. Many statues of Pennycuick can be found in the region, and many of the children born in the Madurai region are named after him. He was seen as a saviour and a god-like figure by the people living in the arid region in southern Tamil Nadu. Pennycuick sold off his family's property in England in order to complete the dam's construction.
6. I was told by informants, both in Tamil Nadu as well as in Kerala, that the shops were also targeted on the basis of the hostility between the local political leaders and the shop owners. The shops whose owners were friendly with the local leaders were vandalised less often than those whose owners were hostile towards the leaders.
7. Christopher works as a sales supervisor in a small-scale garment industry in Pathanamthitta, a town 60 miles from the Peermade tea belt. Muthuraj, who used to be a temporary worker in the

plantation, sought work as a plumber in the valley towns after the collapse of tea production in the Green Valley estate in the crisis context. Robin and his friend Murali work together in a stone crusher unit in Coimbatore, Tamil Nadu. At the time of the incident, Pratheesh and Muthuraj were 28 years old, Robin was 25, Christopher was 24 and Murali was 21.

8   While the police officer implicitly referred to the youths as immigrants, the Tamil population in the tea belt settled in the plantation long before the Malayalam-speaking community. However, not only is this fact well outside the understanding of the Malayalam-speaking population, popular culture in Kerala and the knowledge about Tamils that informs the practice of the bureaucratic state, but also the Tamils themselves are not informed about the specific historical advantage of being early birds in the plantations. This realisation would at least help them in their discourse against the process of their marginality. My intention is not to state that the Tamils are unaware that their ancestors came to the plantations much earlier than the Malayali population. My point is that the socio-cultural construction of state formation in Kerala is so profound that it pervades the imagination of the Tamil minority in such a way that they are unable or forget to use their early bird position to assert their rights in Kerala. The Peermade tea belt is imagined to have been part of Kerala society for longer than the actual period of postcolonial society by the plantation Tamils and particularly by the younger generation in the tea belt. This also means that the minority status of the plantation Tamils is also taken for granted as something that has existed since the initial days of plantation development in the 1860s. This conception significantly informs and influences their relation to the wider Kerala society.

9   A ward member is an elected representative in the Grāma Panchāyat, the local self-governing body. A union convener is a worker-representative of a union in the estate who coordinates the workers.

10 In another incident, the members of the temple council from the Green Valley estate sought police protection for organising the temple festival in fear of a clash between two groups of plantation youth. One of the police officers insulted them by throwing their petition in the rubbish in front of them. The police officer told the temple secretary that plantation youths are drunkards and street goons who do not have anything better to do, so let them fight and die. This incident reveals the dangers of stereotypes and the prejudices of the state officials towards the minority Tamils and how the Tamils have become 'used to' tolerating such insults in the government offices.

11 Doctors are often accused of negligence when the health condition of the patient worsens, and they become subject to public anger. Therefore, referring patients to another hospital is a tactic that doctors use to escape from any legal or moral repercussions in case the patient's health worsens or they die.

6
Crisis of relations

The depressed faces of the workers and their dilapidated houses capture the attention of anyone visiting the Hill Valley estate. Houses in the labour lines were severely damaged, but the company did not repair them. The maintenance of residential lines fell on the workers' shoulders. The work required collective effort by the workers since the dwellings had shared walls and roofs. Many of the workers, however, did not have the money needed to repair their residences. The workers also had a strong sense of the temporary nature of plantation life in the lifeworld of the workers, which was, of course, further intensified by the crisis. This feeling of alienation also may have contributed to their lack of enthusiasm to repair their homes. A worker sarcastically told me that those who could not contribute made up a lame excuse that they would leave the plantation soon and hence did not want to waste their money on repairing the residences. The sarcasm reminded me of the internal differentiation among workers that was intensified as a result of the crisis. This stigmatisation of the poor by other poor indicated a weakening of the solidarity and egalitarian tendencies that had been prevalent among workers before the crisis. In the context of the crisis, it was considered a serious stigma among poor workers when individuals were unable to meet group expectations such as sharing the cost of repairing homes.

Against this background, in this chapter I examine the reconfiguration of social relations by discussing how the crisis led to the disintegration and destabilisation of the solidarity among the workers. Workers have been increasingly polarised based on their affiliations to different groups. Three aspects of social relations in the current context of the crisis are discussed to illustrate this destabilisation of the workers' solidarity. These aspects are the division and antagonism between workers on the basis of trade union affiliations, the intensification of religious polarisation among the workers and an emerging conflict over the status and reputation of workers (I call this process the politics of decency). I have focused on these aspects because they signify the role of the crisis in the fracturing of social relations and not just in changes in material livelihood. Although the crisis created new subsistence relations, the fracturing of social relations involved further alienation of workers from each other and thus aggravated the marginalised existence that resulted from the closure of the plantations.

Solidarity before the crisis

The social order in the plantation, as discussed in Chapter 1, is primarily conditioned by its class structure. The workers in the colonial period, separated from the terms of their previous social life in the villages of Tamil Nadu, developed new socio-cultural forms entirely relevant to the production system in the plantations. Their newly developed culture was integral to the logic of their new situation. For instance, the new plantation order facilitated conversion to Christianity. Many workers saw this as a positive move to break the constraints of ideas and practices that had little relevance in their new situation. Indeed, the logic of the new situation of the plantations facilitated not only radical cultural reconceptualisations of past practices but also the adoption of completely new cultural and ritual forms.

Egalitarianism, where workers from different castes and social origins (in terms of their native villages) were considered relatively equal, featured in the social relations of the production system of the plantations. For example, invitations to wedding ceremonies were often extended to all the workers on an estate. Participation in the wedding ceremony or at least in the tea party that followed the wedding was obligatory on the estate. To not receive an invitation or not attend the function implied some ongoing personal animosity. In the tea belt, temple rituals were generally open to all regardless of caste, unlike in ordinary village society. Temple committees were composed of members of all castes, and the temple priest (*Pūcāri*) was selected mostly from among Dalit castes irrespective of sub-caste identity. The situation in the Thangamalai estate was an exception because each caste had its own temple there. However, no rules restricted entry of other castes into any of the temples, and all castes participated in the festivals in all the temples.[1]

Both Christian and Hindu festivals were celebrated by all families on the plantation, even though particular aspects of worship and rituals were performed only by those belonging to that religion. The affirmation of harmonious social relations can be mainly attributed to the Christians being first- and second-generation converts and the Hindus in the plantations being their relatives. Obligations of kinship, gift-giving and participation in ceremonies contributed to a collective imaginary of egalitarian solidarity, which was further reinforced by their sense of socio-economic similarities. The understanding of the plantation workers that they share similar forms of residence and have almost equal opportunities and lifestyles (Jayawardena 1963) contributed to this egalitarian ideology. In the context of the Caribbean, Samuel Martínez (2007) has discussed analogous forms of solidarity among plantation workers which come partly, as in the Peermade tea belt, from their shared sense of being in a subordinate relationship to management and their view of themselves as people of low status in the wider society.

The egalitarianism that existed in the Peermade plantations contrasts with the caste rigidity and discrimination that the relatives of these plantations workers face even today in the villages of origin in Tamil Nadu. There, access to temples has been increasingly restricted because of the faithful adherence to the practice of the caste system.[2] In the Peermade tea belt, most of the contemporary religious practices of the workers are locally, radically altered forms of practices that have been adapted to conform to the larger Tamil culture. In the context of the crisis, these forms of egalitarianism and solidarity have been undermined by the intensification of various kinds of conflicts and factionalism. New niches of social relations and separate cultural forms have emerged because of the weakening of the relatively rigid plantation system. The following sections discuss the various fragmentations, divisions and factionalism generated and intensified in the crisis context.

Internal factionalism of the unions

Historically, plantation workers in Kerala have been better served than their counterparts in other parts of India. However, I argue here that the trade unions have degenerated. There are several aspects to this degeneration. In the context of the crisis, the unions became involved in organising new patterns of control and work, instead of unifying the workers to radically resist the restructuring. Thus, the unions became agents of the social and political fragmentation of the workers and furthered their economic distress. The polarisation of the workers and the undermining of their collective solidarity in the context of the crisis were due in part to the influential and divisive roles of trade unions and the new cooperative set up to organise tea plucking. Neilson and Pritchard (2009) note in their study that union leaders skimmed profits for their individual as well as the political party's needs by charging dubious commissions and maintaining control of this new cooperative set-up. In line with them and others, I argue that the changes in activities of trade unions were part of a broader emergence of a trade union bourgeoisie in Kerala and its role as a contractor of labour that could hire and fire workers (Rammohan 1998).

Before the crisis, the workers in the plantation system were organised to work according to the date on which they enrolled as a permanent or temporary worker, and not on the basis of their union affiliation. Furthermore, the unions did not play a significant role in the everyday functioning of the plantation system and its social relations because the union leaders were from satellite towns outside the plantations and had hardly any connection with the workers. These external union leaders often relied on local union representatives in the plantations to mediate their relations with the workers. After the closure of the tea estates, however, the union leaders intervened more frequently in the plantations, sometimes on a nearly daily basis, to control the new cooperative setup for tea plucking.

In many closed tea estates, particularly the Killimalai and Pambanar estates, the collective solidarity of the workers was undermined by their new division on the basis of union affiliations in their workplace. Polarisation among workers who had different union affiliations grew when the tea fields were divided up and the work of plucking and selling tea leaves was organised based on union affiliation. The three major trade unions (CITU, INTUC and AITUC) in the Killimalai estate divided up the tea fields into three areas based on the number of workers affiliated with each trade union. The total workforce was divided into three union work groups. Each work group complained about the quality of the tea fields where they were to pick leaves. The amount of money each worker received depended on the quantity and quality of the tea leaves picked collectively by each union work group. That is to say, the amount of money that individuals received each day was linked to their union affiliation, which created a new sense of collective solidarity among workers in a group and also nurtured rivalry between workers from different trade unions.

The conflict between the workers intensified when these antagonisms spread outside the sphere of work and were transmitted into interpersonal relations in the social domain, for example through the informal monthly gatherings, organised by trade unions, of families attached to them. These were known as *family unions* (*kudumba yōgam*). The purpose of these family-based social interactions was to create community bonds among families belonging to a specific union and to celebrate the union-based solidarity that came from being a part of the collective of one's union. However, the various formal and informal actions and arrangements of all three trade unions only served to divide the workers inside and outside the workplace. According to a union leader, these family-based gatherings of union members were intended to create a larger 'family' identity, where members shared their happiness and sorrows in informal settings. While the intent of the unions was to soothe and ameliorate the misery of the workers by generating social solidarity, the antagonisms and rivalries among the unions meant that these social occasions fuelled rivalry and jealousy among the workers. This was partly because the politics of the unions in the region was significantly influenced by the larger conflicts between the political parties to which these unions were affiliated. These larger conflicts informed and reformulated local conflicts, giving them a new meaning.

The conflict among the workers further intensified when two unions and their political parties took different sides concerning the reopening of the tea estates under the MBT tea company. There were seven estates under the MBT and the Killimalai estate was at the centre, with headquarters for all seven estates. MBT was one of the first tea companies in the region to close down because of the crisis. A new company named KABS bought three of the seven MBT estates through an auction conducted by the government because MBT had failed to meet its financial obligations to various government offices. These included the electricity bills of MBT factories, the provident fund for workers' pensions and the pending tax to the government on the income from the tea produced. KABS had wanted to buy the other four estates as well, and it negotiated with the MBT plantations for the same. When the two companies were about to finalise the agreement, one of the unions (referred to as Union A) opposed the handover of the four estates. It argued for the distribution of deferred wages and other benefits (for the period when the estates were closed) to the workers before the commencement of tea production in all seven estates. However, another union (referred to as Union B) wanted the new company to resume production as soon as possible, with an assurance that they would distribute the deferred wages within a year. According to Union B, the recommencement of tea production would help the workers secure their livelihood. This created a conflict of interest between the two unions that was articulated in the souring relations between workers belonging to these 'rival' unions. Both unions, however, belonged to the same political front, and the political parties to which these unions were affiliated were also part of the ruling coalition.

Another union (referred to as Union C) attached to an opposition political party, however, alleged that the real reason for the conflict between Unions A and B was that KABS, the new company, had not paid the amount demanded by Union A in exchange for offering support for reopening the estates. To complicate matters further, the KABS company had a better relationship with the political leadership of Union B. Before expanding into the plantation business, KABS was a prominent timber trading company, and this helped them establish ties by supporting prominent political figures. Union B was the most powerful trade union and provided full support to the KABS company. Although the political party to which Union B was affiliated was the most powerful in the ruling coalition government, the Department of Revenue was with the political party to which Union A was affiliated. Through its influence with the political party, Union A had control over land-related issues, including government processes for registering land transfers. Union A, therefore, used its influence in the Department of Revenue to stop the process of land transfer to KABS and thus dealt a massive blow to the attempt to reopen the closed estates. This infuriated Union B and resulted in a war of words that eventually turned into a major fight between Unions A and B. This conflict was further fuelled when activists from Union B's political party stormed a general meeting of Union A and beat up the participants, including prominent union leaders. The workers fought each other as well, which further damaged the social relations within the plantations. The rivalry between the trade unions in the Killimalai estate meant that the workers were also polarised and became incorporated into broader political and corporate struggles on which their livelihoods seemingly depended.

When KABS finally took over all seven estates, Unions A and B were divided on many additional issues, including the new company's plan to cut down trees for timber. Union A accused the KABS company of conducting massive logging operations and selling plantation timber but only paying the workers half of their deferred wages. Union B defended the KABS company, arguing that it had at least paid a part of the deferred wages and that it would pay the remaining wages after the timber was sold. Union A accused Union B of supporting the company and conspiring with them to loot the valuable assets of the estates (here logging). They predicted that the new company would leave the plantation after it had finished with the logging. This conflict, too, generated hostility between the workers supporting the two unions.

One of my informants in Killimalai told me that during the peak of the crisis, which was roughly between 2001 and 2009, invitations to family functions such as marriages were restricted to those who belonged to the same union. There were, of course, exceptions between families that had shared strong and friendly relationships in the past. The conflicts among workers served to limit the social invitations extended to all workers to attend family functions, which often involved gift exchanges in the form of money. Such universal invitations were widespread and frequent before the crisis. However, after the crisis relations deteriorated to the extent that even the funerals of workers or their family members were attended only by members of the same union. It was considered ethical to attend the funerals of your enemies, and one's absence from a funeral was considered to be insensitive and brutal, an almost dehumanising act. Further, I was told that workers affiliated with different unions did not even exchange smiles when they met at the estate tea shop. The new union-based factionalism was evident in various celebrations such as workers' day, popular cultural festivals including Onam and Pongal, and national holidays such as Independence Day and Republic Day. These celebrations were now organised on the basis of union membership. This meant that customary family, clan and caste solidarities were partly suspended in the light of the overriding importance of new rivalries, which were an amalgamation of corporate and political interests with union affiliation. These amalgamated interests served to create and magnify local conflicts. Personal insult and affront gave a localised intensity to these regional political-economic interests and rivalries.

The violation of family and neighbourhood loyalties introduced its own intense sense of anger to an already anxious situation where the reproduction of plantation communities seemed problematic and precarious. A non-governmental organisation (NGO) representing European trade unions in a fact-finding team looking into the crisis reported the following:

> Although the plantation workers in the Indian tea sector are highly organised, there may be strong rivalry between the various unions on the tea plantations, which is not always to the advantage of the workers. Labour unrest is not always sustained and often turns out to benefit the management. The 'elected' union leaders do not always represent the interests of the plantation's workers. Plantation workers generally belong to the lowest socio-economic groups, while union leaders are often 'outsiders' from the middle class. (Quoted in Neilson and Pritchard, 2009, 144)

Although the antagonism eased once KABS began to run the plantation, it nevertheless continued in milder forms. The prioritisation of trade union affiliation was at the forefront of workers' imagination of themselves as belonging to a 'collective'. To the workers, their trade union affiliation provided their livelihood and secured their future. The new cooperative set up to collect and sell the tea leaves under the supervision of a trade union mediated new ways of being affiliated with it, new forms of corporate membership, new forms of belonging that were closely linked to everyday sustenance. The unions also assumed the role of broker in the relationship with the state and political parties, which controlled the legislative and regulatory environment within which the corporations operated. Unions also operated as the everyday police of a crisis-ridden plantation system, with workers dependent on them to pay their weekly wages and negotiate their annual bonus and other benefits.

The unions themselves were facing a serious membership crisis as many workers had moved out of the plantations. This crisis may have forced the unions to compete more intensely to gain control over the everyday life of the other workers. The control of day-to-day management and organisation of the future ownership of the tea plantations were the primary means through which the unions attempted to sustain their relevance in plantation society. As Anna Tsing (1993, 72) states in the Indonesian context, 'the local leaders are ambitious enough to tell the government that they represent the community and their neighbours that they represent the State'. While this ambiguous and interlocutory role of union leaders as agents between the government and workers is a universal phenomenon, what is noteworthy in the context of the Peermade tea belt is that the union leaders are neither plantation workers nor Tamils. Their unsympathetic intervention and attempts to control the plantation economy in crisis were major contributors to the fractured social relations among the workers.

Brahmanical Hinduism and alienating rituals

In the Peermade tea belt, Hindus form the majority in the eastern part whereas converted Dalit Christians form the majority in the western part. The population of Christians and Hindus in the Peermade tea belt is almost equal, with Hindus having a modest upper hand over Christians (around 60 per cent are Hindus and 40 per cent are Christians), and there is a negligible number of Muslims. The Hinduism followed by the plantation workers is rooted in animism and differs from Brahmanical

Hinduism. Brahmanical Hinduism is dictated by the Vedic texts and rooted in the Brahmanical interpretation of the Vedic texts and Hindu theology. In contrast, the plantation workers belong to Dalit communities, whose religious rituals are rooted in the historically evolved ritual prescriptions of Dravidian or Tamil clan deities, which differ substantially from the Vedic Hindu rituals (Ilaiah 1996).

In the Green Valley estate, out of 130 families, 38 were converted Dalit Christians, three were Nadar Christians and the remaining 89 families were Hindus. All three Nadar Christian families along with eight other families of Dalit Christians were part of the Church of South India (CSI) and another Dalit Christian family belonged to the Salvation Army. Of the remaining 29 Christian families, four were affiliated to the Catholic Church and the other 25 to Pentecostal missions (Siloam Church and Believers Church). The crisis-ridden plantations had provided new opportunities for religious groups to intensify their role in the lives of plantation workers.

With the weakening of the plantation structure as a result of the crisis, a few Hindu nationalist volunteer organisations introduced Brahmanic and Vedic rituals and festivals, which were not familiar to Dalit Hindus in these tea estates. This was meant to bring the Dalits in the plantations into the fold of Brahmanical Hinduism, which promised religiosity as the basis of society's moral order. In early 2011, on the Green Valley estate, I participated in a *vilakku pūjai*, a ritual offering introduced by the leaders of Hindu Mahasabha, a pan-Hindu movement, based in a company town in the tea belt. The ritual was organised on New Year's Eve (31 December). It was to celebrate the successful resumption of production work in the plantation and the partial reopening of the tea factory in the Green Valley estate. During the ritual offering, I noticed that no one in the estate temple knew how to perform this ritual.

A supervisor had a book that explained the procedures of the ritual and its benefits. He was from the Maravar community, a lower caste but ranked higher than the Dalits. He was also one of the local leaders of the BJP, the Hindu nationalist party. His affiliation to the larger Sanskritised Hindu ideology was the reason why he wanted to lead the ritual. He explained the various aspects of the ritual through a microphone. He asked the workers to pray together for the plantation to fully restart operations and frequently advised them on the 'right' time to pray. The supervisor merged his secular economic authority with this new religious *sacred* authority to acquire greater moral authority in the plantation community as a custodian of its welfare. He took custody of the ritual performance, sidelining the local priest, who was ill informed about the various stages of the new ritual. The sidelining of the local priest, who belonged to a Dalit sub-caste, was a symbolic act of alienating the Dalit plantation community from their traditional faith – which was displaced by the Sanskritic prayers. In the Green Valley estate, the incorporation of Dalit workers into Brahmanic Hindu culture mirrors the incorporation of plantation workers into wider political-economic hierarchies.

As the ritual was organised for the successful resumption of plantation production, we can see a clear linkage between the economic crisis and the intensification of Hindu nationalist sentiments (which are also political), that is, an intensification of politics mediated through religious intensification. The introduction of the new ritual was also a way to propagate Hindu nationalism and transform it into a complex form of social governance. The union and political leaders in the company towns were concerned about the recurring visits of the Hindu Mahasabha leaders to the plantations. They regarded this organisation as a potential threat to the trade unions, capable of mobilising workers against the interests of the dominant trade unions and their larger political parties. On the day after the ritual, a few workers were interrogated by a union leader regarding the organisation of new rituals and the presence of Hindu nationalist leaders in the Green Valley estate.

Bhajans (group prayers) and collective chanting of Sanskritic verses were not practised in the plantation temples before the crisis. They were introduced in the Peermade tea belt by a Hindu cultural outfit known as Ayyappa Sēvak Sangh after the first *vilakku pūjai*. For the first few *bhajans*, the outfit sponsored a Brahmin priest (*thirumēni*) and took care of the instruments required. One of my informants, Malathi, a 50-year-old female worker, responded to my curiosity over the new *pūjai* and *bhajans* saying:

> The Christians in the plantations always have group prayers every Sunday morning, and it is a good idea to have group prayers for Hindus, so that we could have a sense of religious identity. The Hindus in the plantation have to learn a lot from the Christians, particularly the Pentecost Christians, on how to generate a sense of belonging among one another.

She thought that the group prayers would help prevent the Hindus from converting to Christianity, especially to Protestant groups with significant numbers of followers in the tea belt. Malathi's concern shows a clear polarisation among the plantation workers based on their religious affiliation. It shows how Hindu religious nationalism emerged in opposition to growing Christianisation among the lower castes.

During my subsequent fieldwork in June 2013, I observed that the performance of *bhajans* had become regular and systematic, with one Hindu household hosting *bhajans* each month. On the advice of Hindu organisations, a communal meal on New Year's Day was also introduced, and this practice went on for six years in the tea belt. Similar practices exist on many other tea estates in the region. In all these tea estates, the pan-Hindu nationalist organisations sent their *thirumēni* (Brahmin priest) to supervise the Vedic-Sanskritised rituals. What can be discerned is the intensified ritualisation of everyday life among Hindus to create a corporate sense of solidarity that, at once, mirrored and surpassed that of their rival, Christian denominations. This ritualisation, which transformed the nature of everyday Hinduism in the plantation, not only generated local solidarity but also incorporated the Hindu workers into a new national imaginary. This new religious national imaginary sought to revive Brahmanical Hinduism, which believes in the varna (caste) system that is fundamentally opposed to the interests of the Dalits. The local priest from the Dalit community, *pūcāri*, became an alien in his own temple when the *thirumēni* took charge on special occasions. The plantation Dalits alienated themselves when they alienated their *pūcāri*.

The Hindu organisations further solidified their presence and reinforced Brahmanical Hinduism in the crisis-ridden plantation by promoting the celebration of *Vināyaka Chaturthī*, the arrival of Lord Gaṇeśa to Earth.[3] At the beginning of the twentieth century, the celebration of *Vināyaka Chaturthi* was popularised by the Hindu nationalist Bal Gangadhar Tilak to bridge the gap between Brahmins and 'non-Brahmins'. Historically, this was an attempt to build unity at the grassroots level among the different Indian caste groups in order to generate nationalistic fervour among the people against British colonial rule (Brown 1991). This historical attempt to bridge the cultural and religious gap was now promoted in a different way by the Hindu elites, particularly by Hindu merchants in the satellite towns of the tea belt – the advocates of this new pan-Hinduism. These processes of cultural incorporation into a homogenised Hinduism are forms of cultural hegemony because local Hindu workers come under the religious control and guidance of external Hindu groups such as urban merchants, who fund some of these proselytising movements and practices.

The Hindu nationalist organisations took advantage of the failure and suspension of welfare activities on the plantations. They tried to reinstitute these welfare measures to attract Hindu workers to their organisation. For instance, when the medical dispensaries in the plantation closed down, the *Ayyappa Sēvak Sangh* recruited Hindu girls in

Figure 6.1: Ruined medical dispensary on the Hill Valley estate

the tea belt who had a high school education and trained them in first aid and essential nursing services to provide free, basic medical services to the plantation workers, in order to attract the workers into Brahmanical Hinduism.[4] When the youth clubs that provided free educational assistance for plantation children disintegrated,[5] the Vivekananda Cultural Society started free evening instruction for estate children, called *Ekal Vidyalaya*. The evening instruction began with a Sanskrit Hindu prayer song to habituate the children of the plantation workers into homogenised Hindu practices and the nationalism of this Hinduism.

    This process of 'learning of faith' created a new cultural hegemony, partially replacing the non-Brahmanical Hinduism that had been practised in the insulated space of the plantation system before the crisis. Pedagogy and the learning of the sacred were always part of the reinforcement of caste power and domination in India. This was now reformulated and remediated through a religiosity that used Brahmanical texts to articulate the growing political and economic power of certain Hindu middle classes. Class and caste powers were intertwined into new desires to cleanse Hinduism and affirm more authentic forms of Hinduism among the lower castes, who were seen as lost in local customs and ignorance. In this process, certain forms of intellectual hegemony and cultural superiority were also articulated through pedagogic religious projects.

The adoption of new rituals by plantation workers emerged during the economic crisis, when the new religious practices became part of their everyday struggles for subsistence. The new rituals could also be considered as an attempt to overcome the fragmentation and division of plantation life while paradoxically contributing to that process. The lack of expertise among the workers regarding the new rituals and their reliance on Brahmins or other higher-caste priests and intermediaries to perform the new rituals further alienated the workers from their own customary religious practices and placed them under the priestly care and hegemony of others outside the plantation. The newly emerged religiosity in the tea belt cannot be captured by the idea of Sanskritisation.[6] While there are elements of Sanskritisation in the processes that emerged on the plantations, I argue that this needs to be understood as the 'learning of faith'. The plantation workers engaged in the new rituals because of the promise that these would bring peace and prosperity to their families during the crisis. This is unlike the idea of Sanskritisation by which lower-caste communities emulate the cultural and ritual aspects of upper-caste communities to acquire higher status in the Hindu caste hierarchy.

The exposure of the workers to new processes of religious homogenisation re-engaged and reimported dimensions of the religion-backed caste hierarchy back into the organisation of everyday life. Hence, the introduction of Brahmanical Hindu practices brought the workers into a larger social and political order that, in effect, resubordinated them within the caste hierarchy that had been partly suspended when the plantation factory system was dominant.[7] Their outcaste status, which had been rendered irrelevant in the day-to-day lives of the workers on the plantations, was reasserted during the crisis. The crisis created ruptures within and outside plantation society that, in turn, created room for the further alienation of the workers from each other and from their local cultural heritage. It was their cultural autonomy that was compromised.

The linkage with larger politico-religious groups politicised and communalised identity, and it led the workers to identify increasingly with others outside the plantation workforce. In other words, plantation workers began to identify with followers of ritualistic religions outside Kerala society and downplayed their linkages with local Tamil Dalit workers. This imagination of being a part of the Brahmanic Hindu fold intensified the process of polarisation among the religious communities in the Green Valley estate. This is evident in the corresponding intensification of religious practices among Christians in the tea belt, to which I now turn.

Pentecostalism and disruptive endogamy

The preaching of Christianity among workers and their conversion dates back to the days of plantation development in Kerala (Kooiman 1991). In the context of the crisis, the Christian religious groups found new opportunities to propagate their faith further. The number of gospel sessions (locally known as salvation festivals) and neighbourhood prayer sessions increased after the crisis began. A local pastor of the Believers Church in the Koolikanam estate mentioned to me that one of the goals of preaching the gospel is to 'heal the wound of the crisis and the economic suffering' of the believers. I met him when he was doing 'fieldwork', that is, propagating Christianity outside the tea plantations in *puthuvēli* the land outside the plantations. He, like many other Christian pastors, feared the opposition of Hindu nationalist outfits who organised against proselytising by the Christian churches, fearing further conversions.

On many estates in the tea belt, the animosity of Hindu groups towards Christian conversions resulted in small-scale acts of violence. For example, in the Maruthamalai estate, Hindus led by Malayalam-speaking Ezhava families vehemently opposed the entry of Pentecostal missionaries.[8] They informed me that one Pentecostal pastor who had tried to convert Hindus was beaten and chased away from the estate. The pastor had been warned a few times after he had converted a family a year earlier. An anti-conversion squad had been active in the estate since its formation under the stewardship of Vishva Hindu Parishad (VHP) in January 1999. Their major objective was to oppose the conversion of plantation workers to Christianity in the tea belts of Peermade and Munnar. The squad brought Tamil-speaking Hindu saints to the plantations to persuade the converts to return to Hinduism. The squad's formation coincides with the period of the economic crisis and rampant poverty in the Peermade tea belt.

The erstwhile muster offices (used for the morning assembly of plantation workers in the Muthukkanam estate), labour clubs (in the Brodley estate) and crèches (in the Green Valley estate) were converted into Pentecostal 'prayer houses'. The Christian groups offered to pay the electricity bills and repair the damage to the buildings. Although the plantation management agreed to this offer only temporarily, these buildings eventually came under the complete control of the Christian groups. Previously the weekly schedule of the workers was strictly controlled by the production processes in the plantation, such that Sunday morning was the only day when workers were free for prayers.

The crisis provided the workers with a more flexible schedule and made them available for prayers on weekdays as well. In the Green Valley estate, the Christian group placed a cross on top of the crèche building. This was a powerful symbol to mark the displacement and irrelevance of the institutions of plantation production because the crèche was a key part of the everyday plantation work. Similarly, another crèche in another part of the Green Valley estate was taken over by a faction of the Pentecostal Church (this faction was formed when three Dalit families fought with their former church and formed their own Protestant group with a new pastor). In 2018, their rival group demolished the medical centre in the plantation and built a prayer house in the same area. They lobbied for this through the cousin of the new pastor.

This intensification of religious practices and divisions shows the extent to which workers sought new forms of identities and material support during the crisis. An incident that occurred during my fieldwork in 2012 shows how the solidarity and friendship that developed through plantation work (or class solidarity) was increasingly displaced by new religious affiliations and by the role of pastors in plantation life. A Hindu couple, Muthu and Saraswathi, who did not have a place to stay on the plantation after their retirement, asked their neighbour, Moses, for a small hut that had been occupied previously by Moses's son and his family. Moses's son had left for Tirupur with his wife in search of work while their children stayed with Moses and his wife. Moses, who was in his mid-50s, was a Pentecostal Christian. Moses agreed to allow Muthu to stay in the hut until his son returned or the company demolished the hut in case the plantation production resumed full operations.[9] Moses decided to help Muthu and Saraswathi because they had been neighbours for around 30 years, and Saraswathi and Moses's wife, Mary, had worked next to each other in the tea fields. Muthu, in fact, had helped Moses with his work when Moses was new to plantation work and did not know how to prune the tea bushes.

In other words, Moses agreed to help Muthu and Saraswathi as a sign of his gratitude. However, a day before Muthu and Saraswathi were to move into the hut, Moses visited them and reluctantly informed them that he had just received a message from his son about his return to the plantation, and that he would need the hut. This shocked Muthu, who was not convinced that Moses's son would return. He believed that Moses's son was living happily in Tirupur and would not be able to get a good job in the tea belt. When Saraswathi asked Mary the real reason for the sudden change in the attitude of Moses, Mary reluctantly told her the truth, that that the pastor had asked Moses to keep the house for Jeevaraj's

Figure 6.2: A crèche converted into a Christian prayer house in 2011

Figure 6.3: The same prayer house in Figure 6.2 in 2019

CRISIS OF RELATIONS 133

Figure 6.4: A muster office converted into a Christian prayer house in 2013

son, Johnson, because Jeevaraj's family were Pentecostal Christians and belonged to their church.

Mary apologised to Saraswathi, and Moses could not face Muthu after the incident. Moses and Mary wanted to continue the friendship with Muthu and Saraswathi, which had developed through the debts and familiarities of the plantation system. However, the intervention by the pastor made Moses indifferent towards Muthu. The pastor prioritised new obligations and solidarities mediated by religion. It should be noted that the high school education of two of Moses's grandchildren was supported by funds from the church. Many of the families in the plantation increasingly relied on charity funds such as those from churches for their children's education as a result of the economic crisis. Furthermore, the churches also provided free rice, vegetables and medical help for chronic illnesses during the peak of the crisis in 2006–7. From 1998, the churches had provided free notebooks, school bags and a small amount of money to buy school uniforms. They also helped the workers get manual labour jobs in the valley towns through church connections. This may be why Moses had to prioritise the church over the friendship and solidarity developed through decades of plantation life.

The intensification of religious practices and the polarisation of plantation workers were also evident in the emerging endogamy among Dalit Christians. Religious identity became a central factor for Dalit Christians when fixing marriages in the context of the crisis. Previously, sub-caste identity was the most crucial factor, and religious identity was less relevant. Therefore, marriages between Dalit Hindus and Dalit Christians were often arranged. This changed with the increasing importance of churches in the everyday lives of workers after the collapse of the plantation system. Between 1998 and 2010, only two inter-religious marriages occurred in the Green Valley estate. One of those was a love marriage and the other was an arranged marriage. However, 13 inter-religious marriages within the same sub-caste had occurred between 1991 and 1997. This may also have been because plantation society made workers arrange their children's marriages within their own estate or with a nearby estate so that their children would live close to them – an important consideration for marriages in the close kinship system of Tamils. This preference disappeared after plantation life was hit by the crisis and opened it up for religious groups.

The increasing focus on endogamous marriages among Dalit Christians can be attributed to various factors including generational changes, with the younger generation increasingly imagining themselves to be part of a religious group more than their parents or grandparents, who may have been born Hindus and later converted to Christianity. However, the economic crisis and the collapse of the plantation system provided opportunities for Christian missions to intensify their proselytising – their role in guiding and steering people towards a morally ordered life. The new marriage patterns articulated the increasing influence of pastors and priests in managing family affairs. I pondered this phenomenon when one of my informants on the Green Valley estate

Figure 6.5: Self-constructed house of a temporary worker

told me that the Dalit Christians were similar to the higher castes because they wanted to marry only those of the same belief system as themselves, namely other Dalit Christians. The Dalit Hindus accepted marriages with Dalit Christians but were a bit more pessimistic about marriages with Dalits from the Pentecostal Church. This is mainly because of the widespread belief in the plantation that Pentecostal Christians were more radical in their beliefs than other Protestant groups and hence difficult to be close relatives with.

Politics of decency

Under the rigid plantation system, the communal solidarity of the workers was produced and protected by their homogeneous occupational identity, which generated class identity of a kind that manifested through shared lifestyle and outlook. This solidarity was threatened by the opening of the plantations to the outside world. Various interest groups from outside merged commerce, political influence, religion, and caste power and influence in new ways. Previously, the differentiation of the occupational identity of the workers was mediated by the value of the various jobs they were engaged in within the plantations. Increasingly, values and experiences outside the plantations formed the basis for workers to differentiate themselves from each other and claim higher status and prestige even within the plantations. The increasing importance of this politics of decency, as I call it, led to a moral crusade that disparaged some workers in terms of their culture and practices. A major aspect of this socio-cultural change was the idea of equality of all human beings based on their essential humanness, their human worth before God or principles of a democratic state. These forms of equality are different from the idea of differentiating people based on socio-economic inequalities including those of caste. However, the new world did not equalise everyone, but instead introduced new differences. For example, the amount of money that workers made through their new-found jobs differentiated the human worth of these workers because the differences in income were seen as a reflection of the workers' effectiveness in finding a manual labour job that paid earned them incomes compared to other workers. Chandra Jayawardena's observation on the Guyanese plantation supports my point about the income of the workers and others' assumptions about their human worth. According to Jayawardena (1968, 414), the two forms of equality (that is, equality based on economic position and equality based on humanness) are not mutually exclusive. They may be interwoven in the ideology of a particular group of people. The presence of Christianity and God's role in providing help in finding a job adds complexity to this picture because on this basis, Christians claimed the superiority of their faith and sacred power.

In plantation society, the value and affirmation of essential human worth is practised and understood through the vernacular concept of *challithanam* (backward/undignified/improper behaviour), which differentiates workers on the basis of their decency. That is to say, if I wanted to differentiate myself from a group of people, I would say that I am more decent or dignified than them and that they are considered to have a *challi* (undignified/silly) attitude. The diversified occupations and consequent inequalities introduced by the crisis bred a new kind of cultural emphasis in plantation life. Increasingly, the idea of decency and dignified properness became a dominant ideology based on which the workers were differentiated.

In late March 2011, I noticed a hoarding on the steep mud wall of the Mariamman temple. It had 'New India' written (in Tamil) on top, followed by the names and photos of a few plantation workers who were part of this new group. Most of the men listed on this hoarding worked outside the plantation, and a few others were the siblings of those who worked outside. I wanted to know more about this group as I had heard people on the estate discussing it. On the same day as this new hoarding appeared, I met Senthil, a 43-year-old male, who was the secretary of this new group. Senthil worked as a mason in a construction firm in the valley town of Ponkunnam, which is located around 40 miles from the tea belt. I walked to *Kēzh layam* (the labour lines situated next to the temple), where his house was located. He was having lunch. He asked me to sit on a plastic chair and wait while he finished his lunch. I asked him about the details of this new group. He told me:

> We have to improve ourselves. Isn't it? Go outside [to the valley town] and see how much money they have. They could have all this money because they behave properly. And they become new members of the group of learned men. So if you need to make more money, you have to grow and behave properly. The valley people do a lot of business and save money, unlike the estate people who spend all the money they get. That is, people in the estate need to stop being silly.

Thus, this group, 'New India', was formed as a platform for members to help one another march towards socio-economic prosperity through hard work and economic prudence. One of the group's activities was to collect money and buy gold ornaments every month for each member. This group seemed to be a revived form of the welfare clubs that existed on the plantation before the crisis and was similar to the micro-credit groups mushrooming all over India. The nature of this group, however, was very different. Its membership was limited to those who worked outside the plantation belt or their close relatives. When I asked the reason for the limited membership, Senthil told me that only those who worked outside the plantations could afford the group's monthly purchase of gold, the cost of which was high and could not be afforded by anyone who stayed back on the estate. He again emphasised the new forms of socio-economic mobility experienced by plantation workers who worked in the valley town compared with those who remained on the plantation and were branded as uncaring. In short, I felt that the new group in the plantation was like the Rotary Club or Lions Club, where membership was limited to the upper classes, and new membership was possible only by invitation of existing members. This is a notable development on the plantation because membership of the micro-credit groups in the Green Valley estate was based on friendships that cut across caste and religious lines.[10]

This strict policy of the New India group, however, irked the families who continued to live on the limited income from the plantation. After a few days, I noticed that the large hoarding had been stoned, apparently by someone who disliked or opposed the new group, and was in a state of disrepair. I met Senthil once again as well as his friend, Madhan, who was also a member of the group. Madhan worked as a cook in a restaurant in the satellite town of Elappara. They both got angry when I asked them about the hoarding. Madhan claimed that people were jealous of the new group and that it was silly behaviour (*challithanam*) by silly people. I suspected that those who vandalised the board were working on the plantation, and hence, I repeatedly inquired about the incident. A few days later, in one of the evening conversations, I brought this incident to the attention of the people present. Three men began to laugh about the hoarding. Shiva, who worked on the estate, claimed that the new group assumed they were of a higher status than others in the plantation. He told me he did not like the idea of a closed group because it could eventually lead to hundreds of such groups being created on the plantation. Shiva's friend, Karthi, sarcastically stated that some kids might have thrown stones for fun and that I should not be bothered about it. Karthi's sarcasm and Shiva's anger towards the new group made me suspect that they might have vandalised the hoarding, which, indeed, proved to be true when Karthi confessed to me two months later, after the tension had died down.

I was interested in observing the use of the concept of *challithanam* some months later, when a few of my friends working in other towns in Kerala and Tamil Nadu visited their home areas. Mahesh, a 29-year-old male, returned home for the Onam festival. Mahesh worked as a salesperson in a well-known textile retail chain in Tiruchirapalli in Tamil Nadu. I had met him on his first day back at the estate, but he seemed to have disappeared within the next few days, and nobody had seen him since. Three days later, while sitting in the compound of a small church near the volleyball ground, I met Muthukumar, a 27-year-old male working as an assistant (*kaiyāl*) to a mason (*mesthrie*). He initiated a conversation, asking if anyone had seen Mahesh after the day of his arrival.

Nikson, a 27-year-old male, teasingly responded that Mahesh might be hiding in his house because he did not want to give them a treat. He added that Mahesh was pretending to be superior to his friends. I did not take this conversation seriously until I met Mahesh again, on my way to Pambanar (company town), when he was waiting with his mother and sister for the jeep that would take them down to the town. Initially, I felt that he might not be interested in talking to me as he had kept himself away from his friends. I greeted him and initiated a conversation, asking where he was headed. He said that he was going to buy new clothes for his sister for Onam. I asked him why he had not been seen outside his house with the other young men in the estate. He responded:

> Well, unnecessary engagement with our boys may create trouble. So it is better to calmly stay at home and leave the estate without making a huc and cry. It won't be right to go with them. Sometimes they behave like *challi* (silly people). When we come home during holidays, we have to just spend time in the house, not outside.

I did not expect this comment from him because he had been an active member of the youth club on the estate and was at the forefront of communal celebrations during festivals before the crisis. As we both got into the jeep to go to the company town, he told me not to tell the others what he had said.

During the course of my fieldwork, I noticed that the term *challi* or *challithanam* was widely used by people to differentiate themselves from others. This was particularly true in the case of those who worked outside the plantation because of the crisis. I often heard parents complain about their children's friendships with *challi,* which got them into trouble. This term was used in a context where those who had gone outside to work sought to create a new social position by differentiating themselves from the moral, intellectual and cultural status of those who stayed back on the plantation. However, it was also used selectively, on particular occasions, to differentiate between people working or staying on the estates. These particular occasions included, but were not limited to, situations where plantation workers accused each other's sons of encouraging the other's sons to consume alcoholic beverages. A sense of moral and intellectual inferiority is associated with this term. The sign of one's intellectual and cultural backwardness is the failure to enter modernity – a world of civilised and polite etiquette.

One could argue that not all the potential plantation workers on the estate would be engaged in plantation work, especially given the changes involving the younger generations, including many plantation youth going outside the plantation for work, which was exacerbated by the crisis. However, I feel that at least 50 per cent of the plantation youth would have engaged in plantation work if the crisis had not hit the plantations. This is because around 50 per cent of the youth were already working in the adjoining areas of the plantations in various informal services. They would have chosen to work on the plantations if the estates were functioning properly. The role of the crisis in accelerating the process of diversification of occupations should be given due consideration when analysing the politics of decency in the plantations.

The crisis of relations

What should be inferred from this chapter is that the differentiation and polarisation of workers and their children intensified and, in turn, alienated them from their local communities, which previously had supported each other in times of crises. The local fracturing of social relations emerged when people were incorporated into new national religious and political groups. This fracturing multiplied, feeding into processes that further perpetuated their alienation. When the workers were alienated from each other by the new religious bodies with resources to buy their allegiance, they were also alienated from their own religious and cultural traditions that had played a key role in generating their sense of identity before the crisis. The allegiance to new groups often results in structural, symbolic and political violence. For example, Jan Breman (2013) reports that 150,000 mill workers became jobless when the textile mills in the Indian city of Ahmedabad shut down. Many of them joined Hindu nationalist organisations that participated in a pogrom against the Muslim minority community. The closure of the mills led to the tearing of the fabric of communal harmony. This experience from the northern part of India is similar to what happened in the tea plantations in southern India.

Fanon (1967) made an interesting observation that de-alienation is achieved only when human beings experience a sense of being part of the larger community, of humanity as a whole. In the fractured plantation society, the workers are alienated not only from the larger Kerala and Indian society, but also from their own community. This alienation was particularly evident when the unions attempted to become powerful by alienating the workers from each other. The unions, who are supposed to represent the workers and bring them together in times of crisis, in fact robbed the workers of their voice. Accordingly, the larger structural processes during the crisis that promised to offer the workers help in achieving their humanity paradoxically prevented them from doing so.

The workers were also alienated when some people distinguished themselves by devaluing others, resulting in their alienation from their kin, their community and their past. As the ethnographic discussion in this chapter shows, the social fabric of plantations society was degraded not only by the larger communal groups and trade unions, but also by the workers themselves. A sense of collective bad faith (Scheper-Hughes 1992; Holmes 2013) developed among the workers to justify their indifference towards others who could not move out of the plantations at the time of the crisis. Their indifference should also be seen as an attempt to reclaim their dignity and recognition, which they struggle to earn when they migrate into the caste-ridden Tamil society or during racist encounters with Kerala society. This could be understood as the banality of evil by workers embroiled in the structural violence perpetuated by the plantation crisis.

Notes

1 In the Thangamalai estate, workers from different castes have their own temples. The Arunthathiar caste (comprising 60 families) worship Kaliamman, their clan deity. The Pallar caste worship Mariamman and were about to build a temple. Workers from the Paraiyar caste have their own temple for their clan deity, Madaswamy. The expenses incurred for the festivals and weekly rituals are divided among members of a particular caste.
2 In rural Tamil Nadu, different castes organise their own temple festivals in the village's common temple, and Dalits are permitted to conduct their festivals only after the upper castes have done so.
3 Lord Gaṇeśa was not popular among plantation Dalits before the crisis. This is evident from the spatial location of the temples associated with these deities. Contrary to the Brahmanical deity-dominated nodal towns, the plantation temples were mainly devoted to the non-Brahmanical deities.
4 See Panikkar (2003), Thachil (2009) and Chithambaram (2011) for a detailed discussion on the concomitant relation between welfare schemes and cultural organisations of Hindu nationalist organisations. The first reference is a newspaper article by a noted historian focusing on the history of communalism in India. The last two references are doctoral theses. Thachil's thesis considers Kerala to lie partly outside the sphere of the welfare schemes of the

    Hindu nationalist organisations and their subsequent success in drawing outcaste/tribal populations into their fold. He credits the Dalit and Communist movements for keeping a check on the growth of the BJP and Hindu nationalism in Kerala. Chithambaram examines how the welfare schemes of these organisations failed to woo the local population.
5   Arts clubs or arts and sports clubs were local associations, mostly managed by the youth, whose primary goal was to strengthen bonds in the local community by promoting cultural activities or organising sporting events. In the plantations, these clubs organised wedding celebrations and took care of funerals. The clubs played a crucial role in sustaining intimate community activities. But these clubs disappeared when youth in the estates sought work outside the plantation.
6   The process of homogenisation is different from Sanskritisation (Srinivas 1952). As mentioned before, in Sanskritisation, the lower castes emulate the cultural and ritual practices of twice-born castes in order to attain a higher social status. Homogenisation refers to the concerted attempt by Hindu nationalist groups and organisations to assimilate the lower castes into 'purified' and more authentic versions of Hinduism by creating a common ritual-based culture based on Brahmanical rituals. However, the process of homogenisation overlaps with Sanskritisation in terms of its consequences because both of these, paradoxically, reaffirm the very value and relational principles vital to the devaluation and exclusion of Dalit populations.
7   The partial suspension of the caste system in its rigid form insulated and protected plantation workers from the kind of caste discrimination and consequent social humiliation suffered by their relatives who lived in Tamil Nadu, or by their Dalit counterparts in the outside Keralan society. I do not mean to imply that the incorporation of Tamil Dalits into the plantation system was a boon to them. The ideology of caste has been an important element in legitimising the creation of a particular system of class oppression related to the plantation economy and its basis in indentured labour. As Omvedt (1980) argues, a pre-capitalist feudal agrarian order formed the basis of a modern capitalist structure. Stoler (1985) presents a similar case for Sumatra's plantation belt, where capitalist production was built on the foundation of non-capitalist peasant orders. However, the relative suspension of these ritually legitimated hierarchical caste relations was an unintended consequence of the insulated nature of the plantation and its strict industrial order.
8   Ezhava is a non-Dalit lower caste and is one of the largest caste communities in Kerala. Hindu groups gained a foothold on other estates by accessing those in a similar position in the caste hierarchy. For example, the Hindu groups were led by families of the Maravar caste in the Green Valley estate. Maravars of Tamil Nadu, similarly to the Ezhavas of Kerala, are a non-Dalit 'lower' caste. They are minorities in the tea estates. Nonetheless, most of them work as supervisors and mechanics in the factories. This higher position in the plantation class structure also gives them more authority and leadership positions in the Hindu social groups.
9   The plantation management would demolish the hut if no temporary workers lived there. Huts such as these were destroyed by companies that took over a few plantations in the tea belt to prevent others from settling there. These huts were built during the heyday of plantation production when many temporary workers were needed to meet the increasing demand for tea.
10 The only exception to this general trend is a new micro-credit group of men belonging to the Catholic Church on the estate.

7
Rumour and gossip in a time of crisis

This chapter examines rumour and gossip within plantation society in the context of the crisis and how they capture social processes that might not be explicitly visible in the social relations of everyday life in the plantation. The explicit and easily accessible social actions of front-stage performance, in Goffman's (1959) term, are in contrast to the backstage performance, where the plantation workers are able to communicate their opinions or circulate rumours mainly through gossip. The rumours and gossip have real consequences for the workers' life situation, and it is irrelevant whether the content is accurate or not.

Rumours about the crisis here refer to those about changes in the control and management of the plantations under crisis. In the crisis context, those who stayed back often engaged in conversations about the troubled times they were going through and about the callous attitude of the plantation company, trade union leaders and state authorities towards their plight. The specific rumours and related gossip discussed here were collected in one such context in the Hill Valley estate. On the plantation, gossip in the crisis context was targeted at the plantation management and the unions, who were considered a rival quasi-group (Mayer 1963) whose interests seemed to be in conflict with those of the workers. Accordingly, this chapter focuses on the varied forms and functions of both rumours and gossip during the crisis and their consequences for the workers' resistance against, or accommodation of, their exploitation and dispossession (Goffman 1967; Handelman 1973).

The significance of rumour and gossip for social relations have long been stressed by anthropologists, but they have mostly been studied from a structural-functional point of view. Max Gluckman, for instance, considers gossip as an integral part of maintaining the social system. For him, 'gossip is the blood and tissue of community life' (Gluckman 1963, 308). In a similar vein, Ann Stoler captures the significance and functional aspect of rumour: for Stoler, rumour is a 'key form of cultural knowledge that … shaped what people thought they knew, blurring the boundaries between events witnessed and those envisioned, between performed brutality and the potentiality for it' (Stoler 1992, 154). This resonates with Raymond Firth's statement that 'rumour is reporting of unverified events' (Firth 1967, 142).[1]

Despite the fact that they are both produced and transmitted in face-to-face interactions, very few studies have focused simultaneously on both rumour and gossip (Goffman 1967; Paine 1967; Handelman 1973; Scott 1990; Stewart and Strathern 2004). The major challenge for these studies was how to distinguish between rumour and gossip. For analytical purposes, one could argue that rumour may be a form of unsigned gossip (Paine 1970). Stewart and Strathern (2004, 38–9) observe that 'gossip takes place mutually among people in networks or groups. Rumour is unsubstantiated information, true or untrue, that passes by word of mouth, often in wider networks than gossip.' While rumour and gossip are often used interchangeably in the Hill Valley estate, there is a distinction between the two in their use and function. In the Peermade tea belt, gossip (*Kicukicu/ vīn-pēchu*) refers to talking (often negatively) about certain individuals with another individual or a group of individuals, while rumour (*vadhanthi*) refers to the spread of unverified information about persons, events and social processes. In the crisis context, gossip by workers and the spread of rumours (by managerial staff/union leaders) appear to be in conflict with each other, but in fact they entered into a dialectic relation, which can be seen in the conversations among the workers and union conveners discussed in this chapter.[2]

I observe that rumours and gossip in the crisis context have distinct consequences with regard to resistance and accommodation in the plantations. The analysis of the gossip shows that the workers are critical of the plantation management, the unions and Kerala state for failing to ensure their means of livelihood during the crisis period. In this context, gossip functions as a form and agent of resistance, which further shows that the workers were conscious of their exploitation. Gossip, as will be shown, often served to sustain criticism of the situation and worked to unify the workers against management. It was part of the resistive potential of the plantation workforce but also integral to processes of ordering and reordering in the plantation society. In other words, gossip here is born within the ongoing texture of social relations in the plantations, and it tracks the fissures and problematics born of ongoing social existence in the plantation during the crisis.

Conversely, the ethnographic data presented here suggests that rumour was an effective instrument for the control and disciplining of workers in the crisis context. Rumours about the possible takeover of the plantations by new companies suggested that the workers would receive work throughout the year in addition to their deferred wages and retirement benefits. Such rumours project the potential for the future in situations of uncertainty and a chronic lack of information. The spread of such rumours, I argue, partly appeased the workers' resistant voice and their expressions of hostility towards management. It soothed the resentment they felt at their increasing sense of displacement and marginalisation. I also suspect that the spreading of such rumours was one of the reasons there were no significant street protests organised against the negligence and callous attitude of the state authorities and company management in failing to reopen the closed plantations or to take steps to ensure the workers' livelihoods.

On the Hill Valley estate, the rumours discussed here tended to be controlled and disseminated by the plantation management. These rumours reflect their authority and function as a controlling mechanism over the growing anger of the working population. Accordingly, in contrast to the nature and function of gossip, the spread of rumours on the crisis generated hope. Such rumours were antithetical to gossip in the sense that they contributed to the sustainment of the workers in the liminal situation that was an effect of the crisis. Nonetheless, rumour and gossip are intermeshed, as will be shown in the conversational encounters that I present. However, the contexts of rumours and gossip are presented separately here for analytical purposes. First, I concentrate on the spread of rumours concerning the possible takeover of the plantations by new companies. Second, I focus on the specific gossip in which the plantation management, the unions and Kerala state were blamed for the depressed condition of the plantation workers.

Major rumours between 2009 and 2012

Throughout my fieldwork there was much rumour-mongering, mainly concerning the possible takeover of the plantations by new companies and the restarting of production in estates where work had ceased. As mentioned earlier, the rumours which circulated in the crisis context provided the impression that the deferred wages and benefits would be paid and that plantation production would return to normal. This impression, I observe, restricted the workers from agitating against the deferral of wages and welfare cuts, or from seeking government intervention through special welfare packages for the crisis-ridden plantation workers. The spread of rumours was directly related to the anticipation of some sort of relief for the plantation workers.

Six major rumours dominated daily conversations in the plantations between 2009 and 2012. They were all related to the possible takeover of the plantations by new companies. Each rumour was displaced and taken over by another when the preceding rumour weakened. The weakening of each rumour refers to the workers' realisation that it was just a rumour and that the plantation was not going to be taken over by a new company. In other words, the displacement of a particular rumour by a new one is related to the loss of faith in the initial one by the workers and thus the lessening of its relevance as a rumour. Each rumour had an active existence of three to six months before it was replaced by a new one. However, there were situations when two consecutive rumours overlapped for specific periods before they were replaced by another.

The first major rumour during my fieldwork in 2009 was related to the takeover of the plantations by Reana Tea Company. This company had previously leased the nine estates (including the Hill Valley estate) of HillTop Company in 1985 for a period of 20 years. A rumour was circulated among the workers that Reana was interested in purchasing the estates it had managed for 20 years. The second rumour was that HillTop would renew tea production under their direct control rather than selling the plantations to Reana. These two rumours circulated for six months. The first rumour began to circulate approximately three months before the second rumour emerged and started to overlap with the first rumour. These two rumours were weakened when the workers became convinced that HillTop was not going to take over control of the tea estates as previously supposed.

These two rumours then gave way to a third one which claimed that two famous tea companies, TTV and TEATA, would lease or rent the plantations through a joint venture for a 20-year period and that the deferred wages and retirement benefits would be paid to the workers from the rent or lease. The rumour further suggested that TEATA would cover most of the cost of the lease, while TTV would be responsible for managing the plantations. This rumour circulated for around four months until another rumour, the fourth, took over. The new rumour was that the TTV–TEATA venture was not going to happen, but that instead, TTV would lease only the factory in the Hill Valley while the field (where the tea leaves are plucked) would be under the control of Reana. These two rumours circulated for around six months in the 2009–10 period.

Although the fourth rumour was closely connected to the third one, I considered them separately because the content of the rumours was distinctive enough that the two survived together for six months as alternative possibilities. I talked to various workers – those who I thought would know about developments concerning the transfer of the ownership of the plantations – to check the veracity of these rumours. In this regard, I often initiated conversations with the security guards in the fields and factory in the Hill Valley estate because they monitor and control the entry of vehicles and people into the estate. Two of them told me that no one from TTV or TEATA had come to visit and assess the fields and the factory. The rumour turned out to be false, and the transfer/leasing of the estates to new companies did not occur. The workers who were hoping for the reopening of the plantations and the payment of the deferred wages felt betrayed and misled once again.

The fifth rumour claimed that the New Travel Company, a real estate firm based in Mumbai, would take over the plantations. While part of the content of the rumour was true, since a real estate company based in Mumbai had paid an advance to HillTop to buy the estates, they were not transferred out of HillTop's control. It was later revealed that a rift had developed between HillTop and New Travel which caused HillTop to back out of the sale. Nevertheless, the representatives of New Travel stayed in the tea belt for further negotiations. This indicated that New Travel was still in negotiations with HillTop and that there was still a possibility of transfer in ownership. This encouraged the rumour and its expectations. A basis was also provided for further rumours when a group of workers raised the idea that New Travel would buy the estates, although many workers remained doubtful. The fifth rumour was sustained for approximately six months.

While the uncertainty of the negotiations between HillTop and New Travel remained, another rumour (the sixth) began circulating that a new company called Batal had entered into the bidding for the purchase of HillTop. This occurred in early February 2011. The entry of the new company created more confusion among the workers, leading to the circulation of more rumours. After one year of negotiations between the companies, by March 2012, Batal had taken over all of HillTop's estates with the exception of the Hill Valley estate, which was left out due to continuing disagreement between New Travel and HillTop concerning the return of an advance payment from New Travel. A settlement was achieved in October 2012, when New Travel was given ownership of the Hill Valley estate in lieu of the advance payment. The workers now expected to receive their deferred or delayed wage payments and retirement benefits. While the deferred wages had been paid by the end of 2012, the retirement benefits were yet to be distributed.

The source of the rumours was very likely the office of the plantation management. It was to this office that the workers directed their enquiries about developments and where they went repeatedly to demand what was owed to them. The managers and office staff fuelled the rumours in order to quell the workers' anxiety. It was easier for the plantation manager or other staff to deny the advances on the basis of these rumours. The rumours started by management were then spread by the workers, becoming for them a discourse of hope. However, it was not these workers who were responsible for validating the rumours. It was the supervisors and the union conveners who corroborated them. The workers only become agents of circulation of these rumours in a fragile situation where they hoped for an improvement in their conditions and feared this was unlikely to happen. As James Scott (1990, 145) has noted, '[a]s a rumour travels it is altered in a fashion that brings it more closely into line with the hopes, fears, and worldview of those who hear it and retell it'.

The rumours bore the tensions that arose out of the crisis-ridden lives of the workers, which is strikingly similar to what Ann Stoler (1992, 179) has discussed in relation to plantation workers in Deli, Indonesia, where rumours bore the cultural weight of social and political tensions. Rumours, in moments of uncertainty, became 'facts', as 'rumours voiced the possible' (Stoler 1992, 180), and rumours about what is 'possible' shape the course of human actions. For the workers in the Green Valley estate, unfortunately, the rumour about the 'possibility' of reopening the estates was important in generating a social reality of passiveness against the callous attitude of the plantation company, the unions and the government bureaucracy. This inaction occurred even when the workers were very much aware of their exploitation, which is evident from their gossip.

As James Scott (1990, 144) has pointed out, 'rumour thrives most, an early study emphasized, in situations in which events of vital importance to people's interests are occurring and in which no reliable information or only ambiguous information is available'. The rumours discussed earlier were created mainly because the workers rarely had access to information related to the negotiations between the unions, plantation companies and the government on the reopening of the partially and fully closed plantations. These negotiations had a direct impact on the workers' future on the plantations but, paradoxically, the workers were not allowed any involvement or access to information about such negotiations. It is the unions which represent the workers in any negotiations with the government as well as with the plantation management. CITU, AITUC and INTUC are the three trade unions that are active in the tea belt. As I have mentioned before, the majority of the union leaders are from Malayalam-speaking upper-caste/class communities and the workers are from Tamil-speaking Dalit communities (though there are a few exceptions in both cases). The majority of the union leaders live in nodal towns outside the plantations and they were not part of the plantation workforce. The workers themselves hardly communicate with these union leaders; it is the union conveners who work as interlocutors between the union leaders and the workers. Therefore, rumours materialised when there was a dearth of information among workers on the negotiations between the authorities.

In such an alienated situation, the workers had to rely on the information given by the union conveners and the supervisors, who maintain close relations with the unions and the plantation company respectively. The union conveners and the supervisors, however, are situated in a low status within the structure of the unions and the plantation companies, so information passed on by them often turns out to be false, as what they claim to be happening does not occur in reality. This observation comes from my personal experience on the plantation when I sought information from union conveners and supervisors regarding the transfer of the plantations from the present company to another. It is possible that the union conveners and supervisors were actually provided with false information on the immediate future of the plantation. However, a few interlocutors have told me that sometimes they have to pretend that they know what is happening in the higher-level talks between the authorities since the possession of valuable information is closely connected to maintaining their higher status among plantation workers. In fact, supervisors and trade union conveners are expected to have such information.

Prospective changes in plantation ownership formed the basis for rumours that became a source for workers' imagination regarding the potential return of plantation production and the revival of ordinary plantation life. The periodic change in the rumours sustained the workers' hopes. When one anticipated solution was not met, another replaced it. This was rumour as a projective fantasy of hope. These rumours were generated in the context of workers being aware that few opportunities existed for them outside the plantations. Hope in the face of despair gave a tragic undertone to many of the rumours.

These six rumours were discussed and circulated both in public spaces and in private households. The rumours often followed me as well as the workers considered me someone who might possess valuable information on the possible reopening of the plantations. Whenever I visited the estate lines (workers' settlements) to interview the workers, they asked me if I knew anything about the transfer of the estates to the new company. I told them what I had heard elsewhere. I became an intermediary, passing on information that I had received from the security guards regarding the possible transfer of the estates. In other words, the workers checked the veracity of rumours through me. I often had the chance to witness all kinds of imaginary scenarios, predictions and claims of authentic information (specifically by the trade union conveners and the supervisors) formulated in the course of the transmission of rumour through gossip. I explore this further in the following section.

Gossip and the circulation of rumours

The crisis has changed the social demographics of the plantation community. The social spaces for gossip reflect this new demography and are composed of groups consisting of persons who, for one reason or another (for example, sickness), are off plantation work or between jobs in one or another of the satellite towns, or else are unemployed. It should be noted that these are the people who continue to rely on the plantations in one form or another and therefore they are deeply concerned about the reopening of the plantations. The concerns of these workers are reflected in the gossip. For more than a decade, the crisis of the plantations had been a major theme of everyday conversations, and gossip took place in public places such as tea shops, work sites, at marriages, funerals and other public gatherings, as well as in the course of commuting between towns and plantations in a jeep. I present three encounters concerned with gossip and the circulation of rumour.

Encounter 1 – Moitheen's tea shop

Daily life in the plantations starts with men assembling in front of *Perattukulam*, the muster office, for their work assignments. Moitheen, the owner of the small tea shop (*chāyākadai*) next to the office, was complaining to me about the collapse of his business when I noticed a few workers moving back to their lines after the early morning muster call. Moitheen's is the only Muslim family in the Green Valley estate. His family came from Malabar in northern Kerala in 1959 in search of employment. His mother became a worker in the plantation so as to feed her five children: Moitheen, his younger brother and three younger sisters.

Moitheen managed to open a tea shop next to the muster office, as the workers had told the management that they needed a tea shop to alleviate the severe cold in the early morning. Moitheen's business flourished. It was to his advantage that (in his own words) each day, he knew exactly how many cups of tea, coffee/black coffee and sometimes even breakfast would be sold. This precision in calculation and Moitheen's hard work had made his tea shop as profitable as those in the nodal towns. However, as the crisis crippled the plantation workers' income, the number of workers who visited Moitheen's shop declined. Moitheen told me that his business was totally ruined by the end of the 1990s. He was further worried that he was unable to support himself in alternative ways such as by undertaking manual labour due to his advanced age and poor health.

As Moitheen voiced his complaint about the ruin of his business, five workers entered the tea shop to have hot tea or coffee before starting the hard labour of pruning tea bushes in the cold morning. One of the five workers – Paramasivam, a 52-year-old male worker – joined our conversation and said that 'the crisis is our fate'. But what is painful is that the government did not give us any support. They only gave 1,000 rupees to buy groceries during an Onam festival a few years ago.[3] But that was only for that particular year. The government does not care because we are Tamils. The union (referring to the trade union) leaders do not ask the government about this. They come to the plantation in a covered jeep,[4] and travel directly to the manager's office and leave without talking to us.

What Paramasivam communicated was that the trade union leaders rarely visit the workers' lines located not that far from the manager's office. By referring to the covered jeep, Paramasivam was commenting on the comfortable, superior lifestyle of the trade union leaders. His comment had other critical implications, specifically that the trade union leaders were more interested in their relations with management than with the workers – and, in fact, that the interests of management and the union were similar. After making his comment, Paramasivam excused himself, saying that he needed to rush to change his clothes and have breakfast before going to the tea fields for pruning. At the time, Moitheen distanced himself slightly from Paramasivam's comment, possibly because, like the management and the union leaders, he is a Malayali, and also because he had rented the tea shop from the company. However, after the workers left he asserted his support for Paramasivam's comment but cautioned that Paramasivam would get into trouble if he kept on criticising the union leaders.

Moitheen entered the cost of Paramasivam's tea and breakfast bun in the accounts register under the latter's name.[5] The conversation continued as a few other workers were still having their tea. The theme of the conversation was the negotiations between the trade unions and the new corporate companies which had taken over the nearby tea estates that were previously closed down. The workers were concerned about a rumour that the trade unions were divided on the issue of supporting the new company, allegedly because the opposing trade unions had demanded a lump sum as a donation to the trade unions and the new company had refused to pay. Manikandan (alias Mani), who was reading the previous day's newspaper, said irately that all the people deceive the workers and make money from them.[6] Everyone was silent for a moment after Mani's angry statement. Moitheen suddenly redirected the conversation by talking about the climate and people of Norway, trying to follow up on an earlier discussion he had been having with me. When Mani left the shop, Moitheen told me that he had shifted the conversation because he did not want anyone to inform the field officer about the conversations that had taken place in the shop. Moitheen did not want the plantation management to know that he had been involved and collaborated in the conversations. Moitheen's concern shows that there are workers who would pass the information on to the field officer, who often acts as an intermediary between the workers and the plantation management. The usual informants for the management were absent from the tea shop during the conversation. Nonetheless, Moitheen wanted to be much more careful about whom he 'gossips' with. This extra caution is the reason for Moitheen's lack of interest in discussing what is locally called 'plantation scandals'. When Mani and the others were leaving the tea shop, Krishnaswamy, a member of the group, told me that everyone has their own troubles and things can slip out from their heart (*manasu*) once in a while. What Krishnaswamy meant was that each and every plantation worker keeps their miseries and anger hidden, although they share them once in a while when they become overwhelmed by their situation. Krishnaswamy's observation was referring to the anger expressed by Paramasivam and Mani. In fact, Krishnaswamy was considered the local savant on the Green Valley estate, one who talks very little while making brief, perceptive comments similar to those mentioned here.

While the tea shop conversation would seem like a casual one, it needs to be considered as gossip because the conversations contained information that was generally agreed upon – it affirmed the commonality of their situation. Furthermore, the workers who were usually suspected of being informers to field officers or the trade union conveners and leaders were absent from the tea shop. The absence of informers provided a perfect backstage – which is an important requirement for gossip transmission (Goffman 1959) – to talk critically about the trade union leaders and the plantation management. As we can see from this encounter, the workers were conscious of the collusion between the trade unions and management and this was a major reason for their exploitation by the company. For many, the collusion between the unions and the management articulated the scandalous nature of management–trade union relations in the plantation. Moitheen understood that the information being circulated was sensitive and this accounts for his wariness about participating. As a tea shop owner, he had to be on good terms with all parties.

The conversations among the workers about the reactions of the management and the unions to the crisis should be understood as gossip since they 'speak the unspeakable' (Gluckman 1963). They took place within a total institution of the plantation, where the participants are under strict surveillance by the management and the unions. Therefore, the workers often express their views only within small groups and they are careful about the membership of such groups. Anyone who participates in conversations about the callous attitude of management and the corruption of unions should be aware of the severe consequences for them if the management or union comes to know about their participation in the 'gossiping'. The popular gossipers are treated as troublemakers by both the management and the unions. Workers who were suspected of participating in 'gossip' will usually be allocated the hardest tasks in the workplace, and the unions would generally refrain from challenging management's decisions related to the 'gossipers'. There were incidents in the past where workers who 'talk too much' (*Nākku Nīlam*) about both the management and the unions were suspended from work for 'lack of discipline', and the unions reprimanded the workers, not the management. The plantation society's disciplinary apparatus is so sophisticated that it makes the workers paranoid about management's informants in their day-to-day conversation about the management–union nexus. In all three cases of gossip discussed earlier, one could see that a few workers distanced themselves from the 'gossiping' although they were present throughout the gossiping sessions. They would dismiss the gossip as unnecessary talk (*vīn pēchu*) and would warn the gossipers about the serious repercussions of participating in gossip (*kicu kicu*). The colloquial term *vīn pēchu* is popular in the plantation among those who denounce (mostly out of fear) gossiping about the management. In the plantation's controlled society, those who were afraid of gossiping about management were in fact considered weak and frightened, not daring to resist the management–union nexus.

Encounter 2 – jeep trip

The second encounter I discuss (recorded in May 2011) concerns gossip during what is locally called a 'jeep trip' from Pambanar town to the Green Valley estate. All the estates represented in the jeep belonged to one company – HillTop – and the gossip represented their general unity of feeling and opinion. The jeep, as usual, was overloaded. It had a carrying capacity of nine persons but 15 were loaded into it. The trip took about 30 minutes. I was sitting in the front seat next to the driver. There were three other passengers sitting with me in the front seat. I could barely stretch my legs or move my body because we were five in a seat made for three. Subramani, who sat beside me, was around 45 years old and was a supervisor in the third division of the Green Valley estate.[7] In the back seat, two women who seemed to be in their mid-30s (one was Saraswathi, a worker from the Green Valley estate, and the other was Ponnuthai from the Kanmani estate, which is located on the way to the Green Valley estate) were chatting about price rises; Saraswathi was complaining that there was no need to bring big bags to buy groceries anymore because, given the monthly income of a family, one is only able to buy groceries that fit in the smaller 50-paise bag (*ambathu-paisa kōdu*). Ponnuthai was nodding her head, indicating that she agreed.

The conversation shifted to the topic of delayed wages, for wages had not been paid for the past two months and Saraswathi was worried. She looked at Subramani (the supervisor) and asked him if the payment of the wages would be made by the end of that week or not. Subramani looked at Saraswathi in the rear-view mirror and told her that the payment of part of the wages would not be made the following weekend, and it was doubtful that anything would be paid for the next two weeks or more. Another worker from the Kanmani estate asked Subramani what had happened to the proposed transfer of the plantations to New Travel. Subramani replied that the transfer would happen soon. The driver of the jeep asked Subramani to give a definite answer rather than hedging his answers (*angēyum ingēyum thodāma solrīnga*). Subramani looked at the driver and told him that what he (Subramani) was saying was true and it was up to the others in the jeep to make their own judgements. When Subramani got out of the jeep in the third division of the Green Valley estate, the driver told me that Subramani was a liar and he did not know anything about the takeover of the plantations by new companies, for Subramani would always repeat the same reply whenever he travelled in that particular jeep. However, those who were listening to Subramani seemed to consider his opinion seriously.

Saraswathi looked at those who were sitting opposite her in the back seat and said that it would be good if the management distributed the wages before the start of school in June, since she needed to buy bags and uniforms for her children who were studying in the high school located in Pambanar town. She then said that her mother-in-law had gone to the manager's office to seek an advance amount from the unpaid pension benefits in order to meet the costs of looking after her grandchildren. The manager had asked her to wait three more months, as a new company would buy the plantations and they would then pay the benefits that were owed. She expressed doubts about whether she would be paid and also doubts as to whether the trade union leaders would force the management to pay the wages. Nallakannu, a retired guard on the Kanmani estate who still had not received his retirement benefits, gave his opinion: 'We will not get anything. Everyone plundered the plantation and left. All the leaders are thieves. I wish the white people still controlled the plantations.' Murugan did not like this comment from Nallakannu as his uncle was the trade union convener in Kanmani estate. Murugan was sitting next to me. Murugan moved close to me and whispered: 'He [Nallakannu] thinks that he knows everything. Old people [like Nallakannu] say insane things.' Murugan then joined in the discussion and, looking at Saraswathi, said that the plantation was going to be transferred soon for sure and that the owed wages would be paid the following month. Saraswathi and the others seemed to believe him, since they knew that he is the nephew of a local trade union activist and that Murugan often travelled to the administrative town of Peermade to meet with trade union leaders. When I asked the driver about Murugan's claims, he told me that Murugan was visiting Peermade town to arrange a subsidised loan to build a house and that he did not have good connections with the union leaders.[8]

I continued listening to the conversations in the jeep. Although other topics such as an auto-rickshaw accident and complaints over rationing shops came up, it was the plantation crisis that was the dominant theme. It should be noted that Saraswathi brought up the topic of the crisis and the criticism of the plantation management and the unions only after Subramani got out of the jeep. Similarly, Nallakannu offered his criticisms only after Subramani left. I suspect this was because Subramani had a reputation for being very close to one of the union leaders and also to an assistant field officer of the Green Valley estate. He was not an accepted member of the group and was perceived as being too close to those in management positions, so he could not be included in the gossip. The gossip, in other words, was as much about affirming solidarity among the workers against the management (see Gluckman 1963; Jayawardena 1968) as it was about communicating unverified information about the crisis.

It should be noted that estate supervisors and trade unionists (as well as those who gained status from association with them) usually rode in the front seat of the jeep. The seating pattern reflected the plantation hierarchy. The supervisors and union conveners were expected to answer questions from the other workers, who mostly sat in the back seat, on issues concerned with the reopening of the plantations. This responsibility of the supervisors and conveners brings them the respect they enjoy as intermediaries between the workers and the controlling institutions of plantation management and trade union leaders. These intermediaries were optimistic about the transfer of ownership when answering the workers' questions. In other words, the rumours were authorised by these intermediaries in these question-and-answer sessions. Although a few (such as the jeep driver and Nallakannu) were sceptical about the optimism of these intermediaries, others such as Saraswathi seemed to be optimistic about the situation and believed what Murugan had said about the negotiation process. In other words, Murugan worked to authorise the rumour, which reproduced hope among the workers. Murugan's intervention shows that the rumours were sometimes used and disseminated by those in power or with perceived access to power. Assumed knowledge reaffirms their position of authority, and so they have an interest in disseminating and authorising rumours. At the same time, many of these rumours functioned to placate the workers, to give them false hope that their unpaid wages would be paid and they would have job security. Accordingly, the reaffirmation of the authority of those in power and the reproduction of the logic of the hierarchical order under the crisis worked together in the circulation of the rumours.

These jeep-trip conversations were very much controlled and mediated by the union representatives or supervisors on the plantations. Murugan, who is the nephew of a union convener, was observing the conversation and would probably report it to his uncle, singling out individuals such as Nallakannu who vehemently criticised the authorities and the unions. This kind of highly graded surveillance system is a potential instrument of discipline that worked to contain unrest in the crisis context. The tension between workers, unions and management in the crisis context made everyone cautious in terms of what or who they gossiped about, and with whom. The jeep trip shows the significance of changes in the constitution of membership (Gluckman 1963) and the rules of conduct (Stoler 1992, 173) for gossiping. Furthermore, the nature of the gossip that could be exchanged and the themes that could be raised within the membership also changed as people got in or out of the jeep.

The workers' condemnation of union corruption is clearly evident in the gossip. Nallakannu's description of union leaders as thieves reflects a popular impression about the unions in the tea belt. This was also evident in the Pembillai Orumai strike. One of the central demands of the strike was to put an end to the corrupt alliance between the union leaders and the plantation companies. The women workers not only went on strike independently, but also actively tried to keep the unions out of the strike. The workers challenged the union leaders' relatively higher social status and economic position mainly because the union leaders became better off than the workers through corruption as they had compromised on challenging workers' exploitation. The union leaders were as impoverished as the workers a few decades ago. However, the union leaders became differentiated from the workers over the years as their socio-economic status improved dramatically, while the plantation workers became poorer. The workers' discontent with the union corruption that is reflected in the gossip was especially severe due to the moral failure of the unions to support the workers in moments of crisis (Raj 2019). After all, moral judgement, especially in moments of uncertainty and crisis, is a major aspect of gossiping (Venkatesan 2009).

Encounter 3 – muster office

The muster office where the workers assemble in the morning for work assignments is one of the places where men come together to sit and chat – an everyday process of socialising. The muster office is a central place close to the workers' lines, the temples and churches, the field officer's bungalow and the labour clubs. When it rains, the group moves to the veranda of the muster office or the fertiliser store or Moitheen's tea shop to sit and chat. Every evening during my fieldwork I joined in the sit-and-chat group. While many themes were brought up including cinema and politics, concerns were often raised over the question of whether there would be a new recruitment of workers (*puthupathivu*) or not, and if yes, who would get the new positions.

On a sunny evening in November 2011, a group of men (Kannan, Mukundan and Michael) were chatting in front of the muster office. My local friend Suresh and myself were on our way to a self-help group meeting when we noticed the heated conversation between the three men. The conversation was about logging on the plantations by New Travel, which had gained control of the Green Valley estate after a year of conflict. The workers were opposed to the logging, arguing that the new management might abandon the estate once they had exploited all the natural resources, mainly the trees in the plantation. Kannan and Mukundan argued about whether the trade union should be blamed for the failure to stop the plantation management from logging. Kannan was a member of one of the left-wing unions (CITU) and Mukundan was a union convener for the right-wing union (INTUC). Michael, who had just become a permanent worker in the estate, did not take a side and was just listening to the argument between Kannan and Mukundan. Kannan expressed his anger at the INTUC leaders for not opposing the logging. To counter Kannan's point, Mukundan argued that CITU should be blamed because they were the most powerful union in the tea belt and their standpoint has major influence over the decisions of the plantation company. Mukundan asked me if I agreed with him or not. I just smiled at him without giving any signals about which side I agreed with, which conveyed that I was just interested in observing their argument. During their argument, both Mukundan and Kannan tried to lure Suresh onto their side.

Suresh, who is a motorbike mechanic in Pambanar, intervened and stated that all the political leaders are corrupt (*ellārum kanakkuthān*) and that it was futile to argue about it. Michael agreed with Suresh, exclaiming *Adhu sarithān* (that is correct). This conversation over logging was not an isolated one. Mukundan did not like Suresh's comment and he informed us how the union leaders of his party had negotiated with the new company to pay the deferred retirement benefits to the retired workers, to reopen the medical dispensary and to repair the workers' lines. Kannan disputed Mukundan's claim and noted that no union leaders had come to the plantation's head office that week. Mukundan was annoyed by Kannan's challenge and stated that Kannan could not see the INTUC leaders going to the administrative office to negotiate with the planters because Kannan had blind faith in CITU leadership. Kannan stood up and walked away after telling me that the conversation was turning bad and that he did not want to fight with Mukundan. After Kannan left, Michael asked Mukundan if indeed the union leaders had negotiated with New Travel to pay the deferred benefits. Michael was convinced after Mukundan told him that he would resign from the convener position if his claims proved to be false.

Michael left after a short conversation about the dam conflict between Tamil Nadu and Kerala. I asked Mukundan to tell me the truth, if the union was indeed negotiating. He told me that he was not sure but there was 'a high probability' that the union leaders were. While Mukundan was not sure about the leaders' visit, he still claimed that the estate lines would be repaired and the deferred wages would be paid. Michael appeared to believe him, and he would probably pass the information on to others. Mukundan, however, told me the truth because he believed that I was not part of the workforce and would not communicate his fabricated story to anyone. Furthermore, I did not take a position in the conflict between him and Kannan. I realised that Mukundan's vow that he would resign if his claims were proved false was indeed a political gimmick that he used to defend his own and his union's sense of moral commitment to the workers. Similarly, Kannan stressed INTUC's failure to counter Mukundan's claim. In a way, by gossiping about each other's political parties and the associated unions, both Kannan and Mukundan wanted to uphold their own (failed) moral convictions. As Soumhya Venkatesan (2009, 85) has observed in another context, 'gossips take it as self-evident that those they are criticizing were free, like themselves, to act in a more moral way but chose not to'.

Many workers defend the unions they are affiliated with in everyday conversation, but a few remain silent and blame all the political parties and the workers who actively support them. While other topics such as cinema and politics were also discussed, themes related to the crisis were always present in everyday gossip and the rumours surrounding the situation of the crisis were the most prominent. Most of the conversations were based on speculation and rumours because the workers and their dependants on the plantations were confused by the situation and did not have access to information about the decisions made by the plantation management, state agencies and the trade unions. It was because of such speculation and rumour that the workers depended on the information from supervisors, local conveners of various trade unions and workers close to the plantation management, such as those who worked as servants or security guards at the plantation bungalows. These individuals often fuelled speculation about the progress of negotiations in the plantations. Gossiping becomes the only source of information in moments of uncertainty. In a crisis situation, 'gossip becomes a way of trying to come to terms with, or negotiate, social situations' (Rapport 1996, 267, quoted in Stewart and Strathern 2004, 4).

It is evident from the discussion that the functioning of the unions was a major theme of the gossip. The unions were supposed to be the representatives of the workers. However, the gossip shows that the workers were often alienated from the unions and highly suspicious and critical of them. The fact that the unions were closely tied to major political parties made them compromise their positions, especially when those political parties were in government. The institutionalised nature of unions in the tea belt made them a legitimate authority to represent the workers. The dilemma of plantation life was that the workers were unable to project and articulate their exploitation and suffering as unjust unless the union approved and authorised this portrayal. In other words, the workers needed the permission of the unions to agitate against their socio-economic insecurity and marginality. Here the norm is that some processes cannot be thought of as unjust until the trade unions accept them as unjust.

As mentioned earlier, the union leaders are from outside the plantations and there was a clear difference in hierarchical status between the union leaders and the plantation workers based on linguistic, class, caste and ethnic differences. There is a fundamental paradox here that the union leaders are imported from outside for trade union activism in the tea belt. The contradictory role of the unions in the plantation belt is also evident in the rivalry between workers of different unions. It could be argued that the workers' slandering and ridiculing of corrupt union leadership through gossip was an attempt to expose the moral failure of the union leadership. In other words, the most common theme of the particular gossips was judging the moral failure of the union leadership. This echoes the earlier analysis of Max Gluckman (1963), John Campbell (1964) and Soumhya Venkatesan (2009) that the element of moral judgement is what underpins gossip across societies.

Rumour and gossip in a time of crisis

Rumour and gossip on the Green Valley estate shed light on the extent to which the crisis conquered the imagination of the workers. Rumour and gossip about the crisis revealed the workers' understanding of the crisis and also their imagination of the immediate future of plantation production. While gossip is integral to the plantation's social life in general, it became increasingly more focused on the economic crisis as it concerned the whole plantation workforce in the tea belt. Similarly, rumours became an important social process in the crisis context, specifically when speculation about the transfer of ownership of the plantations became widespread.

As mentioned earlier, my own impression is that the source of the rumours may have been the company and the unions. The company management used the rumours to deny or stall payment of the workers' outstanding wages. The unions needed to make the workers believe they were actively involved in finding a solution to the suffering and deprivation the workers were experiencing due to the temporary cessation of tea production. Although the rumours were often factually incorrect, they gave voice to real-life suffering in the form of the hope they projected and anticipated. As forms of social control, the rumours were not organised as a conspiracy by the authorities but were more diffused forms of social control mediated and fed by different strategic players who knew the fears and hopes of their audience. Even when they were not sure about the rumours, they recognised the importance of pretending to be sure, and often, I felt, people became entrapped in this role of authorising a new rumour to keep hope alive, to preserve a sense that the plantation community had a future.

The workers, who were uncertain about their future, were very keen to receive updates on the transfer of ownership or relief measures by the management, unions and the government, but only through gossip. Gossip generates solidarity among the workers against their exploitation and it is the practice through which the wounds of the economic crisis are soothed as the workers share their struggle to survive. Goffman rightly observes that backstage performances are events where wounds are licked and morale is strengthened (Goffman 1959). Here Gluckman offers a supporting observation that '[g]ossip and even scandal unite a group within a larger society, or against another group, in several ways … and have the effect of maintaining the village as a village and of preventing it from becoming a collection of houses, like a housing estate' (1963, 313).

He adds that the very phenomenon of gossip is possible only when there is a sense of belonging to a group among those who participate in the gossip. In the plantation society, the recognition of exploitation through gossip regenerated a sense of belonging on the basis of class, caste and linguistic identity. But this process of solidarity did not bring organised resistance from the workforce in the crisis context. The circulation of rumours about the possible reopening of the plantations played a role in the failure to convert that solidarity into active resistance against the lock-out by the company, the non-intervention of the government and the corruption of the unions.

The discussion on rumours and gossip and the conversations in which they are embedded shows that they have different roles in the crisis context. While the gossip discussed here indicates that the workers were conscious of their exploitation, the rumours and their authorisation by the intermediary group of union conveners and supervisors provided hope to the workers. This hope in turn encouraged the workers to remain relatively quiet; very few demonstrations or protests were organised to demand the intervention of authorities such as the state, the plantation management or, to a certain extent, the trade unions to secure the workers' livelihoods. In other words, the (false) hope, while serving as a coping mechanism, also became instrumental in perpetuating the workers' alienation.

Notes

1 Rumour has been studied mostly in relation to anthropological analysis of past events (for example, Thompson 1963; Lefebvre 1973; Guha 1983; Stoler 1992; Tambiah 1996). Anthropological studies on rumour have focused on its potential to instigate political violence (Stoler 1992; Tambiah 1996; Kirsch 2002; Stewart and Strathern 2004) or rebellion and subaltern resistance (Thompson 1963; Guha 1983). Similarly, studies on the functional aspect of gossip have largely discussed it as an instrument of everyday resistance (Scott 1990) or local politics (Besnier 2009) or of realising self-interests (Colson 1953; Campbell 1964; Paine 1967; Brison 1992). Some have also seen it variously as an agent of moral disciplining to maintain social order (Herskovits 1937; Gluckman 1963; Ong 1987) or to control deviant behaviour (Goffman 1967). Anthropologists have been able to capture gossip in its ethnographic present (Haviland 1977; Brison 1992; Besnier 2009), sometimes with a focus on its interactive aspects (Brenneis 1984; Goodwin 1990) or its performative aspects (Abrahams 1970; Bergmann 1993).

2 James Scott and Max Gluckman offer insights on the ways in which rumour and gossip affect resistance against, or accommodation of, exploitation and subordination in various ethnographic contexts. Both Gluckman and Scott approached gossip and rumour from a class analysis perspective, the major difference being that Gluckman focused on gossip within a group. In contrast, Scott focused on gossip by the below group about the above group that is hierarchically located. Scott (1990) argues that both gossip and rumour are processes, similar to others such as slander and backbiting, that the powerless employ to critique the powerful. He emphasises the potential of rumour and gossip for subaltern resistance that is hidden from the powerful and therefore constitutes what he calls the 'hidden transcripts' of resistance. According to Scott, 'gossip is perhaps the most familiar and elementary form of disguised popular aggression. Though its use is hardly confined to attacks by subordinates on their superiors, it represents a relatively safe social sanction' (Scott 1990, 142). With regard to rumour, Scott argues, in line with E.P. Thompson (1963) and Ranajit Guha (1983), that it has the capacity to unleash revolt and powerful resistance from the weaker sections of society. He provides examples of rumour's role in the history of subaltern resistance against the exploitation of the industrial working class in England, slavery in the Caribbean and the caste system in South Asia. In contrast to Scott's analysis, Gluckman (1963) views rumour and gossip as system-maintaining processes (in line with his general framework of structural functionalism, which he developed earlier in writings such as *Customs and Conflict in Africa*, published in 1955). He argues that gossip (and rumour) are employed by those in power to put the weaker sections back in their place, something he refers to as the 'social weapon' of the dominant (Gluckman 1963, 309). It may appear that Gluckman focuses on the functional aspect of gossip for the benefit of dominant individuals, and Scott turns his focus to its use by the powerless. However, Gluckman also discusses the gossip of the powerless against the domination of those who claim higher status *within* their group. Gluckman emphasises how such gossip of the powerless brings solidarity and cohesiveness to the group, thus reproducing the group itself. In a similar vein, Scott also examines the kind of gossip that facilitates solidarity within the working class against the domination of the powerful bourgeoisie. The major difference, however, between Scott and Gluckman is that Scott stresses the rupture of social relations and, therefore, social transformations generated by gossip and rumour, not its reproductions, as Gluckman argued. The ethnographic material I present here suggests that rumour and gossip could lead to contrasting outcomes within a social context.

3 Onam is a traditional festival associated with the homecoming of the mythical ruler of Kerala, King Mahabali. The myth is that, under his rule, the ancient Kerala state was highly egalitarian and prosperous. Various aspects of the festival evoke themes of prosperity, equality and happiness – so that the king will be pleased to see his subjects living a life that he attempted to

provide for them. Kerala state's distribution of 1,000 rupees to buy groceries for Onam taps into this myth of the true hidden potential of Kerala under King Mahabali.
4 A covered jeep is one whose body is covered with metal sheets rather than with cloth.
5 The account register is a credit register to record the debt of each worker in the tea shop. The workers pay off the debt when they receive their monthly wages.
6 By 'all the people' Manikandan was referring to those who make decisions affecting the plantation, namely the plantation owner and management, unions and government representatives, especially the Ministry of Labour.
7 The Green Valley estate is comprised of three divisions.
8 Later, when I visited Peermade town on another occasion, I came across Murugan again but among a different group of workers. When I enquired about the purpose of their visit, one of the workers told me that Murugan also acts as an intermediary for arranging various certificates related to the community, residence and income from various government offices in the town.

8
New companies, new workforce

Many estates in the tea belt remained shut down and other estates were only partially functional, including the Hill Valley estate, until 2010–11 when it was taken over by new companies. In the 2010–12 period, at least 10 other estates were also taken over by new companies and this drastically transformed the way the plantations were run. Most significantly for the workers, new, more exploitative work regimes were put in place. The new companies found themselves with the opportunity to exploit the crisis with a new set of arrangements that favoured them. They found new mediators to bring labourers from other parts of India who are much more vulnerable than the Tamils. Furthermore, the severe labour cuts, the arduous work, the suspension of welfare measures and the increasingly casualised work have resulted not only in greater feminisation of the work force but also a movement of young people out of the plantations, as discussed earlier. Vacancies were not filled and permanent positions were replaced by temporary and, increasingly, casual ones. The plantation companies increased the workload and intensified supervision of the work as well as punishment (such as suspension of workers) for any lapses. The plantation association in South India was successful in forcing the Plantation Labour Committee to increase the plucking rate (daily rate per worker) from 14 kg to 21 kg in January 2011 and then to 25 kg in January 2016.[1]

On the Hill Valley estate, according to a retired field officer, before the crisis in 1995 there were around 700 workers, of whom 500 were permanent and 200 temporary. Casual workers were recruited only during peak seasons, usually amounting to around 50 workers. By 2014–15, two decades later, there were only 174 workers, of whom 133 were permanent workers, 36 temporary and five casual. This decline in the workforce to less than a quarter shows the impact the crisis had on plantation production. The percentage of the temporary workforce declined from 29 to 21 per cent and, in addition, the number of days they were employed fell. This forced the temporary workers to rely increasingly on income from outside the plantation. In other words, the crisis had made the temporary workers' situation more precarious. Meanwhile, although the permanent workers were protected from being laid off, the plantation companies had significantly worsened their terms and conditions.

Although production also declined, workers were having to do more work as a result of the crisis. One field hand told me that he was doing three times the amount of work he did before the crisis since the new company refused to hire the two assistants who had worked with him before the new plantation company took over. Although the Hill Valley estate was not yet employing a significant casual labour force, on neighbouring estates where I also did fieldwork a large part of the labour force was being replaced by casual labour. These were not local Tamil Dalits but more vulnerable seasonal migrant labourers brought from poorer parts of the country, such as Adivasi labourers from Jharkhand on the Auburn and Top View estates. The strategy of employing more temporary workers who live on the Top View estate, and casual daily wage workers from outside the plantation, is carried out in order to reduce what the planters call the social cost of production (since these temporary and outside workers need not be given any welfare benefits) and to maintain the alienated status of labour in plantation production. Different companies thus have employed different strategies in dealing with the temporary and casual workforce given their production needs in the crisis context: Top View estate returned to full functioning after a short period of partial shutdown, whereas the temporary workforce at the Hill Valley estate was cut back because the estate continued to struggle despite a new company taking over.

New companies

The new companies can be referred to as 'new-generation companies' and fall within the genre of larger corporations that prefer subcontracting systems to the wage-labour system. In the case of Tanzanian sugar plantations, Holt Norris and Worby (2012, 356) have noted that liberalisation of the domestic economy has led to vulnerability to price fluctuations in world markets and the entry of new-generation companies arriving from Mauritius who 'exercise a sovereign capacity to shape the conditions of their employees' and have laid off a significant section of the workforce. The new management approach in the Peermade tea belt is strikingly similar to that in the Tanzanian plantations: it involves intensifying contract work, strengthening surveillance of the workforce and increasing the workload in the name of increasing the 'efficiency' of the workforce. The companies have also used the crisis as an 'excuse' to radically alter production relations to their advantage. They have temporarily shut down production units in line with their immediate production needs regardless of the strict labour laws against such moves. In many cases this meant shutting down the tea processing factories where the majority of the men were employed. Each plantation used to have a processing factory on site but more often than not, this is no longer the case.

Wages frequently were not paid on time and workers claimed that the company made money by holding back the wages, often for three additional weeks. The result was that workers often ended up taking out loans from moneylenders at extortionate interest rates to make ends meet. For instance, if a worker was supposed to receive 3,500 rupees after the weekly grocery advance, that worker would lose around 175–200 rupees (at a 5–7 per cent interest rate for 20 days). The payment of 'service pay-outs' to the retirees was also delayed, leading to much distress among the retirees, as discussed earlier.

The new companies also confiscated the kitchen gardens and common yards in the vicinity of workers' lines and fenced them off so that the workers would not be able to use them. They planted tea in these gardens and yards – a reminder that the production of tea is all that matters in the plantations and the workers should not imagine a life outside those production relations. The workers not only lost whatever small material gains they had made but also were socially attacked as the occupation of the kitchen gardens and yards by the company inculcated a sense of psychological alienation in which the workers control nothing in the plantations; they were reminded that they were alienated labour only. In essence, the casualisation of the workforce, the suspension of welfare measures and the withdrawal of the workers' right to use the immediate surroundings of their settlements became part of a quotidian process of material and social dispossession of the workers.

Significantly, as a result of these processes, the Tamil Dalit labour force in the tea plantations was increasingly feminised: the actual tea plucking was mainly done by women and this was, by far, the main task that remained. Whereas previously the gender ratio was around 50–50, by 2014–15, 85 per cent of the workers left on the Hill Valley estate were women (out of 174 workers, 148 were women – 110 permanent workers and 33 temporary workers – and all five of the casual workers were women). For the workers this was also a strategy to make the best of a bad situation: if the women were permanent workers, they would be provided with a (tiny) home for the family in the tea estate labour lines, which would serve as a secure base also for the other members of the household now working in informalised insecure jobs outside the plantation. The female labourers were asked to use handheld shears more than ever before for harvesting tea leaves. The men were asked to use heavier machines for pruning and spraying. While this mechanisation move was exhausting for the workers, the company argued that it was 'imperative' for increasing productivity and to reduce the cost of production in a time of crisis. Whenever the Tamil workforce complained about the increasing workload, the plantation companies in the tea belt threatened to replace them with migrant Adivasi male and female workers from Jharkhand, who were all casual workers.

The plantation companies' engagement with the crisis is in many ways similar to the situation of Sumatra's plantation belt, as described by Stoler (1985), where the Great Depression allowed companies to extract profits on the basis of a more modernised mode of exploitation, with a stronger focus on eliminating waste in the labour force, more efficient mechanisation and an increase in labour's productivity. The costs of the restructuring of the plantation economy were largely borne by the workers. The indebtedness to which they were already prone (because of already low wages, inflation and so on) was intensified because of delays in receiving payment. These delays became a device whereby the planters were able to cover the costs of restructuring, both of production and of the workforce. As the workers were paid infrequently, they usually incurred such debt from accumulating interest that the wages they received would barely meet the demands of the debt repayment. Thus, the workers were forced into a debt cycle due to late payment of their wages, which, as is evident in many cases (for instance, in the tea plantations in Assam), is a common issue among all tea plantation workers in India.

The planters claim that the Plantations Labour Act is an outdated law which should be updated with new amendments that reflect the practical concerns of the planters. Moreover, they are strongly lobbying for the state to share the social cost of production and for exemption from the Minimum Wage Act (*Hindu Business Line* 2008). At the 116th annual conference of the United Planters Association of South India (UPASI), held at Coonoor, then President Mr D.P. Maheshwari, in his presidential speech, called for strong intervention by the planters in urging the state to share the social cost of production and stated that certain outmoded legislations such as the Plantations Labour Act and Minimum Wage Act should be withdrawn because they place many constraints on the competitiveness of plantation products in the international and domestic markets (*Planters' Chronicle*, September 2009). This aspiration of planters to make the government take responsibility for the cost of the workers' welfare is thus internal to a broader lobbying by new-generation multinational corporations to urge the state to ensure all the infrastructural facilities required for flexible capitalist investment and production.

The recent amendment of the Plantations Labour Act to allow the diversification of 5 per cent of the land for tourism and business purposes is antithetical to the logic by which the plantations were excluded from the land reform initiatives. The logic of the exclusion as discussed earlier, is that the monocrop plantations are necessary for the development of the state economy. While it is claimed that the promotion of plantation tourism is intended to stimulate economic growth, it only helps the planters to control the thousands of hectares of land without any obligation to produce cash crops. This is evident from the fact that new-generation companies which take over the plantations from struggling traditional tea companies are primarily associated with real estate developments, as in the case of the Life Time company which took over a plantation in the Peermade tea belt. One of the arguments made for the existence of plantations is that it is the responsibility of the state to kindle economic development through mass production. So plantations, in this sense, became inevitable from the perspective of the state (just as bailing out larger firms is the responsibility of the state so as to secure sustainable economic development). However, what is seen in the case of Kerala today is that plantation production has weakened, but control over the plantation land by individual capitalists has strengthened.

The increasing power of planters and the simultaneous decline in state control over plantations, under an increasingly neoliberal economic system, should be compared with similar developments in north-eastern India where the powerful planters' associations evade state control and earn fair trade certifications even when basic conditions for fair trade are not met, such as safe working conditions and decent wages (Besky 2008). In the crisis context, planters recognised the tourist and real estate value of the plantation lands. In fact, long before the ratification of the amendment by the government, superintendents' and managers' bungalows were being rented out for movie shoots and to Western tourists to re-enact the colonial plantation life. The stay is combined with a trip to the plantations and a safari in the nearby national parks. This venture brought high demand and was very lucrative since the plantation belt is situated within Thekkady, a famous tourist attraction and wildlife sanctuary. Furthermore, portions of estate land in many plantations have been rented or sold to set up new tourist resorts. The estates also earned a considerable amount of money from permitting film and photo shoots. This new plantation tourism is in effect a rediscovery of a colonial connection between tea plantations and tourism (Jolliffe 2007).

Statistics from the Indian Tea Board show that the Indian tea markets had somewhat recovered from the crisis by the end of 2010.[2] However, the workers were ill informed and still considered themselves to be in a condition of crisis, in which indeed they were. The tea companies actively encouraged such a feeling using the very idea of a crisis or the threat of market downturns as an ideological means for continuing to transform the production and social environment of the plantations in their favour. This encouragement was also enacted through negating welfare and generating uncertainty over the monthly distribution of wages, so that workers felt that the crisis was ongoing. For workers, signs of normal plantation life, such as the resumption of services at estate hospitals and the distribution of welfare measures and perks, are what would signal the end of the crisis. However, this did not happen in the plantations, although the price paid for tea had returned to normal. Therefore, the cutting back on welfare measures as an end in itself becomes a means that legitimises the cutting back on welfare measures. The continuing enactment of the economic crisis through these measures gently forces the workers to keep on consuming the myth of economic crisis, which helps the planters weed out any expenditure additional to the mere social reproduction of labour. This is a situation in which a state of exception has been prolonged into an ordinary state of existence, as Agamben would put it,[3] where the crisis continues to be an imagined spectre under which the plantation workers experience their lives today.[4]

The company rationalised the new, much more exploitative labour regime by citing the crisis. Such rationalisations were further supported by the unions and the plantation labour welfare office, who often excused their own failure to confront the plantation companies by saying that '[i]n order to paint the wall, you need to have the wall in the first place', meaning you need to have the plantation system in the first place for the labour to survive. These rationalisations seem to have been internalised by the workers as the crisis became everyday reality for them. The crisis therefore became an event that allowed the plantation companies to generate a discourse that is conducive to the further casualisation and feminisation of plantation labour. Perhaps this is one of the major reasons why there were no everyday protests against the new exploitative labour regimes, with the major exception of a historic strike led by women tea workers in a nearby tea belt. The aggressive exploitation of labour following the crisis has resulted in further expulsion of the Tamil workers, who have been moving outside the plantations in search of work.

New workforce

As the Tamil Dalits are leaving the Kerala tea plantations, the plantation owners are deploying a strategy often used by capital to cut the cost of production and undermine the power of labour: they are bringing in more vulnerable seasonal migrant workers from poorer regions. Adivasi migrant workers from Jharkhand and Muslim workers from Assam form the majority among this new workforce in the Peermade tea belt. There are also workers from Odisha who were brought in to work for smaller estates that cultivate tea, cardamom and coffee. All the migrant workers are maintained, illegally, as casual labour. During my fieldwork I met newly arrived seasonal migrant labourers at Auburn Tea's Top View estate, where Santhali, Munda and Lohra migrants from Godda and Dumka districts of Jharkhand were based.[5] Here they formed almost a quarter of the total plantation workforce. In April 2015, there were 30 families and 12 individual Adivasis from Jharkhand (nine male and three female) at the Top View estate. The Jharkhand workforce constituted 23 per cent of the total workforce (57 workers out of 232). Many of these workers had relatives in other estates as well. In March–April 2016, I visited the Dumka and Godda districts in Jharkhand for two weeks. These are among the most 'backward districts' in the country.[6] Most of the migrant workers were from two villages, Jheratti and Sakri, in Dumka and Godda districts respectively. The field visit was a follow-up on the fieldwork and interviews I had already carried out among the Jharkhandi workforce in the plantation.

There are three major reasons for the recruitment of new workers. Firstly, as Tamil Dalits leave the plantations in greater numbers, the planters often face labour shortages during the high season. Secondly, and perhaps more significantly, the 'social cost of production' of Adivasi migrant labour from Jharkhand is extremely low compared with the social cost of production for Tamil Dalits as the Jharkhandi workers are kept as casual workers while most of the Tamil Dalit workers have permanent status. This denial of temporary or permanent work status for migrant labourers means they do not have a provident fund, annual leave, medical leave and other benefits that are provided to the permanent and temporary workforce. On the Top View estate, although the recruitment of Jharkhandi Adivasi workers began in 2011, by September 2015 not one of them had been promoted to even temporary worker status. While many Jharkhandi workers had left after eight or ten months of work, there were a few who had stayed for more than two years, which technically entitled than to become permanent workers, while those who had stayed for shorter periods should have been temporary workers. While the Dalit Tamils are also exploited, their permanent or temporary worker status shields them from the super-exploitation faced by the Jharkhandi workers.

The final reason why planters are recruiting this new seasonal migrant labour force is that the Adivasi workers are more easily controlled (or 'tamed', to borrow a term from Jan Breman (1989)) compared to the Tamil Dalit workers, specifically as casual labourers. Their lack of recognition in the plantation production system leaves them highly vulnerable as it also denies them facilities and welfare measures outside work. Their living quarters are of poor quality and very cramped. The condition of workers' line houses is bad in general on the estate, but the better ones are provided to the Tamil Dalits, while the Jharkhandi workers received only the 'leftover' houses. In addition, two Jharkhandi families had to share each small tenement house: they are provided only a 'half house', not a 'full house'.

One would have hoped that the trade unions and the labour departments of the state (the inspector of plantations or labour officers) would have challenged or prevented the casualisation of the workforce. Legally (according to the Plantations Labour Act of 1951) casual labour may only be used in the plantations to fulfil tasks outside the daily routine of the plantations and not for routine work or plucking tea – which is what migrant labour is used for. However, the plantation companies, backed by the unions and local officials from the labour department, deny this migrant workforce not only permanent but also temporary status.

The Adivasi labourers do not have access to subsidised rationing of rice, dal and kerosene which is provided through Public Distribution System (PDS) shops for workers who are registered as residents locally. They often demanded that the estate provide them with a certificate of residence in order to apply for the transfer of their ration card, but to no avail. Hospital facilities are available only in the nodal town since the company had reduced facilities in the local clinic, citing the economic crisis. Although they had access to schools, only one child out of at least 10 Adivasi children attended a local school. The workers told me they were not sending their children to school because the languages of instruction were Tamil and Malayalam. Many workers had therefore left their children to be educated back in Jharkhand.

Their linguistic alienation also led to their alienation from the unions and the subsequent inability to negotiate facilities that were due to the plantation workforce. They do not have membership in any unions. The union conveners in the Top View estate told me that the Jharkhand workers are not part of the union because they were casual workers, and that since many of them did not stay longer than 10 months, they could not be considered as part of the organised workforce. During my fieldwork, I noted that the Jharkhand workers were not part of any protest meetings in the estate. In fact, a clash between the local union leaders and the Jharkhand workers escalated when the latter went to work when the unions had called for a strike on the estate. I was told by a local supervisor that the union leaders did not inform the Jharkhand workers about the strike, and therefore they went to work in the field. The supervisor added that the union leaders do not speak Hindi and therefore were unable to communicate with the Jharkhand workers.

While the Tamil Dalits had also lost welfare provisions and suffered in the crisis-ridden plantations, they were members of the unions and had been able to sustain certain important positions such as their temporary or permanent work status. The Adivasis from Jharkhand, in contrast, were unable to negotiate with the management or unions and de facto had no social or legal protection. In sum, the new seasonal migrant workers from the poorer parts of India had become a super-exploited labour force occupying the lowest, most precarious and vulnerable rung in the informal casual occupational ladder of the plantation economy.

The tea companies in the belt bypassed the illegality of casualisation of work by recruiting and maintaining workers through labour intermediaries. It was Thomas, a Syrian Christian contractor from a valley town, who first brought these Jharkhandi workers to the Auburn company. The company instructed Thomas to recruit 100 workers without preference for the ethnicity or social origin of the workforce. Using the connections he had established with Syrian Christian missionaries in Jharkhand, Thomas initially brought in around 40 workers from Jharatti in Dumka district and from the village of Sakri over the border in Godda district. For each worker he delivered to the plantation, Thomas received a commission besides the reimbursement of his expenses for food and transportation of the workers. In addition to this, the company paid Thomas a commission of 20 rupees per worker per day. This, apparently, was not enough. Thomas negotiated an agreement with the management that the migrant workers' wages should be transferred directly to his bank account every month, allowing him to distribute the payment to *his* workers. From these minimum legal wages, Thomas now subtracted a further 20-rupee commission for himself, leaving the daily pay passed on to the workers at just 169 rupees.

Having recruited the migrant workers, Thomas showed little interest in their activities or needs once they reached Kerala. Thomas travelled to the plantation only to distribute the wages – seldom regularly – to the workers. Sometimes, the workers had to wait as long as two months to receive their pay. According to a Tamil worker, 'it was like a festival day for the migrant workers, when they saw Thomas coming with their money'. Thomas used 'delay in payment' as a means to control the workers: those who left the plantation early went unpaid. However, because he rarely visited the plantation, he understood little about the problems arising there.

The role of labour contractor to the Hill Top estate provided Thomas with a handsome income. However, despite the odds seemingly being stacked decisively against the Jharkhandi workers, Thomas's position as a contractor was less secure than he anticipated. Once it was discovered that Thomas was extracting a 'dual commission', his authority (trust) with the workers was lost. The workers complained to a Tamil employee called Anthony. Sympathetic to the migrant workers, Anthony communicated their complaints to the field officer and also to the manager of the estate. At first, the manager told the migrant workers that there was an agreement between the company and Thomas which could not be broken. However, the workers continued to voice their concerns and finally threatened to leave the plantation unless Thomas was removed from the role of mediator. With Thomas's duplicity now made public, the company risked alienating the labour force they had come to rely upon since losing their Tamil workers. Thomas was quickly cut off, deemed expendable by the company. Reneging on their 'gentleman's agreement', the manager of the Hill Valley estate told Thomas that he could no longer act as contractor with the excuse that he did not meet the legal requirement of being registered with the Labour Office in the Peermade tea belt. Thus, Thomas was abandoned by both the migrant workers and the company.

Worker-agents as a buffer

After Thomas's exit, the company was concerned about the difficulties in recruiting new labourers to the plantations. The migrant workers themselves proved to be the agents of further recruitment. The first individual to step into the contractor's shoes was Sagar, a Santali from Jharkhand's Godda district who had been brought to Hill Valley by Thomas. Sagar explained that in February 2013, the company management had approached him with the offer of a bonus for each additional worker he recruited to the plantation. After a short visit to Jharkhand, Sagar returned with 16 new workers including his wife, his sister's husband and his nephew. His reward was a payment of five rupees per person for each day they remained on the plantation. But Sagar was not satisfied with the commission the company gave him. Concerned that Sagar might pull his workers out and move them to another estate, the company responded in two ways. In October 2014, the company upped the commission with an offer of seven rupees per day per worker plus a one-off payment of 1,000 rupees to cover the costs of food and transportation. The company also devised a strategy of extending this offer to other worker-agents. When the company made this new offer, two of Thomas's recruits, Rooplal and Ramadhar, stepped in, promising to bring in more workers for the company. Rooplal, a 40-year-old college dropout, jumped at the chance to make more money. Unlike Rooplal, 50-year-old Ramadhar had never been to school, but he had good village-level connections, having served on the community council in the village. Within a week of the company's announcement of the offer, both Rooplal and Ramadhar had travelled to their native villages to recruit additional workers. Rooplal brought in nine workers while Ramadhar brought in 11 – mostly relatives and friends. The fourth migrant worker who took the chance to act as a worker-agent was Ashok Rana, who also had kin living in Sakri.

A major characteristic of worker-agents is that they continue working as manual labourers alongside those they have recruited. As such, they remain integrated in the kinship and friendship networks that support them and form the basis of the system of recruitment. Worker-agents are more likely to have knowledge of the workers' personal problems and can make attempts to help them. Social expectations based on long-standing relations established back in the village could be used to persuade recruits not to leave and to remain as 'ideal' workers. Compared with the crude withholding of wages by the professional contractor, the worker-agents' knowledge of social context provides a subtler and more sophisticated tool to ensure conformity and commitment. The company appointed Antony, a Tamil worker who speaks Hindi, as an intermediary between the top management and the worker-agents and adjusted the whole managerial structure accordingly. Thus, the companies intensified the continuity of the casualisation of labour through a horizontal contractor system conditioned by kinship and friendship networks.

Casualisation through intermediaries

Initially, the recruitment of Jharkhandi migrants through professional contractors such as Thomas appealed to the companies for a number of reasons. Firstly, the new migrant workers were cheap; they were prepared to accept the minimum wage rates that the previous Tamil workforce had largely rejected. Furthermore, being employed on temporary bases, they were not entitled to the same social security and welfare measures that were available to the Tamils, who were directly and permanently employed by the company. The need for plantation labour spikes twice a year – during the peak plucking seasons – from January to March, and from August to October. Secondly, the supply of labour can be matched to these two peaks without the need to keep workers on in the slack intervening months. That the flow of Jharkhandi workers could be turned up or down according to demand was hugely important to the companies. Having the contractor as a buffer, the workers could be easily abandoned in the event of a crisis in future.

The third motive for using Thomas as an intermediary – and the one that largely explains the first two – is that doing so allowed the plantation company to ignore the legal rights supposedly due to all workers. By using contractors as intermediaries, employers are able to avoid legal responsibilities to labour, for example, the implementation of the Plantations Labour Act of 1951.[7] Legally, casual labour can be used only to fulfil tasks outside the daily routine of the plantations, for example, the cutting of trees. In fact, Jharkhandis of both sexes were engaged in tea plucking; men were also employed in routine 'factory' work such as loading tea leaves into large drums for the crushing machines and carrying the processed tea to the packaging area. Using the contractor as a buffer, the companies were able to deny to their migrant labourers 'permanent worker' status and accompanying benefits including provident fund access, paid annual holidays and medical leave. On any of these grounds, the recognised unions and government officials (such as the inspector of plantations and deputy labour officer) could have intervened in support of the casualised migrant workforce. They chose not to do so. The unions in the tea belt were rarely concerned about the exploitative situation of the new migrant workforce, and the benefits of membership have not been extended to the casual migrant workforce.

Initially, at least, the companies were happy with this arrangement: with Thomas as an intermediary, they hoped to ensure a reliable supply of workers who would remain compliant in order to secure further employment. However, while neoliberal conditions contributed to the initial creation of the niche exploited by Thomas, what happened at the Hill Valley plantation confirms Geert De Neve's view that the same conditions ultimately 'tend to undermine rather than enhance contractors' entrepreneurial success and to reduce rather than intensify their power vis-à-vis both capital and workers' (De Neve 2014, 1306).

Why did the company agree to shift from contractor-led recruitment to making arrangements via worker-agents? The immediate cause was a concern that, following their falling out with Thomas, the migrant labourers might quit the plantation and return to Jharkhand. The company quickly recognised that it is preferable to negotiate with multiple worker-agents than with a single contractor such as Thomas. Furthermore, the worker-agents' superior understanding of the situation of potential workers and their extended social networks in recruiting areas meant they were able to respond to changes in demand and deliver a reliable supply of workers. Even better, as far as the company was concerned, these new recruitment agents were largely unfamiliar with the kinds of bargaining strategies used by employers when negotiating rates of pay. No longer reliant on a single contractor, the company could spread risks while reducing labour costs (compare the seven rupees per worker per day paid to worker-agents with the 20 rupees per worker per day paid to professional contractors). The Jharkhandis were better and cheaper than Thomas and could recruit new labourers quickly and easily. Moreover, one might assume that the worker-agents would side with their fellow Jharkhandis in the event of a dispute, but in actuality, individual worker-agents were reluctant to challenge the company for fear of being sidelined or dismissed. For the company, the figure of the worker-agent has come to play a vital role in the ongoing making and remaking of labour markets.

While the rise of worker-agents provided many advantages for the plantation company, the absence of a professional contractor did expose new tensions in the relationship between the workforce and the company. Previously, the professional contractor would represent the workers and raise their concerns with the management. The company did not want to parley with worker-agents in the same way – to do so would threaten the class order within the plantation. The increasing casualisation of work is supported by the complex mechanism of labour recruitment devised by the company; new layers of management handle the outsourcing of labour recruitment to worker-agents while simultaneously reducing the power of these agents to bargain on behalf of the workforce. The Auburn company chose to refigure the labour hierarchy on the Hill Valley estate by deploying a Tamil, Anthony, to act as a mediator between the new migrant workforce and the field officer of the estate. Previously, Thomas would have to be contacted every time the company wanted to make a decision about the workers' situation. Now, without upsetting the plantation hierarchy, the workers' concerns and complaints and the company's decisions could be communicated directly to the Hindi-speaking Anthony.

On their arrival at the plantation, Anthony would take charge of the new workers, helping them to settle in the plantation. Through Anthony, it was agreed that the company would pay an advance to buy groceries, warm clothes and the tools needed for work.[8] By appointing an informal liaison officer, the company denied further status and power to worker-agents, preventing them from gaining knowledge about the company's economic interests, and discouraged them from organising the workers against the company. Anthony was fondly called *mama* (uncle) by the migrant workers; the company cleverly exploited this close relationship and the workers' vulnerability to exert control over the new labour force.

New ethnic hierarchies of labour

The replacement of some of the Tamil plantation workers with (cheaper) labourers from eastern India is similar to what has occurred in other plantations around the world, where the replacement of earlier workers with new ones has created an ethnic division of labour (Bourgois 1988; Martínez 2007; Holmes 2013) and become a source of ethnic antagonism (Jayawardena 1963; Mintz 1989). As Martínez observes of plantations in the Dominican Republic:

> West Indians replaced Dominicans in the cane fields in the 1880s and 1890s, just as employers switched from paying cutters by the task to ganged day labour. Haitians took the West Indians' place in the 1930s, as gang labour gave way to piece-rate wages. Each of these shifts reduced the workers' bargaining power. Resentment about these upheavals has been directed away from company

management by granting jobs higher up the company job ladder to a few established workers, deporting many others, and letting the reminder find their way towards jobs in port cities. Plantation managers have thus not only circumvented resistance by replacing old labourers with new ones but have promoted ethnic divisions as a strategy of labour control. (2007, 22–3)

In the case of the Peermade tea belt, however, the workers cannot be replaced by force due to the protection provided to the workers by rigid labour laws. Rather, the planters preferred not to recruit new permanent workers and preferred to increase the temporary workforce through accommodating workers from eastern India, probably on a contract basis, so that the planters need not to provide the welfare benefits given to permanent workers.

With worker-agents able to quickly mobilise a reliable workforce, their deployment allows tea companies in Peermade to manage levels of demand for labourers without having to employ workers on a permanent basis. The shift to a *ristedari* (kinship- and friendship-based) recruitment system widened the company's recruitment strategies while allowing them to remain distant from the casual workforce and its representatives. The casualisation of the new Jharkhandi Adivasi workers is reproduced through ethnic hierarchy in the cash crop plantations, as argued by Philippe Bourgois in the case of banana plantations in Costa Rica and Panama. He referred to this ethnic hierarchy of labour as conjugated oppression. At the same time, conjugated oppression primarily dealt with ethnic hierarchy within industrial plantation settings and was not concerned with the blurred boundary between the ethnic hierarchy in and out of workplaces. As Chapter 5's discussion of the dam conflict shows, the workers' experience of plantation exploitation and the crisis should not be confined to an understanding of the workers' identity in relation to the work setting. There is a larger life outside it, and the workers are situated within the larger social hierarchies and power relations between different groups. The larger social hierarchies also normalised the non-intervention of unions, labour inspectors and the larger state bureaucracy against the illegal casual labour regime.

Seth Holmes (2013) further illustrates conjugated oppression in his ethnography about the Triqui migrant berry pickers on a strawberry plantation in the Skagit Valley in the United States. He argues that the Triqui workers' lower status as migrant workers is *naturalised and normalised* through symbolic violence generated by the practices of an ethnic-occupational continuum in the berry farm. Holmes himself provides ethnographic material on the nexus between the ethnic hierarchy inside and outside the fruit farms, although he does not use it to reflect further on the concept of conjugated oppression. I have discussed in depth the extension of conjugated oppression to categorical oppression elsewhere (Raj 2020), not only to show the blurred boundary between the normalisation of their ethnic hierarchy within and outside the workplace but also to understand how Tamil Dalits *experience* the stigmatised categories of identity as an integral element of their lives. This existential dimension of the workers' identity categories exceeds the employment of those categories by the capitalist plantation order.

For the tea companies, the crisis is another excuse for them to expel the workers who demand the distribution of plantation land. And they do it by recruiting workers who do not easily identify themselves with the Tamil tea workers in claiming their demands. It may take another three or four generations for the new workers to make a claim on the plantation land. By then, the companies will have brought in new workers and undermined the claims of the previous workers.

Notes

1 Minimum kilograms of tea leaves to be plucked by the workers to qualify for the daily minimum wage of 320 rupees in 2018, less than half the wage rate in rural India, which is 700 rupees (https://m.rbi.org.in/Scripts/PublicationsView.aspx?id=20083).
2 According to statistics from the Tea Board of India, the average tea production in South India increased to 390.28 million kg in 2008 from 381.87 million kg, and the price at auction increased to 66.27 rupees/kg in 2008 from 49.70 rupees/kg (Statistical Archive, Tea Board of India). Furthermore, the average price of Indian tea in the export markets increased during the year to 136.64 rupees/kg from 117.81 rupees/kg in 2008, and in 2009, South Indian tea-producing states – Tamil Nadu, Kerala and Karnataka – recorded a yield of 244.1 million kg, down from 246.8 million kg in 2008 (http://www.commodityonline.com/news/India-tea-output-dips-exports-up-by-37- percent-25490-3-1.html).
3 According to Agamben (2005), laws related to civic rights suspended for a prolonged period under a state of exception, such as war, will be perpetuated to become an 'ordinary' state of existence through which the contemporary state partially reproduces its sovereign power.
4 Following Veena Das (2006), Henrik Vigh (2008) argues that for much of the global poor, crisis is endemic rather than episodic; crisis needs to be understood as fragmentations within the ordinary life of the poor, not as singular events that generate rupture in their lives. For the Peermade tea workers, the crisis is still a rupture because the intensity with which the crisis hit them practically dictated the conditions of their existence following the collapse of the plantations (see Holbraad et al. (2019) for a recent conceptualisation of rupture). However, Vigh's argument of crisis as a prolonged decline is relevant for the workers in the reopened plantations. For the workers, the dense feeling of deterioration coexists with their attempt to build a life through the prolonged decline and uncertainty.
5 These groups had migrated to different places across India as the scope for their traditional occupation as blacksmiths had declined over the years. Many of them had worked as migrant labourers in other parts of India before coming to the Top View estate. They had worked in road building in Kashmir and Himachal Pradesh, in the construction industry in Delhi and Bangalore, in sharecropping in West Bengal and in meat processing industries in Pune. Migration to the plantation was a new chapter in this long history of migration.

6 In 2006 the Indian government listed Godda and Dumka as among the country's 250 most backward districts (out of a total of 640).
7 The Plantations Labour Act, 1951 is available at https://labour.gov.in/sites/default/files/The-Plantation-Labour-Act-1951.pdf.
8 The company has arrangements with various shops in nodal towns, from which workers can purchase groceries and other necessary things for the first month. However, to do so, they must be accompanied by a supervisor, who is required to approve the items and the bill. The amount spent is deducted from the worker's wages over the next four or five months.

9
The social consequences of crises

Plantationocene and conjugated crises

Before I reiterate the discussion of the book, I want to briefly discuss the ecological crisis that the tea workers experienced directly, which worked together with the economic distress and the dam conflict to further alienate the workers. In the contemporary discussion on globalisation and neoliberalism, plantation capitalism manifests a radical restructuring of global capitalism with disastrous effects not only for the poor but also for human sustainability in general – a process that Donna Haraway (2015) calls plantationocene. Haraway thus places plantation agriculture at the centre of increasing human-driven climate change that threatens species extinction. However, Haraway's multi-species approach to plantationocene keeps plants rather than human beings at the centre of the discussion, thus not paying due attention to racial or casteist capitalism (Davis et al. 2019). The plantationocene discourse should be attentive to the fact that racial- and caste-based plantation capitalism is driven by an elite minority that exposes workers to uneven consequences of the plantationocene. In Kerala's tea belts, it is the Tamil Dalit workers who suffer most from natural disasters. As many of them continue to live in a context in which resources are completely controlled by the plantation company and the state, they are denied autonomy in overcoming the crises.

In the Kerala tea belts, unplanned land clearance and monoculture plantations have led to frequent landslides, especially in the last decade. In the Peermade tea belt, mining companies have been acquiring the rocky hills surrounding the plantations since 2016. When I revisited the plantations in December 2020, I was startled to see that more than 20 per cent of the hills outside Hill Valley are now controlled by companies just waiting to get clearance from the government to commence stone quarrying. Such quarrying will accelerate the destruction of the ecology in the region, which has already been severely affected by monoculture plantations, landslides and floods. In August 2018, many buildings collapsed as a result of floods and landslides, and many families were displaced from their line houses in the Munnar and Peermade tea belts. In May 2021, 15 workers' families in the Peermade tea belt were displaced from their dilapidated, fragile houses in the estate lines due to heavy monsoon rains and floods. They were all housed in the nearby primary school building with little food or protection from the weather. The floods occurred in the middle of the COVID-19 pandemic, and staying together in the school made them more vulnerable to infection. In the Peermade tea belt, the proposed stone quarrying on the outskirts of plantations will further perpetuate landslides and floods, leading to more crises for the workers and endangering their survival.

On 6 August 2020, 70 people from 26 families were buried alive in a deadly landslide in the Pettimudi tea plantation, located only 60 miles from the Peermade tea belt. The landslide also washed away more than 30 line houses and everything inside. To make matters worse, the government of Kerala allocated five lakh (500,000) rupees for the families of the dead, while they allocated 10 lakh rupees for the families of the victims of a plane crash that occurred at Calicut international airport on the same day as the landslide. This discriminatory treatment of the Dalit workers, even after death, provoked a huge public uproar in India. The delay in rescue operations was allegedly a major reason for the high number of deaths. The local government moved the survivors to a relief camp in fear of more landslides. They were not able to settle in a place of their own choosing within the tea belt. Because they do not own or control any land in the tea belt, which is entirely controlled by the tea company, they have to wait until the plantation company and the state intervene to resettle and rehabilitate them. Many workers moved out of the relief camp to their relatives' line houses in other tea plantations due to poor facilities in the camp. I met a few of the displaced families in Munnar town. Manickam, who lost his siblings in the landslide, told me:

> It is so deplorable that we can't even trust the one-room house we had. We have not asked for a bungalow in the town but only a peaceful life in the wild plantation frontier. But it seems even that seems to be too much to expect now. Living in Pettimudi is not only the memory of the dead but also everyday fear of death.

The combined crises have led to further system collapse. At the same time, the economic and ecological consequences of this collapse are highly unequal, for the tea workers are bearing the socio-ecological costs of producing tea for a world from which their lives are detached. Alarmingly, the planters' associations have been lobbying for more dilution of labour laws and land reforms to lift the restrictions placed on land use and labour conditions in the plantations. This lobbying may encourage the 'soft ethnic cleansing' (expulsion) of Tamil workers. The families demanded housing that the state promised to build for them. However, the KDHP tea company controlled by TATA, the world's second-largest producer and distributor of tea, refused to provide the land for the housing project. The tussle between the state and the company over the post-disaster management intensified the workers' precarity. In fact, the state owns the plantation land and the tea company only has leasehold rights. The state could have easily taken over the leasehold estates and distributed the land to the workers, but they apparently chose not to do so. As the issue received nationwide media attention, the state allocated a meagre five cents of land, but only to five of the families affected. The company constructed houses for those five, leaving the rest homeless and landless. This apathy has driven the displaced families to demand distribution of the leasehold land.

On 1 June 2021, the families submitted a petition to the Chief Minister of Kerala raising concerns over the apathy and disregard for the suffering of the landslide victims. They explained how the massive deprivation and merciless displacement of the workers amount to the silent ethnic cleansing of the tea workers. As 'sons of the soil', they claimed the right to own and cultivate the land their forefathers had worked on and developed while fighting deadly diseases and insects. They also filed a case in the High Court of Kerala seeking land distribution, to which the state had yet to respond at the time of writing.[1] In a similar event in 2014, more than 200 tea workers and their families (primarily Tamil-speaking lower castes, referred to as upcountry Tamils) were killed in a disastrous landslide in the Meeriyabedda tea plantation in Sri Lanka. The upcountry Tamils also raised the land question in the aftermath of the landslide. Thus, despite their deep sense of alienation, the workers confronted the loss of life in landslides by attempting to create socio-economic autonomy, a counter-plantation system, that would stand in direct opposition to what the plantation system stands for (Casimir 2020). This counter-plantation society could be achieved, as they rightly realise, only through land ownership.

Crisis of state and struggle for land

It is now clear that land is the most contested resource in the current neoliberal plantation economy in the region. In the larger political scene of Kerala, Dalit and Adivasi (indigenous/tribal) organisations fight the communist-ruled state to redistribute the excess land illegally occupied by the tea and rubber companies. The agitation for the distribution of plantation land started in the early 1990s and continued into the 2000s. This land dispute was revitalised when some of the top officials in the revenue department came up with a series of reports identifying more than 30,000 hectares of land illegally occupied by plantation companies operating from India and the United Kingdom. These reports also found that the land claimed by the tea companies had been granted on lease by a princely state during the colonial period. A high-ranking senior bureaucrat submitted the most critical report, which recommended that the state seize plantation companies' illegal holdings. The companies challenged the recommendation of eviction in the High Court of Kerala, which led to the ongoing judicial proceedings. In 2017, the communist government rejected the report and removed the government counsel (public prosecutor) who had spoken out against the illegal occupation of the plantations. Instead of reclaiming the land occupied by the plantation companies, the state attempted to resolve the land dispute by recreating ghetto housing projects on the fringes of plantations.

When the new companies took over, the workers hoped the plantation would soon return to normal functioning. However, the new companies continued to deny the workers welfare provisions and decent work. The companies argued that tea production was operating at a loss, but they continued to clear land and plant tea on the plantation's fringes so as to later claim the land legally. This increasing state-supported land grab across the global South by corporate plantations has produced immense wealth for a few but has worsened the livelihood options and life chances of many, many millions. Examining the expanding plantation zones in Indonesia, Tania Li describes this contemporary plantation regime as a mafia system that is 'an extended, densely networked, predatory system in which everyone in a plantation zone must participate in order get somewhere, or simply to survive' (2018, 329). Li further reiterates the critical aspects of plantations pointed out by many anthropologists and others who have studied them: plantation systems destroy life, perpetuate violence and monopolise resources (Li and Semedi 2021).

The companies used the crisis to lobby for more state support in rescuing them from the crisis. The state's intervention in the crisis was directed towards the companies in the form of support for replanting, irrigation and the renewal of factories. An astonishing aspect of the tea crisis was that the state institutions did little to help the workers despite a moral call from the workers for state intervention. The state provided workers with a few kilos of rice and a few hundred rupees during the Onam festival so that they would not go hungry, at least during the festival. This intervention by the state was largely symbolic and not an attempt to provide a long-term solution for the workers. As Roitman (2014) observes, state intervention is the only possible way out for the poor in moments of crisis. The state relied entirely on technocrats to interpret the crisis, and the latter were more concerned with saving the tea plantations than saving the workers. The technocrats built their argument on mainstream discourses about the crucial role of plantations in national economies.

The Dalit and Adivasi organisations alleged that the communist-ruled state's intervention was intended to help the plantation companies, including the legalisation of the land occupied by the companies. Kerala state and the dominant political parties attempted to justify their actions by stating that plantation production is vital for the state's economy and therefore the plantation system needs to be supported in times of crisis. This logic of laissez-faire economics, as Naomi Klein (2007, 160) notes, understands crisis as inherent to the free flow of capital and encourages states to protect economic enclaves, triggering further alienation of the workforce. The logic and networks of 'disaster capitalism' facilitate the reinvention of the capitalist market and its ideology during crisis events around the world (Klein 2007, 162; see also Sassen 2014). For laissez-faire economists, any economic distress is a crisis for adjustment, meaning the crisis is a volatility issue that structural adjustment could resolve. This logic rationalises the austerity measures taken by the Indian state system during the tea crisis. The state, therefore, made an anti-human intervention into the economy for the benefit of market capitalism. Such a condition in India is consistent with what Bruce Kapferer (2005c) calls new oligarchic corporate state formations commanded by close-knit social groups that, in the Indian case, include influential planters' associations. Very often the planters have relatives and friends in the high-level bureaucracy who dictate the official discourses of economic crises. While these close-knit social groups existed earlier, the new oligarchs often subjugate the regulative political order of the state (Hardt and Negri 2000).

In these ways, plantation capitalism is rationalised by the neoliberal logic of the post-1990s and by the socialist welfare state at various levels, as is evident in the communist/socialist Kerala state, which is known for its egalitarian credentials. This means both the right and the left consider plantations as necessary in their state's economic planning, and the workers end up bearing the cost of economic growth within both neoliberal capitalist and socialist contexts. This has historical roots in colonial rule, which presented a vision of progress through the inevitability of the plantation system for industrial development. The plantations were one of the key colonial economic projects that the postcolonial state retained, unlike the large steel plants they built in the postcolonial period for a self-reliant modern India (Parry 2020, 9). The economic autonomy of India was chiefly built upon, among a few other sites, the plantations.

However, India's state-led development and the mixed economic approach have mostly retained the plantation system in the private sector, supposedly to enable the plantations to be internationally competitive. The rationalisation of the plantation system by both the social-democratic left and conservative right everywhere generates something closer to Herbert Marcuse's (1964) one-dimensional ideology (of plantation) that legitimises a system that represents one of the most dehumanising institutions in human history in the past five centuries. A globally disconnected workforce, often also located at the bottom of the social hierarchy, is forced to pay the price for the accelerated, globally connected production system, as noted by James Ferguson (1990). The continual displacement of this workforce during crises is integral to the systemic restlessness essential to capitalist accumulation. If the plantations had been nationalised, the workers' lives may have been a little better, with at least a few becoming what Jonathan Parry (2020, 58) calls an 'aristocracy of labour' within India's public-sector undertakings, with a life comparable to that of the lower middle classes in India.

Kerala is renowned for its inclusive development model, whose human development achievements are comparable to those of developed countries. According to the Government of India Census of 2011, Kerala had high rates of literacy among both males (94 per cent) and females (93 per cent), a healthy gender ratio (1,084 women for every 1,000 men), and the highest life expectancy (75 years) and lowest infant mortality (12 per 1,000) of all Indian states. And yet it is clear that the Kerala model maintained long-standing hierarchies of caste dominance and failed to open up possibilities for Dalit socio-economic autonomy (Omvedt 1998, 2006; Prasad 1998; Steur 2017). As Gail Omvedt pointedly summarises in her critique of the Kerala development model and Dalit life, 'Dalit landlessness in Kerala represents a continuation of old patterns that have not been changed by the social struggle and left-led peasant and agricultural labourer movements … and there is still a very high statistical correlation between caste and economic situation everywhere in India: Kerala is no different' (Omvedt 2006, 200–1). Exploring how the Kerala development model undermined possibilities for the socio-economic mobility of Dalit and Adivasi communities in Kerala, Luisa Steur (2017) describes Kerala's development trajectory as a mild form of neoliberalism.

This explains why, in a state that is so often cited as a model of egalitarianism, one finds the kind of oppression and marginalisation faced by the Tamil Dalit communities in the tea plantations.[2] The Tamil tea plantation workers, as seen in the previous chapters, remain the 'other' in Kerala society and an 'outlier' in Kerala's development initiatives. Tamil Dalit workers on the plantations have a long history of marginalisation, discrimination and stigma, although their dynamics and experiences have changed over time. They came to the Kerala plantations as indentured labourers, often escaping the extreme direct oppression of caste discrimination in their native villages in Tamil Nadu. Within the Kerala context, their status was perceived as inferior to that of many other groups. The lack of socio-political organisations that address the specific concerns of the 'Tamilness' and 'Dalitness' of the workers is a significant reason their marginality is neglected in the development discourses.

As I have discussed elsewhere (Raj 2019), the plantation workers were relatively invisible within the development discourse of both India and Kerala state. The official development reports did not acknowledge them even within the list of outlier communities. Kerala's intelligence agency claimed in a report to the government that the Tamil plantation labourers had migrated to Kerala in the 1980s and displaced Malayalam-speaking labourers native to Kerala (*Times of India*, 5 December 2012). This was despite the historical fact that Tamil labour was part of Kerala's plantation system from the time of its establishment. Furthermore, the same report recommended that Tamils be discouraged from owning land in Kerala to avoid ethnic conflict based on linguistic differences. Such exclusionary nationalist egalitarian discourse operated to create a hierarchy of rights that excluded the Tamil plantation workers and fuelled prejudice against them. In such a way, state rhetoric was formed in the enlightenment idiom of the modern Kerala state which actually promotes ethnic division despite legitimating its rhetoric to avoid such conflict.

Just as slavery and caste hierarchy existed side by side with claims of enlightenment and modernity (Fanon 1966; Pandian 2002;

Buck-Morss 2009), so highly prejudicial practices against the Tamils exist side by side with the egalitarian claims of Kerala society. Indeed, certain overtly egalitarian ideas can harbour and obscure some of the most marginalised, stigmatised and powerless people in Kerala, exacerbating their situation, erasing the history that created their circumstances and silencing their voice (Trouillot 1995). To a certain extent, it was the Pembillai Orumai strike that made the miserable life of the outcaste plantation workers visible to the world. The history of the Tamil Dalit plantation workers is a history of struggle to become at least visible at the margins.

Crisis of identity and alienation

Economic enclaves such as plantations and mines operate with exceptions generated by the broader ideological and political-economic norms and practices of state and society. The plantations in India exist within the economistic rationale of capitalism and the social hierarchy of caste, ethnicity and gender. Within the capitalism–caste system logic, the crisis for the tea companies was part of the logic of neoliberal capitalism and the suffering of Dalit workers, particularly women, was inherent to their position at the bottom of the caste/class hierarchy. As Seth Holmes (2013) concludes regarding migrant farmworkers in the United States, the naturalisation of inequalities occurs through the racialisation of bodies. Engaging with Bourdieu's concept of symbolic violence, he articulates how such racialised bodies are associated with specific occupations and how the workers themselves internalise that. In the Indian plantations, caste hierarchy and its racialised forms provide a prearranged naturalisation of occupations for various groups as well as gendered roles, which are sacralised within the Hindu cosmology.

Initially, the tea crisis appeared to me only as a crisis of neoliberal capitalism. Over time, however, I realised that the crisis of capitalism in the plantations translates and feeds into several other crises in the workers' lives. A major predicament that emerged from the crisis is how the plantation workers' economic marginality goes hand in hand with the stigma of Tamil Dalit identity, resulting in their categorical oppression. As discussed throughout the book, the plantation Tamils are crippled with identity and stereotypical characterisations that accentuate them as an inferiorised underclass. Even if some plantation Tamils escape the stigma attached to Tamil identity by learning Malayalam, the stigma attached to Dalit identity continues to haunt them. That is to say that despite the best possible efforts by the workers to escape the system in which they are condemned, the socio-cultural dynamics of India's wider social and political order continue to imprison them and act to reproduce them as economically impoverished and socially disadvantaged. This reproduction through categorical oppression also feeds into situations such as the dam conflict, which developed independent of the plantation crisis but feeds into its implication for the workers.

The naturalisation of suffering during the crisis was also reinforced by the unquestioned folk wisdom generated by academics and journalists that established a *reality* of crisis (Lo 2012). This does not mean that the crisis was not real – it was. However, what is more relevant to the discussion here is how the particular narratives of the reality of crisis produce a conviction about its inevitability and the poor workers' suffering. This enduring presence of crisis for the workers even after the companies returned to normal functioning shows a disjuncture between the narrative of the crisis passed onto the workers, the workers' everyday experience of it and the 'actual' economic crisis. The economic rationale for the crisis is built into the asymmetrical knowledge systems of mainstream economic thought and a historical narrative of crisis consistent with such thought. Drawing on the 2007–8 financial crisis discourse, Janet Roitman (2014, 5) argues that the 'very distinction between expert and lay relies on stable subject positions that are not tenable'. In the plantation case, the workers did not have to produce a crisis narrative. The crisis spread through gossip and rumours initiated by management, political leadership and experts alike, and thus crisis appeared inevitable.

While it might be 'normal' for capitalist plantations to go through cycles of boom and bust, the crisis created a 'radical break' in the workers' lives. Predictably the workers were the worst victims of the crisis, for the plantation is an ultimate human space *only* for the workers – an end in itself. It is a temporary space for the planters and the higher staff out of which they were able to move whenever they wanted to; they owned properties and maintained active social relations outside the plantations. Unlike the workers' children, only a very few children of the managerial staff studied in the tea belt. Most of them attended schools in the plains, occasionally visiting their parents on the plantations. Although somewhat connected to their ancestral villages, the workers did not own land where they could claim a dignified space and life outside the tea belt. This is the primary reason they resisted expulsion with all possible means, as is evident in the retirees' situation. As part of this ethical project, they also had to renegotiate between themselves the 'politics of decency' that threatened the egalitarian space they had generated within the plantations.

The plantation workers are a prime example of a population subjected to expulsion through crises, as formulated by Saskia Sassen (2014, 2016). Sassen talks about the diverse nature of expulsions under global capitalism related to land grabs, advanced mining, international debt regimes and economic crises. Sassen also discusses how these domains of expulsion expel the surplus population to a systemic edge. However, unlike in Sassen's analysis, the plantation workforce at the lowest rung of capitalist production have not been rendered as surplus population useless to the functioning of neoliberal capitalism. Instead, they are forced to move around as a precarious labour force when one crisis pushes them to another, again not to the systemic edge as Sassen observes, but to the very centres of capitalist production, such as Tirupur's global garment production sector. The circular movement from the plantations to the garment sector and back is also an important development in labour migration in Sri Lanka.

In such a context, alienation becomes a key phenomenon of this ontological condition of the workers. As discussed in Chapter 1, nothing in the workers' lives has been left untouched by the plantation system, neither the most intimate processes such as kinship nor structural phenomena such as interconnected aspects of spatiality. As Donna Haraway reminded us in a conversation on plantationocene with Anna Tsing (Haraway et al. 2019), plantations and plantation-like capitalist systems depend on a radical reduction of the labourer's degree of freedom to do anything other than what is demanded by the plantation system. Accordingly, plantations become the epitome of human alienation and are radically incompatible with the capacity to love and care for place (Haraway et al. 2019, 6). The workers remain a perpetually liminal population, although they generate a sense of belonging and ownership of their line houses and the tea fields (Besky 2014; Jegathesan 2019).

This alienation was reproduced when the workers increasingly lost control over their life situation in the crisis context. This was especially so when the collapse of the class order in the plantation gave way to a caste-based social system aggravated by the religiously polarised plantation community, composed of Dalit Hindus and Dalit Christians. Thus, life in the crisis context has demonstrated that the workers are more than exploited as this is an effect of the stigmatised and low value in which they are held. They are alienated by forces within the orders of Indian society and to such an extent that they often come to place little value upon their own lives. Their alienation is of a deep, existential social and political nature – if it is possible to say so, they are alienated to the depth of their being (Sartre 1963) or to the zones of non-being (Fanon 1967).[3]

The idea of alienation, thereby, is essential to impart a fuller sense of the intensity of the experiential situation of the plantation workers, given their history and the contemporary context of the economic crisis. Terms such as abandonment and precarity are helpful to understand the contemporary forms of uncertainty and insecurity brought by the increasing casualisation of work and the uneven impacts of neoliberal capitalism, global conflicts and ethnic violence (see Butler 2004; Al-Mohammad 2012; Millar 2014). However, the idea of alienation is central to the discussion in this book. It helps to bring out the phenomenological dimensions of the crisis and the structural positioning of the tea workers as alienated beings generated by plantation capitalism and categorical oppression.

Economic distress induced a crisis of humanity, removing the essence of human dignity from those at the bottom of the socio-political hierarchy (Fanon 1967, 202). This crisis of humanity is so deep that it even creates a sense of collective bad faith among the workers in justifying their indifference to others who could not get out of the plantations in a time of crisis. The bad faith in the crisis context generated a moral crisis for the workers. Their indifference is directly linked to their assertion of dignity and recognition, which they struggled to achieve when they migrated to caste-ridden Tamil or racist Kerala society. Therefore, the crisis came to redefine significant aspects of the workers' lives. More importantly, the crisis forced the workers to renegotiate their relationship with the plantation system and to contemplate the futility of human life itself. The crisis forced the workers to critically examine their past, present and future, for it created a radical space that was open to various possibilities, negotiations and restructuring. When the resources to retain control of their life situation are exhausted, the workers experience life only as alienated beings. In the end, the crisis conceals itself so that they no longer recognise it as a crisis – it becomes a crisis in disguise. At the same time, the crisis is normalised not through its invisibility but through its excess. Following Foucault's observation (1975, 34) that the excess of violence legitimises violence, we can say that the excess of the crisis legitimises the crisis. This excess of the crisis intensifies the workers' experience of it for a long period, which also significantly contributes to the normalisation of crisis.[4] The crisis, therefore, did not look brutal to many and their suffering appeared to be authorless. Its tranquillity was created by its rationalisation in the logics of caste society, the corporate state and the capitalist market. Such rationalisations and the excess of crisis stand in the way of conceiving of the crisis as a scandal and of dismantling the plantation system.

Notes

1. Incidentally, the workers of Pettimudi were at the forefront of the Pembillai Orumai strike organised against the plantation companies and the unions five years before the landslide.
2. The district of Idukki, where Peermade is located, has one of the highest 'deprivation index' scores among the districts in Kerala (13 out of 14 in 2001) (Government of Kerala 2006, 62).
3. Alienation is a key concern in the emancipatory projects of Frantz Fanon and B.R. Ambedkar, two global thinkers who paid utmost attention to the question of dignity and freedom of the oppressed. Fanon and Ambedkar make strikingly similar calls to overcome the dehumanisation of colonial (plantation) life and the internalisation of the caste/racial order: 'realisation of humanity' (Fanon 1966) and 'reclamation of human personality' (Ambedkar 1942). That is to say, for Fanon and Ambedkar, emancipation is directly linked to the process of de-alienation.
4. Achille Mbembe also discuss the normalisation of crisis through its intense experience. For Mbembe, 'it is in everyday life that the crisis as a limitless experience and a field of the dramatisation of particular forms of subjectivity is authored, receives its translations, is institutionalised, loses its exceptional character and in the end, as a "normal", ordinary and banal phenomenon, becomes an imperative to consciousness' (Mbembe 1995, 325).

Appendix
A short history of the Peermade tea belt

The history of the Peermade tea belt goes back to the 1860s, when the British established plantations there as in the Caribbean, South and South-East Asia and Southern Africa, following the abolition of the slave trade between 1833 and 1848 (Beckford 1972; Hoerder 2002). The workers for these plantations were brought from distant places through the indenture system,[1] and Tamils formed the largest component of the indentured labour from India (Guilmoto 1993). The Tamil workers – who mostly belonged to outcaste communities – were sent to Ceylon (Sri Lanka), Malaya (Malaysia), Burma (Union of Myanmar) and the princely state of Travancore (the South Indian state of Kerala). A comparatively lower number of Tamil workers were also sent to Fiji, Guyana and Mauritius, where most of the workers came from northern India (Mayer 1961; Jayawardena 1963; Lal 1993). Tamil labour, particularly that of the 'Untouchable' castes, had developed a reputation for being manageable, hardworking and able to survive in heavily forested highlands.

Before the establishment of plantations in the region, the Peermade highlands, then called the 'hills of Central Travancore', were inhabited by tribes of Mala-Arayans and Mannans (Lovatt 1972). In 1863 British colonial officials of the Madras Presidency and British missionaries established coffee plantations there as the local tribes were driven away from their land. Tea became a prominent crop when a leaf disease resulted in the decline of coffee cultivation. As tea cultivation was labour intensive, more and more workers from outcaste communities in Tamil-speaking regions of South India were brought to the plantations (Muthiah 1993). They initially came through the indentured labour system. Later, recruitment was done by professional agents of the plantation companies who later became Kanganis,[2] that is, labour contractors-cum-supervisors who recruited workers from their own villages and supervised the workers in the plantations (Heidemann 1992; Hollup 1994). Under the legal contract the workers were provided with an advance to pay off their debt back home as they entered into an agreement to work for specific plantation companies for a period (generally five years) stipulated under the contract. Once an agreement had been made with the company, it was virtually impossible for the workers to free themselves as they were forced to stay with the company even after their contract period expired. The workers under the indenture system thus effectively became bonded labourers.

The workers were presented with an alluring, colourful picture of plantation life and work but when they got to the plantations there was no decent housing nor sanitation facilities. Many of the workers died of malaria, fever and dysentery while clearing the forest (Baak 1997). The labour process was arduous and exhausting. Work was extracted from the labourers with a machine-like precision and any fault detected was dealt with severely (Raman 2010). Many workers tried to run away due to the routine inhuman treatment and the severe work conditions. However, this was rendered virtually impossible by the debt bondage system that was integral to the recruitment of indentured labour, and the sanctions that could be exerted in the case of any attempt to withdraw labour.

In 1865 the Travancore Criminal Breach of Contract Act was passed under which it was a crime for workers to break their contract of employment with the plantation companies. A magistrate's court was established in Peermade by the Travancore state for the purpose of prosecuting workers under the terms of the Act. The Act effectively prevented employees leaving the plantations for alternative work. It advanced no protection against exploitation.[3] On top of that, the Coffee Stealing Prevention Act of 1879 prohibited workers from having any right to the product of their labour. It not only symbolised the dehumanised situation of the labourers, the point of whose existence was solely to labour, but also presented the plantation workers as potential criminals: the coolie beast who needed to be tamed (Breman 1989). The colonial state actively supported the establishment of plantations by providing easy credit, extremely cheap land, bonded labour, botanical knowledge and the infrastructure (roads and railways) required to link the plantation frontiers with ports and metropolis.

International pressure to end the indenture system became stronger across the British colonies in the early 1900s, when the brutality of the system was widely documented and reported (Andrews and Pearson

1916). Indian nationalists, as well as anti-slavery and labour activists in the West, called the indenture system a 'new form of slavery' (Tinker 1974). The legal contract between worker and tea plantation was outlawed by the 1920s, but the Kangani system through which the workers had been recruited and controlled continued. The role of Kanganis did change somewhat after the abolition of the indenture system. They continued to recruit workers but without the control provided by the indenture system, which had given them impunity in punishing the workers, and the workers were more 'free' to shift from one plantation to another. By the late 1940s the Kanganis had ceased to be contractors and their role was limited to that of wage-earning supervisors of the workforce.

While Europeans dominated the plantation economy from its establishment until the beginning of the 1970s, Indian capitalists from dominant caste groups, particularly Brahmins, Syrian Christians and a few from the Nadar caste, had gained access to plantation ownership by the mid-twentieth century. The native planters, as part of their own nationalist discourse, challenged the European monopoly. As the Diwan of Travancore state wrote, 'preference will be given to the *subjects* of the Travancore state in the registration of land suitable for the cultivation of plantation crops' (quoted in Baak 1997, 172). This was directed to benefit the Brahmin, Nair and Syrian Christian communities as they were considered legitimate *subjects*, whereas Dalits were not socially or politically legitimised to own land.

Following the declaration of the Diwan, planters from the high-caste communities were successful in lobbying for huge areas of land for the plantations, involving more than 10,000 hectares. These lands were acquired at throwaway prices or even at no cost at all (Raman 2010). By contrast, the absence of land rights for the plantation workers was never discussed. This historically evolved pattern of landholding in the region, highly influenced by the interplay between land and caste (Kumar 1965; Pandian 1990), ensured that the outcastes were alienated from landownership and continued to be a cheap source of labour for the privileged class of planters.

The formation of Kerala state in 1956 led to a major transition from foreign European control of the plantations to native owners. The structure of control simply moved from foreign elites to local elites (upper-caste Hindus and Syrian Christians) and these effectively continued the same practices. In a few cases, such as Harrison Malayalam plantations, the foreign companies retained shares of plantation companies through their subsidiary companies in India. With the changeover of the plantations to indigenous ownership, the social hierarchy of wider Indian and Kerala society (mainly caste order) assumed more significance in the social and industrial order of the plantations. The new plantation owners – being from the dominant groups – appointed their relatives and other people belonging to their ethnic (caste or religious) community as managers, field officers and office clerks. In one of the estates in the Peermade tea belt, even supervisors – a position that a few experienced workers aspire to – were appointed on the basis of caste identity. Similar to what Jonathan Parry (2020, 23) observes for India's public-sector steel plants, 'inequalities of *class* are lent an aura of inevitability and "naturalness" by the spirit of hierarchy on which the *caste* order is founded'. This was exacerbated by the fact that reforms in Kerala designed to ameliorate caste forces did not apply to the plantations as these continued to be treated as outside state authority.

The plantation system, however, was threatened by the formation of the first communist government in Kerala (and in India) in 1957 as it pressed for land reforms and the redistribution of large landholdings to landless peasants and tenants. The new plantation owners feared the loss of their plantations and other institutional agencies in their control. They lobbied against the communist government and supported the massive political agitation in 1958 known as the Liberation Struggle (*vimōchana samaram*). A significant number of plantation owners in the Peermade tea belt were Syrian Christians and many of their families were at the forefront of this movement. The outcome was that the plantations were exempted from the land reforms. Neoclassical economists supported this by arguing that the plantations were the most productive part of the agricultural economy and that the advantage of economies of scale would be lost in a land reform (Franke and Chasin 1989; Heller 1999). In other words, the abolition of the plantation system was described as *killing the goose that laid the golden eggs* (Baak 1997). Consequently, Dalit plantation workers were largely excluded from the processes of land reform and redistribution, as were the Adivasi (indigenous/tribal) communities whose land it originally was. In this way, land reform legislation did not undermine the historical land-based social hierarchies, contradicting the egalitarian communist ideology that was the new state rhetoric in Kerala.

Plantation workers' attempts to occupy discarded wasteland outside the plantations were vehemently opposed by the planters, who subverted the attempts with the help of local police.[4] In 1984, the wastelands outside one of the estates were occupied by 14 plantation workers to plant cardamom and pepper as an attempt to become independent income earners. But it was opposed by the management of the estate, who threatened the workers with dire consequences if they carried out any planting of their own. They were given written warnings in this regard. When the workers, who were also active in trade unions, carried on in their attempt by building small huts on the occupied land, the estate management filed a case with the police against the land encroachment, although the land did not belong to the company. Tragically, the police intimidated the workers and succeeded in ejecting them from the occupied land.

This again demonstrates that the workers were not allowed or socially legitimised to own land – a strong reminder of their landlessness, which was attributed to their Dalit identity and their position at the bottom of the caste hierarchy.[5] The workers were landless in the places from which they came, and they continued to be landless in the place to which they went. As Eric Wolf (1957) rightly noted for the Caribbean, plantations always tend to inhibit the emergence of small farmers or owners of small property in their sphere of influence (that is, the plantation belt) through keeping the workers in a marginal existence. For Wolf (1957, 138), the plantation 'not only produces its own class structure but has an inhibiting effect on the formation of any alternative class structures outside its area of control'.

The only consolation for the plantation workforce was the Plantation Labour Act that the Indian Parliament passed in 1951, which introduced welfare measures and social security benefits. According to the Act, workers should be provided with housing, water supply, healthcare, school education for their children, crèches, canteens, compensation for accidents and injuries in workplaces and paid maternity leave and annual leave. Benefits, such as compensation for accidents and water supply, were not provided until the 1970s, when the workers organised protests under the auspices of various trade unions. In many plantations, the hard-earned welfare provisions such as healthcare, crèche facilities and paid annual leave were suspended by the mid-1990s, with the plantations citing the economic crisis in the tea industry as the reason. The Plantation Labour Act therefore did benefit the plantation workforce, but only for the period between 1970 and 1990 and that only as a result of the workers' struggle. While the companies often take credit for offering these services, the state and central governments provided significant financial assistance for them. For instance, many plantation companies lobbied state governments to offer school education for workers' children and the companies thus were saved from having to spend money on the schools. Even then, some facilities, such as latrines and electricity, were not made available to the workers until 2000, when the central government funded the construction of latrines and the state government provided electricity to the plantation workforce.

The trade unions emerged as a powerful force in the tea belt in the late 1960s and were instrumental in improving the working conditions of the workers through popular struggle. They also represented workers in the PLC, which determined work conditions and wages. The planters did everything possible to drive away those union leaders who opposed them. Within the plantations, many union conveners who connected the workers with the union leadership were assigned to the hardest work. The planters also filed a number of criminal cases against the conveners in an attempt to demoralise them. However, the union leadership eventually became corrupt and was co-opted by the companies in many tea estates.

A major reason for the union corruption was that the relation between the workers and the union leaders was quite hierarchical since most of the leaders were not of plantation worker background. They were sent by various political parties to set up branches in the plantation belts. As mentioned earlier, the union leadership consisted of people from Malayali-speaking higher castes, which distanced the workers from the unions. Consequently, most Tamil workers supported the Travancore Tamilnad Congress, a party struggling to exclude Tamil-inhabited regions from the new state of Kerala (Baak 1997, 236). However, in due time, the Travancore Tamilnad Congress weakened and the unions affiliated to the Communist and Congress parties became powerful in the Peermade tea belt. The internal rivalry between the unions and their competition for dominance also resulted in division among the workers. In line with what Jonathan Parry (2020, chapter 7) discussed about the unions in the Bhilai steel plant, the unions in the tea belt not only play the workers against the management, but also play the workers against each other. All these processes reproduced the alienation of the workers from controlling the circumstances of their existence.

Notes

1 Under the indenture system, workers signed a legal contract that bonded them to the plantation companies for a certain period. Most often, the workers were unaware of the terms of work until they reached the plantations (Baak 1999).
2 *Kangani* is a Tamil term meaning 'supervisor', equivalent to the North Indian *sardar*. The Kangani system was a form of recruitment and labour control that was common in plantation belts across the world, as Tamil workers were some of the earliest colonial recruits to coffee and tea plantations in Sri Lanka, Malaysia, South Africa, Mauritius, Myanmar, Fiji and the Caribbean islands. For a detailed analysis of the Tamil migration cycle, see Guilmoto (1993).
3 This Act was only repealed in 1935 following pressure from international agencies, especially the League of Nations.

4   The wastelands refer to those lands in the rocky hills located in the outskirts of the plantations which were not under the ownership of plantation companies, mostly because the rocky terrain makes tea cultivation difficult.
5   Murugan, an office peon in the estate office who led the 14 workers in the occupation, was transferred to hard menial labour. According to him, the company tried to eject the workers from the occupied land because they wanted the plantations to remain an enclave and leave open the possibility that they could appropriate the lands in the rocky hills for some purpose other than tea cultivation. When Murugan approached the management to regain his position as a peon, he was told that his punishment should be a lesson for other workers not to 'touch' the land that 'protects' the plantations. He could neither regain his position as a peon nor occupy the land. Murugan was targeted because he was one of the few literate workers in the plantation who realised that land ownership was key for socio-economic progress. He told me that the workers could not even apply for a bank loan because the banks give loans only against land. In fact, the whole incident shows clear continuity with the Coffee Stealing Act of 1879, as in both these cases, the workers were literally barred from possessing or owning material assets, and thus they were to remain in a position of limbo with only the barest means of subsistence.

References

Abrahams, Roger D. 1970. 'A performance-centered approach to gossip', *Man* 5(2): 290–301.

Agamben, Giorgio. 2005. *State of Exception*. Chicago, IL: University of Chicago Press.

Al-Mohammad, Hayder. 2012. 'A kidnapping in Basra: The struggles and precariousness of life in postinvasion Iraq', *Cultural Anthropology* 27(4): 597–614.

Ambedkar, B.R. 1942. Speech at the All India Conference of Depressed Classes, Nagpur.

Andrews, C.F. and W.W. Pearson. 1916. *Indentured Labour in Fiji: An independent inquiry*. Calcutta: Star Printing Works.

Appadurai, Arjun. 1986. 'Is homo hierarchicus?', *American Ethnologist* 13(4): 745–61.

Baak, Paul Erik. 1997. *Plantation Production and Political Power: Plantation development in southwest India in a long-term historical perspective*. Delhi: Oxford University Press.

Baak, Paul Erik. 1999. 'About enslaved ex-slaves, uncaptured contract coolies and unfreed freedmen: Some notes about "free" and "unfree" labour in the context of plantation development in southwest India, early sixteenth century–mid 1990s', *Modern Asian Studies* 33(1): 121–57.

Barth, Fredrik (ed.). 1969. *Ethnic Groups and Boundaries: The social organization of culture difference*. Oslo: Universitetsforlaget.

Bass, Daniel. 2012. *Everyday Ethnicity in Sri Lanka: Up-country Tamil identity politics*. London: Routledge.

Beckford, George L. 1972. *Persistent Poverty: Underdevelopment in plantation economies of the Third World*. Barbados: The University of West Indies Press.

Bergmann, Jorg R. 1993. *Discreet Indiscretions: The social organization of gossip*. New York: Aldine de Gruyter.

Besky, Sarah. 2008. 'Can a plantation be fair? Paradoxes and possibilities in fair trade Darjeeling tea certification', *Anthropology of Work Review* 29(1): 1–9.

Besky, Sarah. 2014. *The Darjeeling Distinction: Labor and justice on fair-trade tea plantations in India*. Berkeley: University of California Press.

Besnier, Niko. 2009. *Gossip and the Everyday Production of Politics*. Honolulu: University of Hawai'i Press.

Best, Lloyd. 1968. 'The mechanism of plantation-type economics: Outlines of a model of pure plantations economy', *Social and Economic Studies* 17(3): 283–326.

Béteille, André. 1965. *Caste, Class, and Power: Changing patterns of stratification in a Tanjore village*. Berkeley: University of California Press.

Béteille, André. 2012. 'The peculiar tenacity of caste', *Economic and Political Weekly* 47(13): 41–8.

Bourdieu, Pierre. 1977. *Outline of a Theory of Practice*. Cambridge: Cambridge University Press.

Bourdieu, Pierre. 1986. 'The forms of capital'. In *Handbook of Theory and Research for the Sociology of Education*, edited by J. Richardson, 241–58. New York: Greenwood.

Bourdieu, Pierre and Loïc J. Wacquant. 1992. *An Invitation to Reflexive Sociology*. Chicago, IL: University of Chicago Press.

Bourgois, Philippe. 1988. 'Conjugated oppression: Class and ethnicity among Guaymi and Kuna banana workers', *American Ethnologist* 15(2): 328–48.

Bourgois, Philippe. 1989. *Ethnicity at Work*. Baltimore, MD: Johns Hopkins University Press.

Breman, Jan. 1989. *Taming the Coolie Beast: Plantation society and the colonial order in Southeast Asia*. Delhi: Oxford University Press.

Breman, Jan. 1996. *Footloose Labour: Working in India's informal economy*. Cambridge: Cambridge University Press.

Breman, Jan. 2013. *At Work in the Informal Economy of India*. New Delhi: Oxford University Press.

Brenneis, Donald. 1984. 'Grog and gossip in Bhatgaon: Style and subsistence in Fiji Indian conversation', *American Ethnologist* 11(3): 487–506.

Brison, Karen J. 1992. *Just Talk: Gossips, meetings, and power in a Papua New Guinea village*. Berkeley: University of California Press.

Brown, Robert L. 1991. *Ganesh: Studies of an Asian god*. Albany: State University of New York Press.

Buck-Morss, Susan. 2009. *Hegel, Haiti and Universal History*. Pittsburgh, PA: University of Pittsburgh Press.

Butler, Judith. 2004. *Precarious Life: The powers of mourning and violence*. London: Verso.

Campbell, John K. 1964. *Honour, Family and Patronage: A study of institutions and moral values in a Greek mountain community*. Oxford: Clarendon Press.

Carswell, Grace and Geert De Neve. 2014. 'T-shirts and tumblers: Caste, dependency and work under neoliberalisation in South India', *Contributions to Indian Sociology* 48(1): 103–31.

Casimir, Jean. 2020. *The Haitians: A decolonial history*. Chapel Hill: University of North Carolina Press.

Chatterjee, Piya. 2001. *Time for Tea: Women and post-colonial labour on an Indian plantation*. Durham, NC: Duke University Press.

Chaudhuri, Soma. 2014. *Witches, Tea Plantations, and Lives of Migrant Laborers in India*. New Delhi: Cambridge University Press.

Chithambaram, Soundarya. 2011. 'Welfare, patronage, and the rise of Hindu nationalism in India's urban slum'. PhD Thesis, Ohio State University, Columbus.

Clifford, James and Goerge E. Marcus. 1986. *Writing Culture: The poetics and politics of ethnography*. Berkeley: University of California Press.

Colson, Elizabeth. 1953. *The Makah Indians*. Manchester: Manchester University Press.

Daniel, Valentine. 1996. *Charred Lullabies: Chapters in an Anthropography of violence*. Princeton, NJ: Princeton University Press.

Das, Veena. 1995. *Critical Events: An anthropological perspective on contemporary India*. New Delhi: Oxford University Press.

Das, Veena. 2006. *Life and Words: Violence and the descent into the ordinary*. Berkeley: University of California Press.

Davis, Janae, Alex Moulton, Levi Van Sant and Brian Williams. 2019. 'Anthropocene, capitalocene, … plantationocene? A manifesto for ecological justice in an age of global crises', *Geography Compass* 13(5): 1–15.

Deleuze, Gilles. 1992. 'Postscript on the societies of control', *October* 59 (Winter): 3–7.

De Neve, Geert. 2008. '"We are all *Sondukarar* (relatives)!" Kinship and its morality in an urban industry of Tamilnadu, South India', *Modern Asian Studies* 42(1): 211–46.

De Neve, Geert. 2014. 'Entrapped entrepreneurship: Labour contractors in the South Indian garment industry', *Modern Asian Studies* 48(5): 1302–33.

Dirks, Nicholas B. 2001. *Castes of Mind: Colonialism and the making of modern India*. Princeton, NJ: Princeton University Press.

Dumont, Louis. 1953. 'The Dravidian kinship terminology as an expression of marriage', *Man* 53(1): 34–9.

Dumont, Louis. 1977. *From Mandeville to Marx: The genesis and triumph of economic ideology*. Chicago, IL: University of Chicago Press.

Dumont, Louis. 1980. *Homo Hierarchicus: The caste system and its implications*. Chicago, IL: University of Chicago Press.

Empson, Rebecca M. 2020. *Subjective Lives and Economic Transformations in Mongolia: Life in the gap*. London: UCL Press.

Epstein, A.L. 1958. *Politics in an Urban African Community*. London: Manchester University Press.

Fanon, Frantz. 1966. *The Wretched of the Earth*. New York: Grove Press. Original: 1961.

Fanon, Frantz. 1967. *Black Skin, White Masks*. New York: Grove Press. Original: 1952.

Ferguson, James. 1990. *The Anti Politics Machine: Development, depoliticization, and bureaucratic power in Lesotho*. London: Cambridge University Press.

Ferguson, James. 1999. *Expectations of Modernity: Myths and meanings of urban life on the Zambian copperbelt*. Berkeley: University of California Press.

Firth, Raymond. 1967. *Tikopia Ritual and Belief*. Boston, MA: Beacon Press.

Foucault, Michel. 1972. *The Archaeology of Knowledge*. New York: Pantheon Books.

Foucault, Michel. 1975. *Discipline and Punish: The birth of the prison*. New York: Vintage Books.

Foucault, Michel. 1980. 'Body/power'. In *Power/Knowledge: Selected interviews and other writings, 1972–1977*, edited by Colin Gordon, 55–62. New York: Pantheon Books.

Foucault, Michel. 1982. 'The subject and power', *Critical Inquiry* 8(4): 777–95.

Franke, Richard W. and Barbara H. Chasin. 1989. *Kerala: Radical reform as development in an Indian state*. San Francisco, CA: The Institute for Food and Development Policy.

Geertz, Clifford. 1972. *Interpretation of Cultures*. New York: Basic Books.

Genovese, Eugene D. 1976. *Roll, Jordan, Roll: The world the slaves made*. New York: Vintage.

Gluckman, Max. 1955. *Customs and Conflict in Africa*. Oxford: Basil Blackwell.

Gluckman, Max. 1958. *Analysis of a Social Situation in Modern Zululand* (Vol. 28). Manchester: Manchester University Press. Original: 1940.

Gluckman, Max. 1963. 'Papers in honor of Melville J. Herskovits: Gossip and scandal', *Current Anthropology* 4(3): 307–16.

Goffman, Erving. 1959. *The Presentation of Self in Everyday Life*. Garden City, NY: Doubleday.

Goffman, Erving. 1961. *Asylums: Essays on the social situation of mental patients and other inmates*. New York: Anchor Books.

Goffman, Erving. 1967. *Interaction Ritual: Essays on face-to-face behavior*. Garden City, NY: Doubleday.

Goldstein, Donna. M. 2003. *Laughter Out of Place: Race, class, violence, and sexuality in a Rio shantytown*. Berkeley: University of California Press.

Goodwin, Marjorie Harness. 1990. *He-Said-She-Said: Talk as social organization among Black children*. Bloomington: Indiana University Press.

Gouldner, Alvin. W. 1954. *Patterns of Industrial Bureaucracy*. New York: Free Press.

Guha, Ranajit. 1983. *Elementary Aspects of Peasant Insurgency in Colonial India*. Delhi: Oxford University Press.

Guilmoto, Christophe Z. 1993. 'The Tamil migration cycle, 1830–1950', *Economic and Political Weekly* 28 (3/4): 16–23.

Handelman, Don. 1973. 'Gossip in encounters: The transmission of information in a bounded social setting', *Man* 8(2): 210–27.

Haraway, Donna. 2015. 'Anthropocene, capitalocene, plantationocene, chthulucene: Making kin', *Environmental Humanities* 6(1): 159–65.

Haraway, Donna, Anna Tsing and Gregg Mitman. 2019. 'Reflections on the plantationocene', A conversation with Donna Haraway and Anna Tsing moderated by Gregg Mitman. *Edge Effects Magazine*. Accessed 25 January 2020. https://edgeeffects.net/haraway-tsing-plantationocene/.

Hardt, Michael and Antonio Negri. 2000. *Empire*. Cambridge, MA: Harvard University Press.

Harriss-White, Barbara and Nandini Gooptu. 2001. 'Mapping India's world of unorganized sector', *Socialist Register* 37: 89–118.

Harvey, David. 2010. *The Enigma of Capital: And the crises of capitalism*. New York: Oxford University Press.

Haviland, John B. 1977. *Gossip, Reputation, and Knowledge in Zinacantan*. Chicago, IL: University of Chicago Press.

Heidemann, Frank. 1992. *Kanganies of Sri Lanka and Malaysia.* Munich: Anacon.

Heller, Patrick. 1999. *The Labor of Development: Workers and the transformation of capitalism in Kerala, India*. Ithaca, NY: Cornell University Press.

Herskovits, Melville J. 1937. *Life in a Haitian Valley*. New York: Octagon.

Hoerder, Dirk. 2002. *Cultures in Contact: World migrations in the second millennium*. London: Duke University Press.

Holbraad, Martin, Bruce Kapferer and Julia F. Sauma (eds.). 2019. *Ruptures: Anthropologies of discontinuity in times of turmoil*. London: UCL Press.

Hollup, Oddvar. 1994. *Bonded Labour: Caste and cultural identity among Tamil plantation workers in Sri Lanka*. New Delhi: Sterling Publishers.

Holmes, Seth. 2013. *Fresh Fruits, Broken Bodies: Migrant farm workers in the United States*. Berkeley: University of California Press.

Holt Norris, A. and E. Worby. 2012. 'The sexual economy of a sugar plantation: Privatization and social welfare in northern Tanzania', *American Ethnologist* 39(2): 354–70.

Ilaiah, Kancha. 1996. *Why I Am Not a Hindu: A Sudra critique of Hindutva philosophy, culture and political economy*. Kolkata: Samya.

Israel, Joachim. 1971. *Alienation, From Marx to Modern Sociology: A macro sociological analysis*. Boston, MA: Allyn & Bacon.

Jain, N.K., F. Rahman and Peter Baker (eds). 2008. *Economic Crisis in Tea Industry*. New Delhi: Studium Press.

Jain, Ravindra.K. 1970. *South Indians on the Plantation Frontier in Malaya*. New Haven, CT: Yale University Press.

Jayawardana, P.L. and M. Udupihille. 1997. 'Ventilatory function of factory workers exposed to tea dust', *Occupational Medicine* 47(2): 105–9.

Jayawardena, Chandra. 1963. *Conflict and Solidarity in a Guianese Plantation*. London: Athlone Press.

Jayawardena, Chandra. 1968. 'Ideology and conflict in lower class communities', *Comparative Studies in Society and History* 1(4): 413–46.

Jayawardena, Kumari and Rachel Kurian. 2015. *Class, Patriarchy, and Ethnicity on Sri Lankan Plantations: Two centuries of power and protest*. Hyderabad: Orient BlackSwan.

Jeffrey, Craig, Roger Jeffery and Patricia Jeffery. 2004. 'Degrees without freedom: The impact of formal education on Dalit young men in North India', *Development and Change* 35(5): 963–86.

Jeffrey, Robin. 1992. *Politics, Women and Well-Being: How Kerala became 'a model'*. London: Macmillan.

Jegathesan, Mythri. 2019. *Tea and Solidarity: Tamil women and work in postwar Sri Lanka*. Seattle: University of Washington Press.

Jolliffe, Lee. 2007. *Tea and Tourism: Tourists, traditions and transformations*. Clevedon: Channel View Publication.

Kapferer, Bruce. 1995. 'The performance of categories: Plays of identity in Africa and Australia'. In *The Urban Context: Ethnicity, social networks and situational analysis*, edited by Alisdair Rogers and Steven Vertovec, 55–80. Oxford: Berg Publishers.

Kapferer, Bruce. 2005a. 'Introduction'. In *Retreat of the Social: The rise and rise of reductionism*, edited by Bruce Kapferer, 1–16. New York: Berghahn.

Kapferer, Bruce. 2005b. 'Situations, crisis, and the anthropology of the concrete: The contributions of Max Gluckman', *Social Analysis* 49(3): 85–122.

Kapferer, Bruce. 2005c. 'New formations of power, the oligarchic-corporate state, and anthropological ideological discourse', *Anthropological Theory* 5(3): 285–99.

Kapferer, Bruce. 2010. 'In the event: Toward an anthropology of generic moments', *Social Analysis* 54 (3): 1–27.

Kar, Sohini. 2018. *Financializing Poverty: Labor and risk in Indian microfinance*. Stanford, CA: Stanford University Press.

Kirsch, Stuart. 2002. 'Rumour and other narratives of political violence in West Papua', *Critique of Anthropology* 22(1): 53–79.

Klein, Naomi. 2007. *The Shock Doctrine: The rise of disaster capitalism*. New York: Metropolitan Books.

Kooiman, Dick. 1991. 'Conversion from slavery to plantation labour: Christian mission in South India (19th century)', *Social Scientist* 19(8/9): 57–71.

Koselleck, Reinhart. 2006. 'Crisis', *Journal of the History of Ideas* 67(2): 357–400. Translated by Michaela W. Richter.

Kumar, Dharma. 1965. *Land and Caste in South India*. Cambridge: Cambridge University Press.

Lal, Brij V. 1993. '"Nonresistance" on Fiji plantations: The Fiji Indian experience, 1879–1920'. In *Plantation Workers: Resistance and accommodation*, edited by Edward D. Beechart, Doug Munro and Brij V. Lal, 187–216. Honolulu: University of Hawai'i Press.

Latour, Bruno. 2005. *Reassembling the Social: An introduction to actor-network-theory*. Oxford: Oxford University Press.

Lefebvre, Georges. 1973. *The Great Fear of 1789: Rural panic in revolutionary France*. Princeton, NJ: Princeton University Press.

Li, Tania M. 2014. *Land's End: Capitalist relations on an indigenous frontier*. Durham, NC: Duke University Press.

Li, Tania M. 2017. 'The price of un/freedom: Indonesia's colonial and contemporary plantation labor regimes', *Comparative Studies in Society and History* 59(2): 245–76.

Li, Tania M. 2018. 'After the land grab: Infrastructural violence and the "mafia system" in Indonesia's oil palm plantation zones', *Geoforum* 96: 328–37.

Li, Tania M. and Pujo Semedi. 2021. *Plantation Life: Corporate occupation in Indonesia's oil palm zone*. Durham: Duke University Press.

Lo, Andrew W. 2012. 'Reading about the financial crisis: A twenty-one-book review', *Journal of Economic Literature* 50(1): 151–78.

Lovatt, Heather. 1972. *Above the Heron's Pool: A short history of the Peermade/Vandiperiyar district of Travancore*. London: Putney.

Lukács, Georg. 1971. *History and Class Consciousness: Studies in Marxist dialectics*. Cambridge, MA: MIT Press. Original: 1923.

Luxemburg, Rosa. 2003. *The Accumulation of Capital*, translated by Agnes Schwarzschild. London: Routledge. Original: 1913.

Luxemburg, Rosa. 2013. 'History of economic crises (chapter 8)'. In *The Complete Works of Rosa Luxemburg. Economic Writings*. Vol. 1. London: Verso. Original: 1911.

Macfarlane, A. and I. Macfarlane. 2004. *The Empire of Tea: The remarkable history of the plant that took over the world*. New York: Overlook Press.

Madhusoodhanan, C.G. and K.G. Sreeja. 2010. *The Mullaperiyar Conflict: Backgrounders on conflict resolution*. Bangalore: National Institute of Advanced Studies.

Marcus, George and Michael M. Fischer (eds). 1986. *Anthropology as Cultural Critique*. Chicago, IL: University of Chicago Press.

Marcuse, Herbert. 1964. *One Dimensional Man*. London: Routledge.

Marriott, McKim. 1955. *Village India: Studies in the little community*. Chicago, IL: University of Chicago Press.

Martínez, Samuel. 2007. *Decency and Excess: Global aspirations and material deprivation on a Caribbean sugar plantation*. Boulder, CO: Paradigm.

Marx, Karl. 1959. *Economic and Philosophic Manuscripts of 1844*, translated by Martin Mulligan. Moscow: Progress Publishers. Original: 1844.

Marx, Karl. 1981. *Capital*, Vol. 3. London: Penguin. Original: 1894.

Marx, Karl and Friedrich Engels. 1964. *The German Ideology*. Moscow: Progress Publishers. Original: 1846.

Mauss, Marcel. 2011. *The Gift: The form and reason for exchange in archaic societies*. Mansfield, CT: Martino Publishing. Original: 1925.

Mayer, Adrian C. 1961. *Peasants in the Pacific: A study of Indian rural society*. Berkeley: University of California Press.

Mayer, Adrian C. 1963. 'The significance of quasi-groups in the study of complex societies'. In *The Social Anthropology of Complex Societies*, edited by Michael Banton, 97–122. ASA Monographs 4. London: Tavistock Publications.

Mbembe, Achille. 1995. 'Figures of the subject in times of crisis', *Public Culture* 7(2): 323–52. Translated by Janet Roitman.

Meinert, Lotte and Bruce Kapferer (eds). 2015. *In the Event: Toward an anthropology of generic moments*. New York: Berghahn Books.

Mészáros, Istvan. 1970. *Marx's Theory of Alienation*. London: Merlin Press.

Millar, Kathleen. 2014. 'The precarious present: Wageless labor and disrupted life in Rio de Janeiro, Brazil', *Cultural Anthropology* 29(1): 32–53.

Mintz, Sidney W. 1966. 'The Caribbean as a socio-cultural area', *Cahiers d'Histoire Mondiale* 10(4): 912–37.

Mintz, Sidney W. 1978. 'Was the plantation slave a proletarian?', *Review* 2(1): 81–98.

Mintz, Sidney W. 1985. *Sweetness and Power: The place of sugar in modern history*. New York: Viking–Penguin Books.

Mintz, Sidney W. 1989. *Caribbean Transformations*. New York: Columbia University Press.

Mishra, Deepak K., Vandana Upadhyay and Atul Sarma. 2011. 'Invisible chains? Crisis in the tea industry and the unfreedom of labour in Assam's tea plantations', *Contemporary South Asia* 19(1): 75–90.

Mishra, Deepak K., Vandana Upadhyay and Atul Sarma. 2012. *Unfolding Crisis in Assam's Tea Plantations: Employment and occupational mobility*. New Delhi: Routledge.

Mitchell, J. Clyde. 1956. *The Kalela Dance: Aspects of social relationships among urban Africans in northern Rhodesia*. Manchester: Manchester University Press.

Mollona, Massimiliano. 2005. *Made in Sheffield: An ethnography of industrial work and politics*. London: Berghahn.

Morris, Chris. 2010. *Diet of Mud and Despair in Indian Village*. ISKCON web portal. 20 May. Accessed 14 April 2012. https://iskconnews.org/diet-of-mud-and-despair-in-indian-village/.

Mosse, David. 2010. 'A relational approach to durable poverty, inequality and power', *Journal of Development Studies* 46(7): 1156–78.

Mosse, David. 2020. 'The modernity of caste and the market economy', *Modern Asian Studies* 54(4): 1225–71.

Muthiah, S. 1993. *A Planting Century: The first hundred years of the United Planters' Association of Southern India*. New Delhi: Affiliated East-West Press.

Narotzky, Susana and Gavin Smith. 2006. *Immediate Struggles: People, power, and place in rural Spain*. Berkeley: University of California Press.

Nash, June. 1979. *We Eat the Mines and the Mines Eat Us: Dependency and exploitation in Bolivian tin mines*. New York: Columbia University Press.

Neilson, J. and W.E. Pritchard. 2009. *Value Chain Struggles: Institutions and governance in the plantation districts of South India*. Chichester: Wiley-Blackwell.

Ollman, Bertal. 1971. *Alienation: Marx's conception of man in capitalist society*. Cambridge: Cambridge University Press.

Omvedt, Gail. 1980. 'Migration in colonial India: The articulation of feudalism and capitalism by the colonial state', *Journal of Peasant Studies* 7(2): 185–202.

Omvedt, Gail. 1998. 'Disturbing aspects of Kerala society', *Bulletin of Concerned Asian Scholars* 30(3): 31–3.

Omvedt, Gail. 2006. 'Kerala is part of India: The Kerala model of development, Dalits and globalisation'. In *Kerala: The Paradoxes of Public Action and Development*, edited by Joseph Tharamangalam, 188–214. Hyderabad: Orient Longman.

Ong, Aihwa. 1987. *Spirits of Resistance and Capitalist Discipline: Factory women in Malaysia*. Albany: State University of New York Press.

Paine, Robert. 1967. 'What is gossip about? An alternative hypothesis', *Man* 2(2): 278–85.

Paine, Robert. 1970. 'Informal communication and information-management', *Canadian Review of Sociology and Anthropology* 7(3): 172–88.

Palomera, Jaime and Theodora Vetta. 2016. 'Moral economy: Rethinking a radical concept', *Anthropological Theory* 16(4): 413–32.

Pandian, M.S.S. 1990. *The Political Economy of Agrarian Change: Nanchilnadu 1880–1939*. New Delhi: SAGE.

Pandian, M.S.S. 2002. 'One step outside modernity: Caste, identity politics and public sphere', *Economic and Political Weekly* 37(18): 1735–41.

Panikkar, K.N. 2003. 'Communalising Kerala', *The Hindu*, 13 May.

Parry, Jonathan. 2020. *Classes of Labour: Work and life in a central Indian steel town*. London: Routledge.

Pattenden, Jonathan. 2010. 'A neoliberalisation of civil society? Self-help groups and the labouring class poor in rural South India', *Journal of Peasant Studies* 37(3): 485–512.

Piliavsky, Anastasia (ed.). 2014. *Patronage in South Asia*. New Delhi: Cambridge University Press.

Polanyi, Karl. 2001. *The Great Transformation: The political and economic origins of our time*. Boston, MA: Beacon Press. Original: 1944.

Prasad, Chandra Bhan. 1998. 'EMS is no more: Long live socialism', *Communalism Combat* (Mumbai), May.

Raheja, Gloria. G. 1988. *The Poison in the Gift: Ritual, prestation, and the dominant caste in a North Indian village*. Chicago, IL: University of Chicago Press.

Raj, Jayaseelan. 2019. 'Beyond the unions: The Pembillai Orumai women's strike in the South Indian tea belt', *Journal of Agrarian Change* 19(4): 671–89.

Raj, Jayaseelan. 2020. 'Categorical oppression: Performance of identity in South India', *Australian Journal of Anthropology* 31(3): 288–302.

Ram, Kalpana. 2007. 'Untimeliness as moral indictment: Tamil agricultural labouring women's use of lament as life narrative', *Australian Journal of Anthropology* 18(2): 138–53.

Raman, K. Ravi. 2010. *Global Capital and Peripheral Labour: The history and political economy of plantation workers in India*. London and New York: Routledge.

Ramaswamy, Sumathi. 1997. *Passions of the Tongue: Language devotion in Tamil India, 1891–1970*. Berkeley: University of California Press.

Rammohan, K.T. 1998. 'Kerala CPI(M): All that is solid melts into air', *Economic and Political Weekly* 33(40): 2579–82.

Rankin, Katherine N. 2001. 'Governing development: Neoliberalism, microcredit, and rational economic woman', *Economy and Society* 30(1): 18–37.

Rapport, Nigel. 1996. 'Gossip'. In *Encyclopaedia of Social and Cultural Anthropology*, edited by Alan Barnard and Jonathan Spencer, 266–7. London and New York: Routledge.

Robinson, Cedric J. 1983. *Black Marxism: The making of the Black radical tradition*. Chapel Hill: University of North Carolina Press.

Roitman, Janet. 2014. *Anti-Crisis.* Durham, NC: Duke University Press.

Sangren, Steven P. 1991. 'Dialectics of alienation: Individuals and collectivities in Chinese religion', *Man* 26(1): 67–86.

Sangren, Steven P. 2000. *Chinese Sociologics: An anthropological account of the role of alienation in social reproduction*. London: Athlone Press.

Sanhati, 2011. '20 suicide attempts a day – Tirupur, Tamil Nadu: Textile workers in a globalised workplace'. 18 June. Accessed 28 May 2021. http://sanhati.com/excerpted/3787/.

Sartre, Jean-Paul. 1963. *Search for a Method*. New York: Vintage Books.

Sassen, Saskia. 2014. *Expulsions: Brutality and complexity in the global economy*. Cambridge, MA: Harvard University Press.

Sassen, Saskia. 2016. 'At the systemic edge: Expulsions', *European Review* 24(1): 89–104.

Scheper-Hughes, Nancy. 1992. *Death without Weeping: The violence of everyday life in Brazil*. Berkeley: University of California Press.

Schroyer, Trent. 1972. 'Marx's theory of the crisis', *Telos* 14(Winter): 106–25.

Scott, James. C. 1985. *Weapons of the Weak: Everyday forms of peasant resistance*. New Haven, CT: Yale University Press.

Scott, James. C. 1990. *Domination and the Arts of Resistance: Hidden transcripts*. New Haven, CT: Yale University Press.

Seeman, Melvin. 1959. 'On the meaning of alienation', *American Sociological Review* 24(6): 783–91.

Selvaratnam, V. 1988. 'Theoretical perspective in the study of plantation system: The Malaysian case', *Economic and Political Weekly* 23(21): 1080–8.

Sennett, Richard and Jonathan Cobb. 1972. *The Hidden Injuries of Class*. New York: Vintage Books.

Shah, A., J. Lerche, R. Axelby, D. Benbabaali, B. Donegan, J. Raj and V. Thakur. 2018. *Ground Down by Growth: Inequality in twenty-first-century India*. London: Pluto.

Smith, Raymond T. 1967. 'Social stratification, cultural pluralism and integration in West Indian societies'. In *Caribbean Integration,* edited by S. Lewis and T.O. Mathews, 226–64. Rio Pedras: University of Puerto Rico Press.

Srinivas, M.N. 1952. *Religion and Society among the Coorgs of South India*. London: Asia Publishing House.

Srinivas, M.N. 1966. *Social Change in Modern India*. Berkeley: University of California Press.

Steur, Luisa. 2017. *Indigenist Mobilization: Confronting electoral communism and precarious livelihoods in post-reform Kerala*. Oxford: Berghahn.

Stewart, Pamela J. and Andrew Strathern. 2004. *Witchcraft, Sorcery, Rumour and Gossip*. Cambridge: Cambridge University Press.

Stoler, Ann Laura. 1985. *Capitalism and Conflict in Sumatra's Plantation Belt*. New Haven, CT and London: Yale University Press.

Stoler, Ann Laura. 1992. '"In cold blood": Hierarchies of credibility and the politics of colonial narratives', *Representations* 37(Winter): 151–89.

Stoler, Ann Laura. 2008. 'Imperial debris: Reflections on ruins and ruination', *Cultural Anthropology* 23(2): 191–219.

Tambiah, Stanley J. 1996. *Leveling Crowds: Ethnonationalist conflicts and collective violence in South Asia*. Berkeley: University of California Press.

Taussig, Michael. 1980. *The Devil and Commodity Fetishism in South America*. Chapel Hill: University of North Carolina Press.

Thachil, Tariq. 2009. 'The saffron wave meets the silent revolution: Why the poor vote for Hindu nationalism in India'. PhD Thesis, Cornell University, Ithaca, NY.

Thompson, Edgar T. 1959. 'The plantation as a social system', *Revista Geográfica* 25(51): 41–56.

Thompson, Edgar T. 1975. *Plantation Societies, Race Relations, and the South: The regimentation of populations; Selected papers of Edgar T. Thompson*. Durham, NC: Duke University Press.

Thompson, Eric P. 1963. *The Making of the English Working Class*. New York: Vintage.

Thorat, Sukhdeo and Paul Attewell. 2010. 'The legacy of social exclusion: A correspondence study of job discrimination in India's urban private sector'. In *Blocked by Caste: Economic discrimination in modern India*, edited by S. Thorat and K.S. Newman, 35–51. New Delhi: Oxford University Press.

Tinker, Hugh. 1974. *A New System of Slavery: The export of Indian labour overseas, 1830–1920*. London: Oxford University Press.

Trouillot, Michel-Rolph. 1995. *Silencing the Past: Power and the production of history*. Boston, MA: Beacon Press.

Tsing, Anna, L. 1993. *In the Realm of the Diamond Queen: Marginality in an out-of-the-way place*. Princeton, NJ: Princeton University Press.

Tsing, Anna, L. 2005. *Friction: An ethnography of global connection*. Princeton, NJ: Princeton University Press.

Tsing, Anna, L. 2015. *The Mushroom at the End of the World*. Princeton, NJ: Princeton University Press.

Turner, Victor. 1967. *The Forest of Symbols: Aspects of Ndembu ritual*. Ithaca, NY: Cornell University Press.

Turner, Victor. 1969. *The Ritual Process: Structure and anti-structure*. New York: Aldine de Gruyter.

Van Velsen, J. 1979. 'The extended-case method and situational analysis'. In *The Craft of Social Anthropology*, edited by A.L. Epstein, 129–49. Oxford: Pergamon Press.

Veblen, Thorstein. 2007. *The Theory of the Leisure Class*. Oxford: Oxford University Press. Original: 1899.

Venkatesan, Soumhya. 2009. 'Charity: Conversations about need and greed'. In *Ethnographies of Moral Reasoning: Living paradoxes of a global age*, edited by Karen Sykes, 67–89. New York: Palgrave Macmillan.

Vera-Sanso, Penny. 2006. 'Experiences in old age: A South Indian example of how functional age is socially structured', *Oxford Development Studies* 34(4): 457–72.

Vera-Sanso, Penny. 2007. 'Increasing consumption, decreasing support: A multi-generational study of family relations among South Indian Chakkliyars', *Contributions to Indian Sociology* 41(2): 225–48.

Vigh, Henrik. 2008. 'Crisis and chronicity: Anthropological perspectives on continuous conflict and decline', *Ethnos* 73(1): 5–24 .

Viswanathan, S. 1999. 'The Tirunelveli massacre', *The Hindu Frontline* 16 (13 July–13 August).

Wolf, Eric W. 1957. 'Specific aspects of plantation systems in the New World'. In *Plantation Systems of the New World*, edited by Angel Paler and Vera Rubin, 136–46. Social Science Monograph 7. Washington, DC: Pan American Union.

Wolf, Eric W. 1966. 'Kinship, friendship and patron–client relations in complex societies'. In *The Social Anthropology of Complex Societies*, edited by Michael Banton, 1–22. London: Tavistock.

Wolf, Eric W. 1982. *Europe and the People without History*. Berkeley: University of California Press.

Government statistics and reports

Human Development Report 2005, Kerala. 2006. State Planning Board, Government of Kerala.
Kerala Development Report. 2008. Planning Commission, Government of India.
National Census Data; 2011. Government of India.

Newspapers and magazines

The Hindu
Hindu Business Line
Planters' Chronicle
Times of India

Index

abandonment 191
   by company 21, 173
   by contractor 173, 175
   during crisis 6, 42
   its legitimisation 21
   nature of 19
   of plantation workers 5, 7–10
   of plantations 23, 46, 48, 78, 158
   by the state 21
Adivasi
   from Jharkhand 7, 170, 172
   from Kerala 16
   See also tribal
alienation 19, 25, 42–3, 64, 68, 71–4, 76–9, 80, 85, 87, 89, 93, 104, 111, 113, 130, 141, 203, 205–7
   anthropological approaches to 13–14, 192
   definition 12, 190
   history of 11
   from land 195
   linguistic 172
   multiple 115, 140, 181, 185, 190
   psychological 165–6
   through rituals 125, 127–8
   through rumour 149
   in the tea belt xvi
   from unions 159
   of workers xi–xii, 4, 10, 20, 32, 62, 66, 70, 96, 98–9, 118–19, 130, 162, 173, 183, 188, 198
Ambedkar, B.R. 59, 192
aristocracy
   African labour 26
   of labour 30, 186
autonomy 76–7, 186
   cultural 130

denying 181
   loss of 66, 68,
   to regain 74
   socio-economic 183

Bourdieu, Pierre x–xi, 25, 43, 87, 96, 114, 188, 200–1
Bourgois, Philippe 24, 26, 177–8, 201
Breman, Jan 12, 53, 140, 171, 194

capital
   forms of 96, 200
   socio-cultural ix, 36–7, 41, 43, 63, 87, 110–11, 114
   symbolic 36, 43
capitalism 13, 43, 62, 95, 203–4, 206–7
   agrarian/industrial 9, 21
   disaster 185
   extractive 6, 9
   history of 22, 71
   neoliberal/modern/global 2, 6–9, 181, 188, 190–1
   plantation 7–8, 19, 21, 181
caste ix, xi–xiii, 19, 43, 52, 55, 76, 80, 84, 87, 93–4, 97, 105, 113–16, 119, 124–30, 135–8, 141–2, 149, 160–2, 181, 183, 186, 190–3, 195–8, 200–8
   and class 90, 95, 187
   discrimination based on 2–6, 54, 59, 60–2, 65, 68–72, 78, 81, 120, 188
   disguising of 88–9
   hierarchy of 1, 31–4, 41, 98–9
   system of 11–16, 21–5
casual
   labour 2–5, 9, 20, 28–30, 52–3, 58, 62, 83, 164–7, 170–2

casualisation as a process 10, 62, 164–6, 169, 172, 175–8, 191
categorical
　oppression 11–13, 89, 93, 179, 188, 189, 191
　relationship xii, 11, 21, 94, 114–16
Christian 92, 96, 101, 119, 204
　Dalit 60, 87, 120, 125–8, 130, 190
　Nadar 61, 88, 126
　Pentecostal 131–7
　Syrian 22, 32, 41, 44, 57–8, 172, 195–6
class xi, 4, 11, 25, 28, 42–3, 45, 60, 84, 142, 162
　capitalist class 23
　class order 50, 59, 89, 177, 190, 197
　Dalit working class 12, 14–16, 20, 26, 69, 99, 115
　relation with caste 31–8, 76, 95
commodification
　of land 90, 93
comparative advantage 8, 22
conflict xii, 113–16, 120, 158, 178, 187, 189
　over dam 4–6, 14–15, 99, 102, 104
　global 191
　among the workers 42, 59, 119, 121–4, 143–4, 159
contract
　social 23
　sumangali 53
　types of 29
　workers 3, 166
counter-plantation system 183
COVID-19 182
crisis
　economic ix–xiii, 1–15, 19–22, 125, 42, 45–7, 62, 64–6
　as an excuse 166–9
　of identity 188–92
　intensifying 49, 53, 80, 93, 118–19
　Marxist theory of 21–2
　multiple 68, 71, 79, 98, 130–2
　phenomenology of 96
　of relations 141–1, 145, 161

Dalits xiii, 1–2, 4, 12, 15–16, 22, 31–2, 44, 52, 59, 61–2, 69, 84, 87–9, 94–6, 126–8, 188
dam 4, 14, 98–104, 113–15
decency, politics of 5, 119, 136–7, 140, 189
dignity
　moral 66
　struggle for 12, 76–7, 104, 141, 191–2
discrimination
　caste 2, 12, 14, 54, 59, 61–2, 65, 68–71, 80–1, 187
　linguistic/ethnic 4, 99, 105
　multiple 15, 79
dispute
　among workers 28, 36, 41, 79
　between states 98–100
　over dam 4, 14–15, 20, 103–5, 113–16
　over land 184
Dumont, Louis 21–2, 26, 31–2, 43, 97

egalitarian
　relations among workers 59, 70, 118
　system 22, 31, 104, 120, 162, 186, 188, 196
egalitarianism 119–20, 187
ethnic
　division of labour 177, 179
　oppression 19, 183
　slur 104
　stereotyping 15, 20, 98, 102, 116
ethnicity 4–6, 11, 13, 94, 172, 188
event
　crisis as 14–15, 22, 35–6
　dispute as 104–5

factionalism 120, 124
factory
　tea 28, 34–8, 43, 48, 73, 75, 147, 166
Fanon, Frantz 14, 89, 141, 187, 190–2
Ferguson, James 7, 22, 42, 186
Foucault, Michel 15, 25, 34, 191
fracturing
　of social relations 5, 20, 119, 140

garment work 2, 51–4, 63, 80, 116, 190
Gluckman, Max 14, 22, 143, 153, 156, 160–2
Goffman, Erving 25, 35, 43, 143–4, 153, 161–2
gossip 15, 20, 66, 68, 112, 143–4
gratuity 29, 64–8, 72, 75, 77, 79
　deferral 19, 66, 74, 76, 78

hierarchy
　caste 1, 14, 22–3, 25, 31–4, 41, 44, 61, 95–6, 98–9, 130, 142
　occupational 24, 27, 35–7, 40, 43, 87, 156, 177
　racial/ethnic ix, 8

210　PLANTATION CRISIS

spatial 38–9
Hindu
   cosmology 21, 188
   festivals 119
   nationalism 140–2
   pilgrimage 22
   rituals 125–30
homogenisation
   religious 130, 142
humiliation, of workers
   caste 69, 142
   social 73
   racial 94, 104

Idukki 16, 96, 100, 192
indenture
   workforce 1, 31–2, 62,
   system 65, 193–5, 198
Indigenous 5, 16, 90, 184, 196

Jharkhand
   workers from 5, 7, 20, 165, 167, 170–6, 178

Kapferer, Bruce xii, 10, 14–15, 20, 98, 114–15, 185
Kerala model 22, 186–7

land grab 184, 190
Latour, Bruno 5
laughter 86
layam 31, 38–9, 137
leisure
   class 36

Malayalam 4, 21, 32, 41, 82–4, 86, 96, 98–9, 104, 107, 116–17, 131, 149, 172, 187–8, 195
Martínez, Samuel 6, 26, 36, 90, 120, 177
Marx, Karl 10, 13, 21, 22, 40, 78
MGNREGS 48, 66, 68, 72
Mintz, Sidney 7, 21, 32, 43, 177
Mitchell, Clyde 11, 14, 26, 44, 95, 97–8, 114–15
mobility 57, 81, 138, 187
   economic 54
   gendered 3
   social 87, 94
   social vs economic 20, 95
moral
   economy 5, 23, 37, 42, 66

expectation 23
   failure 23–4, 157, 160, 191
   order/relationships 23–4, 42, 126, 135
   society 4, 70, 76, 90, 107, 112, 136
morality, relational 33
Mullaperiyar 4, 20, 98–101, 105–6
Munnar xvi, 11, 22, 41–2, 55, 96, 112, 131

neoliberal
   capitalism 2, 6, 8–9, 188, 190–1
   austerity measures 22
   economy 90, 93, 168, 184
   logic 8, 10, 50, 186
   policy 7, 25, 73
   regime 5
   structural readjustment reforms 1, 62
neoliberalism 7, 10–11, 21, 26, 95, 113, 176, 181, 187
non-being 14, 190

Omvedt, Gail 142, 186–7

Pāndi 20, 95, 104, 107, 116
Peermade
   tea belt xvi, 1, 6–8, 12, 16–18, 21–2, 26, 31–3, 38, 48–9, 52, 60, 82, 90, 96, 102–3, 107, 112, 115–17, 120, 125, 127, 144, 155, 163, 166, 168, 170, 173, 178–9, 181–2, 192–4, 196, 198
periphery
   plantation as 18–19
polarisation
   religious 119, 130
   of workers 120–1, 127, 134, 140
poverty
   experience of 76
   rationalise 22
   to reduce 50
   stories of x, 69, 84, 86–7
   of workers 62, 67, 131
power 6, 15, 37, 40–1, 156
   of caste 129, 136
   of deities 13, 137
   of ethnographer xiii
   of labour 20, 170
   of planters 21, 27, 168
   political 24
   of sorcery 71
   symbolic/social 24, 31, 34, 36, 43
   of unions 123, 141, 158, 198

powerlessness xi, 27, 78, 113, 162, 188
prejudice
    caste 79, 89
    linguistic–ethnic 4, 14–16, 20, 98–9, 102, 104, 112, 114, 116–17, 187
protest
    against dam 100–6
    lack of 145, 161, 170, 172
    occupy 9
    by retirees 66, 75
    by workers 23, 197

racial
    capitalism 22, 181
    discrimination 14
    identity 32
    slurs 88, 95
respect
    lack/loss of 66, 77, 84
    to retain 19, 64, 66, 74
retirees 5, 62, 64, 66–8, 166, 189
    alienation 71, 74, 76–8
    struggle 19, 65, 72–4
rumour 15, 68
    authorise 156, 159–62
    as a form of control 20, 143–9

sanskritisation 96, 126–8, 130, 142
Scott, James C. 112, 144, 148, 162
situational analysis 14–15, 44
solidarity
    against dam 101, 111
    destabilisation of 20, 36, 118, 134, 136
    through gossip 155, 161–2
    of workers 26, 84, 116, 119–22, 128, 132
sorcery 69, 71
spatiality 26, 38, 40, 190
state
    abandoning workers 21
    corporate/neoliberal 9–11, 42–3, 96, 113–14, 117, 184, 186, 191
    Kerala 1, 4, 5, 18, 26, 98, 163, 187
    nexus with unions 11, 40, 64, 66, 125, 143–5, 168, 178, 181, 183–5
    plantation as 25
    princely 16, 43, 99–100, 116, 193–6
    regulation 2
status
    through caste 31–3

differentiation/conflict 37, 43, 119, 138, 140
    of managerial staff 36, 40
    struggle for 5, 95–6, 130, 136, 142
    of unions 149, 156–7, 160
    of workers 4, 26, 66, 80–2, 98–9, 114, 120, 165, 187
stereotyping
    cultural 87
    ethnic 20, 98, 104
stigmatisation 4, 7, 11–13, 15–16, 18, 21, 57, 65, 68, 71, 78, 85, 89, 93–5, 98–9, 112, 114, 118, 179, 188, 190
strike
    against dam 100–1
    by workers 11, 23, 42, 157, 170, 172, 188, 192
Stoler, Ann Laura 19, 142, 144, 148, 156, 162, 167
suicide 45, 53, 69, 86

Tirupur 7, 19, 47, 52–5, 57–8, 61–2, 80, 90–1, 132
total institution 18–19, 25, 35, 43, 45, 116, 153
trade union 3, 11, 20, 23–4, 40–4, 46–7, 62–3, 114–16, 120, 122–5, 141, 145, 151–3, 159–63, 169–76, 178, 192–3, 197–8
    convenors 41, 107, 117, 148–50
    leaders xii, 10, 101, 108–10, 121, 127, 143–4, 155–7
    membership 42, 118
tribal 5, 16, 20, 44, 95, 142, 184, 196
    See also Indigenous
Tsing, Anna L. 6, 125, 190

welfare
    benefits 3, 30, 34, 36, 43, 96, 126, 138, 141–2, 146
    claims 14, 175
    denying 24, 128, 164–6, 168–9, 171–2, 178, 184, 186, 197
Wolf, Eric 7, 21, 24, 34–5, 38, 43, 197

Zambia
    copper belt 22, 26, 44